D. Mac   9/23   HIST (Brit)   £3-00

Flora M. Watherspoon.

1948

MRS GLADSTONE

The Portrait of a Marriage

by the same author

CHARLOTTE MARY YONGE.

Catherine Gladstone, 1849. From a watercolour drawing by George Richmond now in the possession of Mr. C. A. Gladstone at Hawarden Castle.

MRS GLADSTONE

The Portrait of a Marriage

by

GEORGINA BATTISCOMBE

"Marriage is the greatest earthly happiness when founded on complete sympathy."
DISRAELI to GLADSTONE

CONSTABLE · Publishers · LONDON

LONDON
PUBLISHED BY
Constable and Company Ltd
10–12 ORANGE STREET W.C.2

·

INDIA
Orient Longmans Ltd
BOMBAY CALCUTTA MADRAS

·

CANADA
Longmans, Green and Company
TORONTO

·

SOUTH *and* EAST AFRICA
Longmans, Green and Company Ltd
CAPETOWN   NAIROBI

First published 1956

Printed in Great Britain by Butler & Tanner Ltd., Frome and London

TO MY HUSBAND

Illustrations

CATHERINE GLADSTONE, 1849

From a watercolour drawing by George Richmond now in the possession of Mr. C. A. Gladstone at Hawarden Castle

[frontispiece

CATHERINE GLYNNE, Rome, 1839

From a bust by Laurence Macdonald now in the possession of Mr. C. A. Gladstone at Hawarden Castle. Photograph by J. Burge, Birkenhead

[facing page 22

Author's Note

THIS book is chiefly based on hitherto unpublished letters and diaries to be found among the Hawarden papers, now in the possession of Mr. C. A. Gladstone. To him, and to Mrs. Gladstone, I owe a deep debt of gratitude, not only for permission to examine these papers but for unfailing encouragement and hospitality. I would also like to express my gratitude to the trustees of the British Museum for allowing me special access to the Hamilton Papers, and to His Grace the Duke of Devonshire for permission to quote from unpublished portions of Lady Frederick Cavendish's Journal deposited at Chatsworth.

I have to make grateful acknowledgement of permission to quote copyright material from the following works: *The Life of Sir James Graham*, by C. S. Parker (John Murray Ltd.); *Lord Rosebery*, by the Marquess of Crewe (John Murray Ltd.); *Gladstone to His Wife*, edited by A. Tilney Bassett (Methuen & Co. Ltd.); *Mary Drew*, by Lucy Masterman (Methuen & Co. Ltd.); *Catherine Gladstone*, by Mary Drew (James Nisbet & Co. Ltd.); *A Diary with Letters*, by Thomas Jones (Oxford University Press); *After Thirty Years*, by Viscount Gladstone (Macmillan & Co. Ltd.); *Autobiography of Lord Morley* (Macmillan & Co. Ltd.); *Reminiscences of Lord Kilbracken* (Macmillan & Co. Ltd.); *The St. Deiniol's Library Memorial Lecture*, by the Hon. George W. Lyttelton (privately printed).

A detailed bibliography of published material would make tedious and somewhat unprofitable reading, since inevitably it must include most of the standard works and books of memoirs dealing with the Victorian period. The two primary authorities are, of course, Lord Morley's great *Life of Gladstone* and the more recent biography by Sir Philip Magnus. I have been specially dependent on two short books, both of them entitled *Catherine Gladstone*, the one, by Mary Drew, a brilliant sketch rather than an accurate biography, the other, by E. A. Pratt, valuable chiefly for the account it gives of Catherine Gladstone's charitable activities and her connection with the Women's Liberal Federation. Two or three of Gladstone's letters are here printed for the first time, but most of the quotations from his letters are taken from the volume edited by Mr. A. Tilney Bassett and entitled *Gladstone to His Wife*.

My thanks are due too to Professor W. L. Burn for his kindness in reading and correcting my manuscript, and to the many people who have supplied me with reminiscences of Catherine Gladstone, in particular to the Viscountess Cobham, Dame Meriel Talbot, D.B.E., Susan Lady Tweedsmuir, Mrs. Parish, Mrs. C. F. Masterman, Sir Walter Moberly, Mr. A. Tilney Bassett, Mr. Albert Gladstone, and finally to the Hon. Mrs. Alington. This is her book in very special manner, since it was she who made live again all the peculiar brilliance of that famous family circle, re-creating for me the figure of the beloved Auntie Pussy, and turning legend into reality.

G. B.

Foreword

A READER who glances through the biography section of a library catalogue may perhaps be struck by one curious omission. Women achieve fame, and with fame a biography, because they are notable as artists, authors or actresses, as explorers or aviators or social reformers, as saints or courtesans, but never because they are notable as wives. Yet matrimony remains the most usual, as it is by far and away the most popular, of feminine careers. Why then does it go unhonoured and unsung? Even the Christian Church seems to countenance this attitude; the calendar is liberally besprinkled with the names of virgin saints, but the number of "godly matrons" can be counted on the fingers of one hand. Many famous women were, of course, married, but they are famous for reasons which have nothing to do with their marriage. Elizabeth Fry, for instance, would have been equally renowned had she remained Miss Gurney, and Elizabeth Barrett Browning's claim to fame does not rest upon the fact that she was Robert's wife.

Marriage, however, can of itself become a woman's life-work, and there is no career more exciting or exacting than marriage to a great man. Catherine Gladstone is a remarkable instance of a brilliant woman married to a brilliant man and finding in marriage the ideal outlet for her energy and talents. Her husband was one of the greatest men of the century and she herself possessed something of this quality of greatness. Her beauty, charm and originality made her an outstanding figure in any company; she was a little of a genius and rather more of a saint. In her own right she deserves remembrance, but she is chiefly important as affording a new means of approach to the somewhat baffling and distant figure of Gladstone himself.

ix

Considerable difficulties, however, beset the way of Catherine Gladstone's biographer. Her life was so much bound up with her husband's career that to write an orthodox biography would merely be to repeat the story which has already been told with such fullness and brilliance by Lord Morley and Sir Philip Magnus. The obvious answer to this problem would be to print a selection from her multitudinous letters. In practice, however, this has proved impossible because, interesting and witty though her letters may be, they are also extraordinarily inconsequent. Passages of personal or political interest are embedded in page after page of domestic detail, or lost in a maze of small talk about friends and relations whose very names are today forgotten. If her letters were to be made comprehensible to the general reader they would either have to be disfigured by a mass of bulky and trivial footnotes or subjected to such drastic excision as to leave very little of the originals remaining. It seemed best, therefore, to use the more interesting passages from the letters as a basis for a consecutive narrative.

The resulting story does not pretend to reveal any new facts; instead, it attempts to look at familiar facts from an unfamiliar angle. Through his wife's eyes we can see Gladstone as a person, not as a personage. Without Catherine, William Gladstone's life would have been comfortless and unhappy; without William, Catherine's life would have been emptied of its essential significance. This book is not an exhaustive biography of Catherine Gladstone, still less is it any sort of biography of her famous husband; rather, it seeks to describe the entity which these two remarkable people made out of their lives. It is, in fact, the portrait of a marriage.

FAMILY TREE

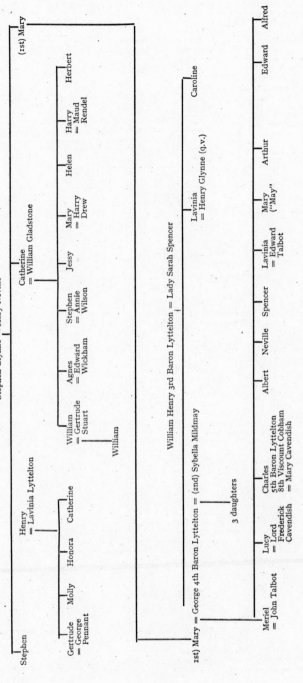

Chapter One

THE old castle of Hawarden stands sentinel where the foothills of the Welsh mountains roll down to the flat Cheshire plain. Lord Morley was to describe Catherine Glynne's husband, William Gladstone, as a Highlander in the custody of a Lowlander, and Catherine herself was the child of a similar alliance of Celt and Saxon. Today, standing on the ruined ramparts, it is possible to see on the horizon the dark smudge of smoke which hangs over Liverpool, distant only half-an-hour's journey by modern means of transport. A hundred and fifty years ago, when wild roses grew in the hedgerows of Bootle and Liverpool was a small clean harbour filled with white-sailed ships, the actual journey was longer and more difficult, whilst the spiritual distance between the two places was immense. Although they were born within twenty miles of each other there was no reason why young William Gladstone, living in a handsome brick house in Rodney Street, the typical home of a Liverpool merchant, should ever meet the little daughter of the great house standing in the shadow of ruined Hawarden Castle. A few years earlier any contact between them might have seemed surprising, but this was the nineteenth century, golden age of trade and commerce. The mercantile Gladstones were going up, the land-owning Glynnes were as certainly soon to go down, and inevitably one day their paths would cross.

Meanwhile the Glynnes and their kind were still on top of the wave, blissfully unconscious of the trough into which they were to be hurled. Money was plentiful and the Glynne house stood surrounded by well-kept grounds and resplendent in the glory of its newly-erected castellations. Some eight years before Catherine's birth a renovating architect had completely changed the outward appearance of the house, but he had had the good sense to leave the interior more or less untouched, and the fine new library which he had added harmonised surprisingly well with the eighteenth-century decorations of the original rooms. All these alterations and improvements had been planned by Sir Stephen Glynne to grace the home-coming of his bride, Mary Neville, daughter of Lord Braybrooke, but now, in 1816, another and sadly different home-coming was preparing. Young and handsome Sir Stephen was dead in foreign parts, where he had gone in a last hope of arresting the consumption which was killing him. As he lay dying in Nice, Napoleon escaped from Elba and the adventure of the Hundred Days began. The newly-widowed Lady Glynne found herself stranded in the south of France in company with six-year-old Stephen, now a baronet and master of Hawarden. Lord Braybrooke set out at once to rescue his daughter, only to find his coach stopped, his horses commandeered and he himself sent ignominiously home again. Meanwhile, Lady Glynne was making her own way back by a circuitous route through Genoa and Germany, and at last, in the summer of 1815, arrived in Essex at her own family home of Audley End.

The letters which passed between husband and wife—"What a good, kind Mary you are for writing to your Stephen!" one of them begins—make it clear that the Glynnes were a devoted couple. Now in her widowhood Lady Glynne found her chief comfort in devoting herself to her young family and for many years she kept careful records of health, education and character. She took particular pleasure in noting the growth and development of the three small children she had left behind at Audley End in the care of their grandfather and devoted aunts. Changes there were in plenty after her eight months' absence, but neither Henry, Catherine nor Mary presented her with such an interesting study as did young Stephen. She was pathetically anxious to see in this elder son a replica of his father but here she had to admit herself baffled. Stephen was clearly something of an original. He was a child who cared little or nothing for other people's opinion, "having taken a line of his own from two years old". Precociously clever, and possessed of an astonishing memory—"one evening he read through the list of the books in the Bible and the next morning knew perfectly and distinctly how many chapters each book contains"—he made not the slightest pretence of interesting himself in the outdoor games and occupations which delighted the other children, but instead remained "wholly engrossed in Botany, Conchology and Optics". Even at this early age Stephen stood, as it were, a little apart from life, a gentle, religious-minded child, capable of intense concentration when his interest was aroused but otherwise a little indolent and, inevitably, a little spoilt.

Next in age came four-year-old Henry, the exact opposite of his brother. Stephen was a handsome little boy but nobody could say more for Henry's appearance than that he had "a pleasant, honest countenance and will probably improve when his teeth appear". But plain though he may have been the glimpses we have of Henry show a most engaging small boy, proudly helping Mamma in the garden by trundling around a toy wheelbarrow containing real grown-up flower-pots, or playing at journeys, a favourite game with these much-travelled children, when he would walk solemnly round an imaginary coach, bending down at each imaginary corner to inspect an imaginary wheel. Again unlike Stephen, Henry took a very poor view of learning and letters—"his countenance glooms the moment his book is taken and the idea of spelling appears to shut up his faculties"—and although he had inherited his full share of the family talent for music he refused to sing because he did not regard singing as a manly occupation. To appear manly was the height of Henry's ambition and it was a great day for him when on his brother's seventh birthday he was allowed to shed his childish petticoats and appear in more masculine garb.

Stephen was openly bored by horses and carriages—it is as if a small boy of today should glory in his ignorance of cars and aeroplanes—but Henry delighted in such things and so did his sister Catherine. This child had neither Stephen's intellect nor Henry's equable temper, but even now, when little more than a baby, she was possessed of a brilliance and a buoyancy that were all her own. She was a superb physical specimen, with a mass of curling hair, and wide-apart, deep blue eyes; her mother described her as "one of the most thriving, magnificent children that can be seen, with a remarkably animated, pretty expression of countenance". "Pussy" was her nickname, and when she liked she could be gentle and caressing as a kitten, but she had a very strong will and on occasions she could fly into the most tremendous tantrums. "Pussy's passions" became proverbial in the Glynne nursery, but fortunately these outbreaks were rare. A tremendous tomboy and "perfectly fearless", she could even face a dentist with equanimity, unlike the small William Gladstone who later recorded that at the age of six or seven "I remember praying earnestly but it was for no higher object than to be spared the loss of a tooth". She was, however, a most feminine pussy-cat in her love of ribbons and finery, and her mother must have been sorely tempted to indulge her passion for dressing up, so bewitchingly pretty was the result. She was a very woman too with her beguiling wiles, so that her mother could note with amused severity that already Pussy was "a sad flirt". Lady Glynne had to admit that she herself found Pussy's charms very hard to resist—"As for Catherine, she is really quite beautiful, and her sweet childish manner and winning way with her eyes is quite bewitching. She talks more than Henry and is less shy, that is, I should think she never knows the sensation."

All the young Glynnes were devoted to one another and to their widowed mother, but Pussy's warm heart positively overflowed with demonstrative affection. Later on her loving spirit was to lavish itself especially upon her younger sister, Mary, but at present Mary was only a very delightful baby, rather more delicate than her robust brothers and sisters, and Pussy's devotion was chiefly given to her mother, "nothing's too *dood* for Mamma". Among her more distant relatives, and they were many, she was particularly attached to an elderly aunt whom she addressed as "Dear Chat". This lady was no less a person than Lady Chatham, daughter-in-law of the Great Commoner and sister-in-law to Pitt. Catherine Glynne was in fact a very well-connected young woman, unlike William Gladstone, whose father had served in the family corn store; she could count no less than five Prime Ministers of England among her forbears and her family tree included such famous names as Grenville, Wyndham, Cholmondeley, Neville, Vane, Stanhope and Stanley. Her mother traced her descent back to a companion-in-arms of William the Conqueror, whilst her father came of a still more ancient family supposedly descended from one of the Seven Kings of Wales.

This galaxy of relations played an important part in the lives of the Glynne children who spent more than half their time on visits to the homes of uncles, cousins or grandparents. On her return from Nice Lady Glynne lingered long at Audley End, perhaps dreading the return to Hawarden, a house overful of memories. In February 1816 the family at last set out for Hawarden. The return to the scene of her brief married happiness was made less dreary to Lady Glynne by the presence of her brother George Neville [1] at Hawarden Rectory. Uncle George's churchmanship would not have been approved by a later generation at Hawarden Castle; when offered the living by his brother-in-law he had written a grateful letter of acceptance, outlining his plans for the future, "once I can get through this bother of ordination".

The young man who took such a casual view of Holy Orders made an excellent parson, becoming in due time Master of Magdalene College, Cambridge, then Dean of Windsor. As Rector of Hawarden he at once set about the business of reforming his parishioners, who were indeed in sad need of reformation. "Hardeners" had an unenviable reputation for rowdyism and drunkenness. The village lay on the main road between Chester and Holyhead and the chief local excitement was the passing of the mail coach four times a day. The passage of Hawarden was a moment much dreaded by coachman and outside passengers, for the villagers would assemble outside the innumerable public-houses and pelt the coach with the most unsavoury objects that they could collect from the village middens. Parson George determined to put a stop to this and similar unruly practices and in all his efforts his strongest supporter was his sister.

Lady Glynne interested herself greatly in village affairs, spending hours at the Rectory discussing schemes for opening schools and poring over plans of churches to be built on outlying portions of Hawarden estate. Churches and schools were all very well, especially when attendance was rewarded with a substantial gift of clothes or coal of a Christmas, but the villagers were less pleased when they found many of their favourite inns closed, and discovered that in no inn at all could they get drunk of a Sunday. Protest, however, was useless; Squire's widow and parson formed

[1] In 1825 he assumed the surname of Neville-Grenville.

an omnipotent combination and Hardeners had sobriety forced upon them.

There was constant coming and going between Castle and Rectory, distant hardly a mile by the path which wound uphill past the ruined castle and along the edge of the Park to the great gates in Hawarden village. In 1816 Uncle George married Lady Charlotte Legge, and soon there were babies in the Rectory nursery to delight Pussy's maternal heart. In spite, however, of her liking for her brother, her interest in village affairs and her absorption in estate business, Lady Glynne could never bring herself to settle permanently at Hawarden. She would come for a brief three months or so, generally in the summer, when the children could be sent to the neighbouring resort of Hoylake to benefit from the fashionable tonic of sea-bathing. (A few miles away, across the Mersey, young William Gladstone was riding, racing, and generally running wild on the sands at Seaforth.) For the weak or cowardly there were warm sea-water baths but Lady Glynne mentions the delicate baby Mary as bathing in the sea itself during the chilly month of October. Pussy was always to be an intrepid and fanatical bather; when she was over sixty she still delighted in bathing before breakfast. The rest of the year would be spent staying in Lord Braybrooke's two houses, Audley End and Billingbeare, in the family house in London, or on a round of visits to relations at Escrick in Yorkshire, Butbury in Somerset, Vale Royal in Cheshire, and many another famous home.

In essentials the children's life went on much the same wherever they might happen to be. There would be lessons to be done, the multiplication table, some words of French and Italian, a little geography, and reading out of the little books by Mrs. Trimmer, *The History of the Robins* or *The Perambulations of a Mouse*, which were staple literary fare in the nurseries of the period. Out of doors, according to the season, there would be swings, snowhouses, games of "I spy", and, most delightful of all to Pussy, rides on an old horse whose manners presumably justified his curious name of "Polite". On Sundays there was church twice a day for the elder children. Church-going was a real pleasure to Stephen; the service appealed to his inborn sense of religion and the singing delighted his musical ear. In the early nineteenth century hymn-singing was hardly known in the Church of England

and Stephen had to be content with the somewhat dry musical fare of the metrical psalms—"he raves of the new and the old versions and is acquainted with the words and tunes of most of the psalms". At Audley End and at Billingbeare, as at Hawarden, the ladies of the great house were on the most friendly terms with their tenants, and often Pussy would accompany Mamma or Aunt Nooney on a visit to one of the cottagers. Far from living in splendid isolation the children grew up in close intimacy with their neighbours, feeling themselves to be part and parcel of the life of the countryside.

School-teaching was the most popular of good works with the fashionable ladies of the day and the Glynne children saw and heard a very great deal of the schools which were the especial concerns of their mother and aunts. With Stephen "the school is just now his great rage" and of course he must needs perform one of his prodigious feats of memory—"he knows most of the girls, one hundred and twenty-five in number, by name and knows their number and classes; yesterday he wrote out the register which he understood much more readily than the school-mistress". A charming letter from Aunt Neville to Stephen gives a little picture of Pussy's daily life and tells of a very early visit she paid to the village school:

"We are a little less lonely, having dear Pussy's company; she fell asleep upon Uncle Neville's lap just beyond the place where we left you and slept without intermission until we reached Broughton Hall, and there the young lady began to bump until she got home. She has been at *The Stool*, as she calls it, this morning and enjoyed very much watching the children dance the Mulberry dance—Pussy has been in the garden and planted some mignonette, her peas are very much grown, she has tied them up with a string and made the garden quite tidy. In the morning she said a very good French lesson, but we were puzzled for words, as we could not make out more than seventy this morning."

Clearly Aunt Neville was not altogether pleased with Pussy's linguistic attainments although a vocabulary of seventy words in a foreign language might be considered something of an achievement for a young lady of four or five years old.

7

This happy, healthy life would seem an ideal existence for children, but Lady Glynne was a little less than satisfied with its effect on her two young sons. It was perhaps inevitable that Stephen should become the king of the nursery, "where he continues to bully the maids and to name trumps upon every occasion". (In Lady Glynne's pungent metaphors it is possible to see the germ of that witty and esoteric private language known later as "Glynnese".) His lessons too were not progressing in the satisfactory manner that might have been expected; "he wants method, and to learn to learn". As for Henry, he was still the same endearing little boy, "remarkable for kindness of disposition though he is often naughty", observant of all that went on around him, and blessed with a keen sense of the ridiculous. But, alas, he made but slow progress with his books, and in 1817 Lady Glynne decided that there was nothing for it but to send him to school with Stephen. "It is full early at six years old," she noted, "but dear Henry is full able to take care of himself"—Henry was always to be more adequate than Stephen to the task of taking care of himself—"and at home had contracted so many idle habits, living out of doors or with his whip in his hand driving his cart in the hall". It seems hard that at the age of six Henry was not to be allowed to enjoy a few more months of idleness but in 1817 education was a business which even the youngest child must take seriously, and poor Henry was torn from whip and cart to be packed off to school at West Bromwich.

Pussy was now a great girl between five and six years old, growing, as Lady Glynne put it, "much more rational". Her pretty hair was all cut short and her beauty sadly diminished thereby which was no bad thing in the opinion of her Spartan mother, since Pussy had now the less temptation to vanity. A French governess had taught her to read and write French tolerably well. When in London she delighted in her lessons at the "accademy" of dancing, to use her own spelling, but above all else she loved music and riding. Although "comically ignorant of the notes" she could pick out simple tunes by ear, and she would sit quietly for hours together listening to anyone playing the piano. She was an admirable little horsewoman—"What a saucy Puss," exclaims her mother in one letter, "mounted upon Fairy!"

During her frequent absences from home Lady Glynne wrote

charming affectionate letters to the children and by the time she was six Pussy was old enough to write back in reply. Her earliest letter is to brother "Ste" who has just gone to school for the first time. It is an artless little letter that might have been written by any happy child, of any place or period, giving news of pet animals and the small but infinitely important happenings of nursery life. "Now for Cathy's letter", it begins in Lady Glynne's hand, "Cathy" herself being as yet too unskilled with her pen to attempt letter-writing. "My dear Ste, I hope you are very well. Nurse sends her best love. Baby says 'Good dear Ste best love'. Whittingham has lost four ferrets. Pray are there prayers at West Bromwich? I was very good at prayers this morning and Henry and I said the belief and Baby whispered a little. A great pheasant came to Hands' window to be fed. Dash was shot in the ear and is lame. Hands made him up a warm bed when he was shot. I am dear Ste your affectionate sister Catherine Glynne." Her earliest letter in her own handwriting is addressed to "Mamma" and in a covering note Lord Braybrooke justly praises it as "beautifully written". Alas, that in later life the exquisite copy-book hand should have degenerated into an all-but-illegible scrawl!

The Glynnes were a great family for letter-writing. Taken as a whole their letters are far more unstilted and spontaneous than most children's letters of the period and they are wholly free from that strain of conventional piety which runs through all the writings of the youthful William Gladstone. Some letters, of course, are clearly composed with a governess looking over the writer's shoulder, as when Pussy writes laboriously to Mamma "We really do not lose a moment of our time, Miss Williams says we are improved in our work", but when Mamma and not the governess is in charge, or when the letter is addressed to a school-boy brother, the tone is much more carefree. "Having told you all I know," Catherine ends one letter to Stephen, "I must conclude hoping that Fudge's low fits will keep off"—Fudge was a drawing-master—"and his big wig give him no further trouble". The letter finishes with a series of childish exclamations and "doodles" which would never have passed the eye of the vigilant Miss Williams.

As the boys grow older and move on to Eton their letters become more revealing of individual tastes and character. Henry

9

is chiefly concerned with everyday happenings and like the Fat Boy he enjoys making the readers' flesh creep with gruesome stories, such as a dreadful tale of poisoned pigs and stomach pumps. In one letter from Eton he mentions that Arthur Hallam, Gladstone's especial friend, "is Captain of m'tutor's house", and in another and later letter written to Stephen at Oxford, he refers to a visit which the family proposed paying him at Eton; "Miss Hawtrey hopes that you will not pay a shabby visit, as I do also. I wish you would persuade Mamma to bring the Pussies to Montem as they would enjoy it very much." Miss Hawtrey was sister to the Eton master to whom William Gladstone "first owed the reception of the spark, the *divinae particulam aurae*, and conceived a dim idea that in some time, manner and degree, I might come to know", and that Montem of 1826 was the ceremony which he described as "a day miserably wasted, the whole thing a most ingenious contrivance for making us appear as baboons". Unfortunately no letter tells us whether or not Pussy had a glimpse of William Gladstone baboonlike in his gay Montem costume.

Different as they were, the two brothers were devoted to one another, Stephen taking the greatest care of young Henry, helping him with lessons, and only occasionally "bursting out laughing at dear Henry's slowness which it must be owned is very great". Stephen himself had grown into a very good-looking boy with a curiously precise, almost priggish manner of speech. His appetite for knowledge was insatiable. Much of his time was spent sticking in cuttings and copying out extracts into a commonplace book— "his selections are very curious", wrote Lady Glynne—and on occasions he would compose little poems of his own, complete with notes. His letters to Catherine reflect his interest in churches and architecture, which was to become the ruling passion of his life. "Churches have been going very well," he writes, "but some occasional *dowdy* ones will sometimes appear." Brother and sister shared a passionate love of music, and especially the music of Handel. As quite a small child Pussy writes to Stephen, "I am trying to learn the Hallelujah Chorus for you but it is very difficult and you must not expect too much", and in a later letter Stephen asks, "Have you been applying much to Handel and Gardiner's Sacred Melodies lately? You cannot think how much I longed for you to hear the beautiful music in Exeter cathedral, especially that on Easter Day, when a great deal of the Messiah was sung." Stephen, however, could unbend when he wished, and the same letter ends in more frivolous vein, "My kind benedictions to Miss Mary Glynne."

That young lady, the "Missykins" of early letters, grew up so inseparable from her sister that the two were almost always referred to collectively as "the Pussies". In everything Catherine was the leader although the elder only by a year. At archery, a sport at which both girls excelled, it was Catherine who invariably made the best score, and when it came to riding it was Catherine who chose the more spirited mount, Mary's preference being for an animal with the suitably sedate name of Dowager. In fact Catherine, rather than either of her elder brothers, was the natural leader of the family, but neither Stephen nor Henry seems to have felt any jealousy on that score. They were both of them deeply devoted to her and she to them. The series of "The Gentleman's Pocketbook" in which Catherine somewhat inappropriately wrote her childhood diaries are full of such entries as "Merry with thought of dear brothers' coming" or "Dull without the dear boys".

She started keeping a diary in 1823, a few days after her eleventh birthday, and the series runs unbroken till 1831. The little books are not very revealing; like many another child diarist Catherine conceived that her task was to fill the space allotted to each day, no matter how, rather than to note down significant events. Whilst in London she records visits to the British Museum and to "the Panorama", also a visit to the theatre to see *Cymbeline*. At Brighton, where the Glynnes often stayed for the sake of sea air, the favourite sights were the Pier and the Pavilion, and "the French Giant". But more interesting are the entries which set imagination picturing the day-to-day life of two little girls a hundred and thirty years ago. "Danced in the evening, rode the hobby-horse", Catherine writes of a Christmas house-party, and, of more ordinary occasions, "We went to Chester, had our hair cut", "The Poor People came, Ste gave them clothes", "Dressed up as May chimney-sweeps", and, prettiest of all, "We sat under the lime-trees at our lessons", those lime-trees which still stand to shelter a later generation of children at Hawarden.

The pictures are lit with a curiously steady radiance; never, in letter or diary, is there a complaint, a quarrel, a cross or even an unhappy word. Catherine is a little sad because her mother has written twice to Mary with never a letter to her, and poor Henry returning to school, feels sadly "in ye dumps", but no greater shadows seem ever to cross the paths of these happy children. Sorrows, of course, come, but they are gentle and inevitable. "Poor grandfather died", so runs one entry in Catherine's diary, and a letter to Stephen gives an account of the old man's last illness, a quiet ending which could not frighten even the most sensitive child. "I am afraid that I cannot give you a better account of poor dear Grandpapa, who is worse", she writes, but she takes comfort in "the great treat" of dining late with Mamma and in Aunt Neville's gift of a pretty gold seal engraved with the name "Catherine". She is sad because "It is melancholy not to see dear Grandpapa and you cannot think how dull the house looks without him, it is seven weeks since he has ridden out", but she herself thoroughly enjoys her ride on Grandpapa's black "ponny".

As the children grow older and Stephen leaves Eton for Christ Church a faint, very faint cloud appears on the horizon, ominous of storms to come. Nature had played an unkind trick in fastening the headship of the family upon Stephen rather than upon his sister or brother. Stephen's gentle, scholarly temperament and deep religious sense would have fitted him exactly for the role of country parson for which Henry was destined, whilst Catherine's energy, common-sense and keen interest in everyone about her were the very qualities required of a great land-owner. Towards the end of his Eton career Lady Glynne began to feel that the time had come for Stephen to take some leading part in local affairs, and she wrote to urge him to take command of a Yeomanry troop. She was met by a blank refusal, and a year or two later he was equally unaccommodating over the question of the celebrations to be held to mark his coming-of-age. The letters which passed between mother and son show Stephen trying his hardest to wriggle out of the ordeal of presentations, parties and speeches, and Lady Glynne firmly holding him to his duty in these respects. On this occasion victory lay with Lady Glynne, and Stephen's twenty-first birthday was duly celebrated at the cost of £874. 17. 3½ with ale and feasting for the tenants and a great ball for the local gentry.

This last item had been the one to which the hero of the occasion had objected the most strongly, but sister Catherine would have been bitterly disappointed had it been omitted. From her earliest days she had delighted in parties and dancing, and by the time she is sixteen or so such entries as "another delightful ball" occur frequently in her diary. Lady Glynne had decided that once the birthday celebrations were over she would take the two Pussies to spend a winter in France, so to Paris Catherine duly went in the autumn of 1829. The journey marked the ending of childhood, for Paris was to the Pussies, as to so many other young English girls, at once an education in itself and a door leading to the gaieties and interests of adult life. Catherine enjoyed everything, from the very first day in Paris when she went shopping for a new velvet bonnet. She "lionised" the sights, she attended balls and operas, she had the honour of being presented to Charles X and the French Royal Family, and she took piano lessons from the great Abbé Liszt.

Back again in England the Pussies embarked on their first London season, a typical week in Catherine's diary recording a ball, a visit to the theatre to see Fanny Kemble, two operas, and an evening at Almacks. It is not surprising that it also records frequent headaches. Life at Hawarden was hardly less gay. The house would be filled with young people passing their days with "shooting matches" when Catherine was almost invariably the winner, and long horse-back expeditions, or of an evening fishing in the pool above the old mill with its curious inscription: "This Mill was Built 1767 by Sir John Glynne, Bart., Lord of the Manor, Charles Howard, Millwright. Wheat was this year 19/– the bushel and barley 5/– a bushel. Luxury was at a great height and charity extensive but the poor were starving, riotous and Hanged."

The poor were still starving and riotous. Generous landlords may have given oxen to be roasted whole on occasions such as Stephen's coming-of-age, but for many poor people meat was an almost unknown luxury. One Sunday morning Catherine was stopped on her way from church by an old woman who begged the pitiful dole of two rabbits in order to make a funeral feast after the burial of her only son, and when Catherine stayed at

Escrick in Yorkshire with her aunt Lady Wenlock her diary constantly recorded serious trouble with poachers. At home at Hawarden difficulties arose with the pitmen who worked in the coal pits which were the chief source of the Glynne fortune. In December 1830 a strike broke out which Henry described as "the sanguinary menace of the colliers"; mysterious fires occurred, and roving bands of strikers forcibly prevented workmen from turning "blackleg". Special constables "marched about everywhere, headed by respectable persons", and there was even talk of calling in the military. The roads were not considered safe for travelling and the Pussies had to abandon their proposed visit to Vale Royal. Catherine ended her diary for 1830 with the heartfelt wish, "How I hope our anxieties will end with the year!"

These distresses and disturbances were indicative of the new age of industrial revolution in which Catherine grew up. Other signs of the times were less unpleasant, the "steam-carriage", for instance, being a most amusing novelty. Catherine records that "Uncle George [Neville-Grenville] returned from the opening of the railroad when poor Mr. Huskisson was killed", the railroad being the Liverpool–Manchester railway which William Gladstone's father helped to finance. Steam was the fashionable topic of the day, and Catherine's especial friend, Harriet Brooke, wrote her an amusing account of railroad travel:

"On Tuesday we prevailed upon Papa to let us have an expedition to the Railroad and most excellent fun we had. We breakfasted early and got to Newton just in time to catch the Steam Carriage. I had no idea it was anything half so grand and we almost screamed with delight when first the Engine came in sight. I did not think the pace we went particularly fast going to Liverpool; they said it was about 15 miles an hour and they stopped so often to take in Passengers which was rather tiresome, but coming back it was quite delightful. We whizzed along quite to our hearts' content. We took luncheon with us which we ate upon an immense stone a little way out of Liverpool but could scarcely eat for laughing at the romantic spot we had chosen."

For the most part the letters which passed between the Pussies, or between the Pussies and their various girl friends, were not concerned with such matters as railroads but with the question as to whether a blue calico slip would look well under a muslin gown or whether feathers should be worn to a ball at Devonshire House, the type of problem which has always exercised the minds of fashionable young ladies. "Fashionable" in the worst sense of the term the Pussies were not nor ever could be, for Lady Glynne was a serious-minded woman who had brought up her children to take life seriously. When Stephen was at Oxford she wrote of her delight at hearing that "young men of fashion nowadays are expected to furnish their heads, and idleness and ignorance are not tolerated as formerly", adding how pleasant life would become if this were indeed so and "country houses will no longer be filled with sportsmen and dandies". After this outburst it is a little surprising to find her positively urging idleness upon her son and discouraging him from reading for honours—"Everybody says you will take a creditable degree so pray do not harass your mind so much". In the same year that Stephen took his "creditable degree", William Gladstone, his contemporary both at Eton and Christ Church, took a brilliant Double First.

Henry followed his brother to Christ Church, and there, in the summer of 1831, Catherine paid him a visit. Suddenly tiring of London gaiety she took it into her head to accompany Stephen to Hawarden for a fortnight of country peace and quiet, afterwards returning by Cheltenham and Oxford. Her departure left Mary desolate—"Naughty little Pussy, you would go!"—but Catherine thoroughly enjoyed the adventure of travelling through the night with Stephen in the briztska—and she even made a jest of finding herself "actually accomplish dressing without any assistance whatsoever". "My petticoat", she continues, "was the most difficult and very tiresome to tye but as for the stayes that was quite a joke." In reply Lady Glynne remarks, "A little roughing it without a maid makes one both handy and independent."

Catherine and Stephen's journey took place in the middle of the General Election of 1831 at the height of the Reform agitation. At Coventry they came in for the excitement of chairing the newly-elected member and Henry wrote a long letter from Oxford to urge them not to put off their visit because of disturbances due to the Election, adding, "You have no idea of the noise, racket and din which is going on at the minute, what with bands of music, shouts, drunken men etc." This was the Election in which William Gladstone made himself so conspicuous on the Tory side that ardent reformers pelted him with mud as he rode down the High. A friend of Gladstone's, Robert Phillimore by name, was sharing rooms with Henry, and to Henry's letter he added "an impertinent interpolation" begging Catherine on no account to put off her visit to "the happy pair in the untidy room" and ending with the plea, "*pray—do—come!*"

Other young men besides Robert Phillimore found Catherine's company most attractive—among others, a character known as "Kittums", son of Lord Skelmerdale, and an admirer who went into rhapsodies over her likeness—"I showed him your miniature, I thought he would never have done looking at it." Mary too had her swains and some of them were most persistent. Various letters of proposal still survive, together with drafts of answers written by her uncle and guardian, Lord Braybrooke, whose manner with undesirable suitors was more firm than polite. The family, however, were much perturbed when Mary persisted in refusing the eligible Lord Gairlie. To her plea that she could not and would not love the young man in question, her Aunt Neville replied with more sense than sensibility: "Women are not like men, they cannot chuse, nor is it creditable or lady-like to be what is called in love; I believe that few, very few, well-regulated minds ever have been and that romantic attachment is confined to novels and novel-readers, ye silly and numerous class of young persons ill-educated at home or brought up in boarding-schools."

This same aunt had rigid ideas on the subject of decorum; wishing success to a bazaar in which her nieces were interested, she adds the caution "I heartily hope that nothing may turn you and Mary into shopwomen. I declare I do not know which I should dislike most, to hear of your waltzing or your selling, those who practise the one would shine at the other." Some suitors found it difficult to make up their mind as to which of the two Pussies they preferred. "If only I had been there", wrote one of the Brooke sisters of such a young man, "I would have managed to find out by hook or by crook which of you it is."

Neither Pussy, however, was as yet to be persuaded into matrimony. The two sisters were devoted to one another and to their happy home at Hawarden. A letter from Mrs. Howard Stanley to

Mrs. Augustus Hare, aunt and adoptive mother of the diarist, gives a pleasant picture of their family life.

"We have all enjoyed our visit to Hawarden. You recollect the place perhaps, on the Conway road, eight miles from Chester. We have always longed to go into the grounds and up to the castle. It is a house of about eighty years old, castellated and very well done, no pretension inside to anything but comfort, a 'library', ante-room and billiard-room opening into one another, the library large and well filled with books. From the end window you see the old castle within gunshot, a pretty sloping lawn up to it and fine trees, the whole within the compass of one's [illegible] just the sort of place one would like to have. We arrived early, found Lady Glynne writing. After salutations were gone through I begged not to interrupt her, which she acceded to and so went on writing, leaving me at liberty to do the same, and she manages everything in this way so as to set everybody at their ease. We had the Stanleys of Hooton, Wilbrahams of Delamere Hall, Mr. Grosvenor, Sir Philip Egerton, and a young Mr. Frankland-Lewis and Charles Mytton. Wednesday was a beautiful day and Sir Thomas Stanley had ordered the hounds over. Miss Glynne mounted and habited Mary[Stanley], Owen rode Dragon, and away they all went. Mary says she never enjoyed anything so much, the park and country so pretty. The Miss Glynnes were so good-natured and took such care of her. They went out at eleven and came back at three, having found and hunted and had no disasters. Sir Stephen walked with Edward, very glad to escape the hunting party; he is something like Arthur in appearance, pretty, small, shy, kind, gentle-looking, only I do not think Arthur would ever speak so deliberately or so gravely. His study and pursuit is Antiquity and Cathedrals; there are only two in England that he has not seen, and that so thoroughly as to know all their details by heart. He has made a good collection of topographical works and seemed very happy to find anybody who cared about them and liked to be shown the fine prints. My friend, Rickman's *Architecture* lay upon the table interleaved with observations of his own. He never rides, or shoots, or dances, or likes any young man's pursuit, so that he keeps quite aloof in his own

17

home except just the going in to dinner. He seems aimiable and much respected and loved by his own people—'such a good young gentleman'. He reads prayers and a psalm and a chapter every morning to the family about half-an-hour before breakfast in the dining-room to which some of the guests come and some do not; he did not seem to be at all shy about that. Thursday was a wet day. Mr. Grosvenor took the command directly after breakfast, and kept the party going from one sort of fun to the other the whole day, round games of billiards, all sorts of games of cross-questions, singing and at last dancing. The topographical baronet sat immoveable in one armchair, the geological baronet [Sir Philip] in another. I made myself useful playing quadrilles, galloppes, and they all got a ride in the middle of the day in the rain, which was also quite charming. The Miss Glynnes are just as nice as they look, such sweet manners, and an air of ingenuous youthfulness that is quite refreshing—and so Mr. Grosvenor thought, I guess."

This letter would have caused considerable horror to Aunt Neville who disapproved strongly of young ladies going out hunting. "I hope you will *never* allow your daughters to 'meet ye hounds'," she had written to Lady Glynne. "It would indeed grieve me most sadly to hear that they joined in such practices . . . it lowers women in ye eyes of all and renders them what I am sorry to know many young ladies are—cheap."

Among the visitors to Hawarden at this time was the young Princess Victoria, who stopped there for an hour or so to make a break in a long journey. Years later Catherine could remember vividly all the details of the Princess's visit, and could show exactly where the Royal carriage had stopped and how the terrace had been arranged for the great occasion.

In 1834 Lady Glynne suffered a slight stroke, which left her bodily powers impaired and her mind clouded with melancholy. Her brain remained quite clear, and some of her letters show a tragic awareness of her own condition of mind. Her mother's illness made Catherine the effectual if not the nominal head of the family; her brothers and sisters revolved round her "like planets round a sun", and Uncle Braybrooke was moved to remonstrate with her for setting herself too obviously against Stephen's wishes.

So the years went by, busy, happy, each one much like the last until at length Pussy fell in love. Nothing now remains of this century-old romance but the name of the man, Colonel Francis Harcourt, and the fact that he jilted Catherine for Lady Charlotte Jenkinson. The general opinion seems to have been that Lady Charlotte was much to blame, and Catherine must have smiled ruefully to think that the respectable and strait-laced Aunt Neville had strongly urged her nieces to cultivate that lady's acquaintance. "I am pleased to think you have heard from the Lady Jenkinsons," she had written approvingly, "I like you to have friends who are not missy or pushing and I think Lord Liverpool has taken great pains in educating his daughters."

That it went deep with Catherine is clear from a letter written by her especial friend, Harriet Brooke, who was then in the full tide of joy at her own engagement to Lord Brabazon. (Harriet was nicknamed "Fuchsia" and this letter ends with the shame-faced remark "Don't laugh; he always wears a fuchsia in his button-hole!") "My own Pussy, How I do think of her! The marriage is, I believe, quite generally known. Can such a match be productive of any real happiness? Must there not be mutual mistrust now and mutual recrimination hereafter? Thank God our dearest Pussy has been spared such a fate, reserved, we may dare to trust and believe, for one more worthy of such perfection, more worthy of appreciating the treasures of her heart." The blow had indeed been severe and one not easily to be forgotten.

Years later, when Catherine was the supremely happy wife of a man infinitely more talented and famous than Colonel Harcourt, she was invited with her husband to pay a visit to the Harcourt family home at Nuneham Courtenay, and wrote in agitation to Mary that the bare idea of a possible encounter with her one-time suitor seemed to her "a nightmare". Meanwhile she remained unconsoled, and Harriet, now happily married, wrote again to comfort her.

"As surely as there is a God in Heaven so surely do I feel that sooner or later he will reward you for all you have gone through so unrepiningly. There are blessings yet in store for one who has the blessings of so many on her head. I shall live to hear you one day say you are thankful to have escaped the lot you once carved out for yourself. Why, even now, my own Pussy, if the love of every creature who knows you can bring satisfaction you are more to be envied than any person I know! and though you have as yet been denied the love of *one* that you can live for and love again, it will yet come, and the feeling that all men are not sincere will make you more eager to return the one true love when it does come."

Catherine could do nothing but turn as brave a face as possible to the world, whilst her many friends waited hopefully for the fulfilment of Harriet's prophecy.

Chapter Two

THE marriage of Catherine's faithless suitor took place in 1837 and in September of that year the two Pussies set out with brother Henry on a tour of the great houses of Scotland. Travel is an age-old specific for broken hearts and it may be that the desire to distract Catherine from thoughts of her unhappy love-affair had something to do with Lady Glynne's proposal to undertake a more extended journey and to spend the next winter travelling on the Continent. The party, which consisted of Lady Glynne, Stephen, Catherine, Mary, two maids and two couriers, left England at the end of August 1838, travelling by way of Antwerp down the Rhine towards Germany and Switzerland. At Ems, whether by chance or design, they fell in with a young man, by name William Gladstone. Catherine had already made his acquaintance at London dinner parties and in 1835 he had stayed at Hawarden as Stephen's guest. Handsome, clever and industrious, he was making such a name for himself in the House of Commons, where he sat as Tory member for Newark, that gossip at the *table d'hôte* in the Ems hotel had it that he would one day be Prime Minister.

William Gladstone was nevertheless rather an unhappy young man at heart. Underneath his Scottish reserve lay the temperament of the born orator, emotional, responsive, highly-strung, and although he had his own nature well under control he had not yet acquired that self-mastery which in later years was to enable him "to dismiss all but the great central aim, to put aside what is weakening and disturbing". However, so little did Catherine realise of the fires burning below the surface that she wrote him down as being somewhat too "matter-of-fact".

William Gladstone had enough work to absorb the energies of

any ordinary man with his parliamentary business, which he took very seriously, and with his membership of various religious societies and committees—he had recently forsaken the evangelicalism of his youth to become an ardent High Churchman— but to all this he must needs add a programme of study which would not disgrace a University professor, and cap it with the writing of an abstruse and closely argued book entitled *The State in its Relations with the Church*. Added to this burden of work was the weight of personal trouble. Like Catherine, William had recently been disappointed in love, not once but twice. The speed with which he transferred his affections from one lady to the other might be thought to prove him fickle and frivolous. In fact, it was a symptom of his need for female companionship and his craving for the security of wedded love. The sister to whom he had been specially devoted had died in her early youth, he had recently lost his dearly-loved mother, and his one remaining sister was an eccentric nervous invalid.

His father, John Gladstone, loved William with a warm affection which the son was quick to return, but this ambitious self-made business man, wise and benevolent though he might be, was not the best company for a young man who needed to be soothed rather than stimulated. In the circumstances it was not surprising that he should have found himself suffering physically from a threatened breakdown of his eyesight and mentally from a series of black fits of depression. The doctors had ordered a complete rest from reading or writing, and suggested foreign travel.

So here was William Gladstone, in attendance on his eccentric sister, delighted to find himself once more in company with congenial friends, and especially in company with a young and attractive woman. A bust now at Hawarden gives the best idea of Catherine as William saw her that autumn day at Ems. It is odd that cold marble should give the impression of glowing life that the painters so conspicuously fail to capture. The best of the portraits shows her wearing a classic wreath of ivyleaves which suits well with the clear lines of her features and the loveliness of her wide-apart eyes, but no picture can give the soft contours of throat and cheek or the warmth of her finely-modelled mouth, the lips always a little parted as if in the ghost of a smile.

Catherine Glynne, Rome, 1839. From a bust by Laurence
Macdonald now in the possession of Mr. C. A. Gladstone at
Hawarden Castle. Photograph by J. Burge, Birkenhead

Catherine was now twenty-six, only a year younger than that Anne Elliot whom Jane Austen relegated as a matter of course to the ranks of the faded and middle-aged; she was no longer a young girl but a woman, who had known something of responsibility, something too of the heartbreak of love, but nothing at all as yet of the discipline of submission to the will of another. She was a better man than Stephen, a more energetic one than the indolent Henry, her mother was a semi-invalid, her sister her devoted shadow. Though she was neither wilful nor disobedient, in her little world it had always fallen to her to give orders and to make plans. William Gladstone too had been the darling of his family circle, the favoured child of fortune. What would happen when these two young people, both of them handsome, gifted and strong-willed beyond the ordinary, chanced to take serious notice of one another? One thing, of course, was self-evident; William Gladstone would fall in love.

Catherine's reaction was not so certain. She recorded the meeting with William Gladstone in the journal of her travels, contenting herself with remarking that she had been "much struck by his pretty attentions to Miss Gladstone who is an invalid". The Glynnes spent only one night at Ems before setting out again for Naples by way of Switzerland, the Italian lakes, Bologna, Florence and Rome. A week or so later William set out alone on a similar tour, but a less enjoyable one. Unable to read or write, unable even to study pictures with any concentration for fear of damaging his eyesight, he wandered solitary, bored with hotel life, bored with his own company until at last he betook himself to Sicily and then came back to settle in Naples. There the Glynnes found him when they arrived on November 13th to take rooms in the same hotel.

The next act of Catherine's love story was played out against the romantic background of the Bay of Naples. Her diary is full of such remarks as "Mr. Gladstone dined with us, a very agreeable evening", "shopped in spite of a tremendous storm of rain with Stephen and Mr. Gladstone", "to the church of San Ferdinando with Mr. Gladstone and heard a most extraordinary sermon". Listening to sermons was one of William's favourite forms of relaxation. Serious-minded he certainly was, although he was no longer quite the stern young puritan of his evangelical days. On

Good Friday of this very year, 1838, he had relented sufficiently to draw up a table of thirty-nine good reasons, for the most part as obscure as the Thirty-Nine Articles, showing why a religious young man might be permitted to attend balls and dances. Article Nine was calculated to find an echo in many a masculine heart: "Some of us might add, and that not from superior spirituality, that to them these are not pleasures but upon the whole a burden." The young man who found balls so burdensome had not yet fallen in love with Miss Catherine Glynne to whom dancing was sheer delight.

Catherine does not mention whether or not William Gladstone was among her partners at a grand ball which she attended on November 26th, but she records that he accompanied the Glynne party on various excursions, including an ascent of Vesuvius and a visit to the museum. He came to dinner and entertained them with an account of his recent encounter with the Italian poet Manzoni, who had said to him on parting, "You must allow me to pray for your conversion"; he dined or drank tea with them nearly every day, and he was on such familiar terms that the Glynnes gave him the playful Italian nickname of "Già". On December 11th the Glynne party left Naples for Rome, and Catherine wrote that "we turned our backs on Naples with feelings of regret, retracing in my mind the many pleasant days we had passed there". The majority of those pleasant days had been passed in company with William Gladstone.

Their separation was to be of the most temporary nature for Gladstone had also left Naples for Rome and the day after her arrival in that city Catherine's diary records the fact that "Mr. Gladstone called". The next day they all went to church together in quest of an Italian sermon, but Catherine discovered to her discomfiture that no women were allowed to remain in church after the saying of the *Ave Maria*—"I was compelled after all my pains to walk out, half ashamed at finding myself doing an unusual thing, half angry at my disappointment." Catherine rejoiced to find that Harriet Brabazon was also staying in Rome and William Gladstone was glad to encounter his Oxford friend, Henry Manning. Together Gladstone and Manning listened to innumerable sermons, together they called on Wiseman, as head of the English Roman Catholic community, little thinking that Manning would one day be Wiseman's successor, together they visited Richmond's studio in search of a picture and returned empty-handed, William's financial prudence triumphing over his artistic sense. Manning was now a Rural Dean, but William evidently did not consider that his behaviour was always sufficiently ruridecanal, for one Sunday he found occasion to reprove his friend for breaking the Sabbath by buying a pound of apples.

A prude and a prig? Perhaps; but the remedy was close at hand. Catherine was to bring out a side of this young man's character which was unsuspected by his friends, she was to discover a William Gladstone who was not afraid to laugh at himself, a person equipped with a sense of the ridiculous and an appetite for the small and simple gaieties of life. For all her commanding presence, her almost classic beauty, there was nothing either static or statuesque about Catherine; a relative, asked for recollections of her, replied immediately, "she always twinkled". The earnest young Scotchman, William Gladstone, wandering through Rome in company with rural deans and Cardinals, could never be said to twinkle. The idea verges on the blasphemous. Yet this twinkling pussy, this untidy, unmethodical, entrancing creature was the woman who finally won his heart and held it until the end. She was to help him to relax, to teach him some of her own gaiety; in a word, she was to make him human.

During the months spent in Rome William's name appears nearly every day in Catherine's diary but unfortunately it appears wholly devoid of comment. She remarks, "We live completely in one small circle, Brabazons, Ellisons, Mr. Gladstone and Mr. Boothby", a circle to which Manning was soon admitted on Gladstone's introduction, but for any indication that she may give it would seem just as likely that her preference was for Mr. Boothby, who presented her with a copy of *Corinne*, a book to which she declared herself *"devoted"*.

Gladstone often acted as guide on the expeditions which the Glynne family described as "church-hunting", and in the course of their visits to the various Roman churches he would sometimes find opportunity for a few words alone with his Catherine. Recording a visit to a New Year's Eve service in the Gesú, she notes "an interesting talk with Mr. Gladstone whilst sitting waiting for the *Te Deum* to commence". He was coming to know her better and to realise that under all the gaiety and sparkle lay a heart whose sympathies were wide as the world and a soul which shared his own innermost convictions. One day, whilst admiring the gilded splendours of Santa Maria Maggiore, the two young people fell to contrasting the small sums given to the cause of religion with the amount habitually spent on personal luxury. No woman had less to reproach herself with on that score than had Catherine. All her life long her impatient refusal to spend more than the smallest fragment of her time or money on dress and adornment made her the despair of long-suffering but devoted ladies' maids, and if her purse was always empty it was not because she was extravagant but because she could never resist any appeal to her charity. Nevertheless, the question of wealth troubled her, as it has troubled many a young creature born to a position of ease and comfort ever since the days of the Rich Young Man of the Gospel story, and she turned to William Gladstone with the anxious query, "Do you think that we can possibly be justified in indulging ourselves in so much luxury?" "I loved her for that question", he wrote that night in his diary.

Love her he certainly did, but she was not at all sure that she loved him in return. In spite of its romantic setting in the moonlit Colosseum his first attempt at a proposal was a fiasco; she could not or would not listen to what he had to say and he for all his reputation for eloquence was tongue-tied and bashful as a schoolboy. He waited a fortnight, meanwhile seeing Catherine nearly every day, and then decided to write a letter, but his pen was scarcely more explicit than his tongue. The letter he produced lamentably failed to fulfil his declared intention of expressing himself "in the simple words which I believe in any event will be most acceptable to you", but out of the welter of qualifying and conditional clauses one sentence emerged, clear, brief and unequivocal, "My heart and my hand are at your disposal."

Catherine's reply was temporising. It began with the slightly disingenuous statement, "Your letter has so completely taken me by surprise." A young woman, well practised in the ways of suitors, must have guessed what was passing in Gladstone's mind, more especially after that abortive proposal in the Colosseum. However, she was gracious enough to propose a meeting— "Should it be any satisfaction to you to see me we shall be at the

Porta Maggiore soon after twelve." This visit to the Porta Maggiore had as its ostensible purpose the inspection of a newly discovered tomb, where Catherine's diary records that "the bas-reliefs are in good preservation, they depict the ——" What they may have depicted is left significantly blank. Catherine's mind was on other things than bas-reliefs and when William left next day for England he went with a heart not altogether devoid of hope.

From Marseilles William wrote another one of his long and involved love-letters. Apparently Catherine had suggested that they should continue to meet each other without any commitment on her side and she had also asked his leave to confide in Harriet Brabazon:

"Dear Miss Glynne, Do not be afraid that this is the commencement of a series of intrusions; the limits of my rights are too close to allow any such temptation to prevail. At least I persuade myself that my object is simply to state with clearness one or two points which on Friday last I may have left more or less obscure, as one is often incapable of making use of a small interview just in proportion to the sense entertained of its value. First, I am not sure whether you understood me fully about Lady Brabazon; that is to say, not as giving a qualified or reluctant, but a hearty consent—to what indeed was fully within your own sole discretion, had your delicacy allowed you to use it. My meaning was this; that I thought any declaration from myself upon the point superfluous because it seemed as if implying a disposition to interfere with your free will in a matter where I was entirely sure that it would be its own best and safest rule.

"I asked you also not to do yourself injustice by considering the pain which it might hereafter be your duty to inflict, as injury. The truth here as elsewhere is delicate and easily missed on this side or on that; but true it is, and I would say fearlessly that you may feel it, you are already my benefactress and I am your debtor for pure and delightful recollections, for an elevating intercourse in a period which has the freshness of childhood renewed, and for a hope which, though it be slender, is dearer to me beyond all comparison than any other earthly object, if indeed I do not do it injustice by placing it in that class, for it

27

has a higher aspect (you may guess at my meaning if you take the trouble to look at a beautiful sonnet of Michael Angelo's near the commencement of his volume to which I give you no other guide) and which renders me happy at this moment of return to the place of cares, happy indeed by comparison with what I might have been. And if your generous indulgence were finally to fail of effect, I would myself beseech you not to reproach the act with having done me injury, knowing well by experience that the sharpest events of my life have been the least injurious, though with others of a better mould it need not perhaps be thus. In the meantime be assured that so far from having to question your own proposal on the charge of selfishness, you are conferring upon me a daily blessing of no common value.

"May I add one word more, and answer in more formal terms the question of the Corsini? I have only to answer in the name of a man; and to adapt the reply to the query as it was put, must be added so much more of time, difficulty, and suffering, as is the difference between *him* and *her* in the depth of the spirit of affection. For a man my answer is that I do not believe that transfer can really be accomplished without considerable interval and sharp and piercing pain; or that even thus it can be many times repeated. Farewell, and may God bless you; and if I close in the terms which alone are at my choice, pray interpret them not in their common and exhausted sense but in their real significance and so believe me, your most truly, W. E. G."

To this letter Catherine replied with a message sent through Henry, who had travelled home with William Gladstone. "I appreciate very much the generous feelings which are expressed in his letter to me", she writes to her brother. "I cannot take Michael Angelo's beautiful sonnet to myself, but the sentiments contained in it are so lofty it was impossible not to read it without the greatest delight. Please read this yourself to Già, as I particularly want the message to be given exactly"; then, in a postscript, "Tell me how you get through my message to Già and any rebound*; nothing could express more honourable feelings and taste than the letter he wrote me."

* Wherever an asterisk occurs, see Extracts from *Glynnese Glossary*, pages 231–3.

Arrived home Gladstone found that his book on State and Church, which he had left in proof form only, had been published some weeks before his arrival and had met with a very mixed reception. He was naturally anxious to learn what might be the opinion of his political leaders about his work. "Not a word from Peel, Stanley or Graham yet," he wrote anxiously, "even to acknowledge my poor book." The perturbed author would have been still more agitated had he known what in fact had been Peel's reaction; that good but undogmatic Christian threw the book on the floor with the exasperated query, "With such a career before him why should he want to write books?"

There was one person whose opinion mattered to Gladstone even more than did Peel's, and her verdict was not for a moment in doubt. Until the spring should bring them both together again in England Catherine beguiled her time by reading William's book, copying out her favourite passages and even endeavouring to learn some of them by heart. Many years later her daughter Mary was to cite this to prove that in her youth Catherine was something of an intellectual, although when she grew older she was seldom seen to read either a book or a newspaper, but in hard fact her absorption in the learned pages of *The State in its Relations with the Church* must be put to the credit of her heart rather than of her head. A woman in love will read anything, however dry, if it is recommended to her by the man of her choice, and she will read it the more eagerly if it is written by that very man. It must be admitted that Gladstone's book is dry indeed. In spite of its virtues, and they are more than is generally supposed, *The State in its Relations with the Church* suffers from one fatal and fundamental defect; it is unreadable.

In his authoritative analysis of the book [1] Canon Vidler makes mock of Macaulay's remark that "a book which is not readable wants the highest of all recommendations", but even Canon Vidler admits that Gladstone's treatise "cannot be said to be exciting on the surface", and a woman would have to be very much in love with the author before she could find excitement anywhere in it, however deeply she might plunge into its rather turgid profundities. All this talk of truth and toleration, of establishment and government, might have been of interest to Stephen Glynne when

[1] *The Orb and the Cross*, by A. R. Vidler.

suffering from one of his frequent attacks of "the Churchums",* but of itself it was not calculated to appeal to the very different tastes of his sister Catherine. Her sudden interest in the question of Church Establishment is clear proof that "Già" was in fact very much nearer to her heart than she was at present prepared to admit.

In April the Glynnes returned to England and established themselves in London, where William and Catherine were soon meeting as frequently as ever they had done in Rome. He dined with her family at their pleasant house in Berkeley Square, he danced with her at balls, he squired both Pussies out riding in the Row, and soon the position became so clear to interested onlookers that Stephen Glynne wrote to enquire as to William's intentions and prospects: "It is impossible for me to see the interest you take in my sister's society without feeling deep anxiety as to the result of your attachment. . . . There is no one to whom I would so gladly entrust my sister as to you, feeling convinced that there is no one who would be so worthy of such a prize." However, William himself remained despondent—"What I ask for is next to an impossibility." Catherine was still haunted by the ghost of former love and she exclaimed to William that she had but half a heart to give him. "Give that to me", he answered, "and I will give you back a whole one."

Private anxieties were interspersed with political alarums and excursions. Early in May the Whigs resigned, and Gladstone looked for a place in the new Tory administration, but Peel found himself thwarted by the famous and foolish "Ladies of the Bedchamber" crisis, and by May 10th Melbourne was back in the saddle. The cares of office were not to distract William Gladstone from the cares of love. On June 8th he accompanied his Catherine to a garden-party at Fulham, where he found occasion to lead her away from the crowd to a quiet path beside the Thames. Two days later, answering an invitation from Samuel Rogers, he wrote to excuse himself: "A deranging incident has occurred. I am engaged to be married."

As they walked together by the river William had explained to Catherine that his real desire had been to take Holy Orders rather than to enter politics, and in telling her this he had put into her hand the key to the complexities of his life and character. Though he had subordinated his desire for ordination to the declared wish of his father, who was perspicacious enough to see where his son's real talent lay, he still considered himself a dedicated person, vowed to the service of the Church, and as a dedicated person he was to live all his long life. Catherine's religious opinions were much less clear-cut; she had experienced neither his strict Evangelical upbringing nor his conversion to Tractarianism, and moreover, where religion was concerned she was always to be extremely reticent. Yet essentially she was, as Gladstone described Arthur Hallam, *"Anima naturaliter Christiana"*, a soul turned instinctively towards God. To her it did not seem strange or incongruous that her lover should talk of such matters in their first moments of mutual happiness, nor that he should choose for her, who was already a lover of Dante, a motto which was to sound the keynote for their married life—*"In la Sua voluntate e nostra pace."*

This "deranging incident" of an engagement gave great pleasure to both families concerned. The Gladstones could have had no possible objection to the match but the fact that the Glynnes approved so enthusiastically is clear evidence of the position which William had already made for himself and the opinion generally held as to his future prospects. Had it not been for his exceptional personality and the brilliant future which so clearly lay before him, Catherine's family might have expected her to find herself a more aristocratic husband than the son of a Liverpool merchant. Even money was lacking to gild Wililam's birth; his father was indeed a very wealthy man but a fourth son had no great expectations and could never hope to find himself rich according to the lavish standards of the age. Years later, when financial stress made necessary the sale of their London house, he remarked to Catherine that their £5000 a year made but poor showing against the £25,000 or so enjoyed by all the other inhabitants of Carlton House Terrace.

Nevertheless, Catherine's friends and relations welcomed William with open arms. Her formidable great-uncle, Thomas Grenville, wrote, "I am very fond of the nephew you are giving me", and described himself as "exulting in a marriage so promising of all that I could wish for you", whilst Harriet Brabazon sent somewhat pointed congratulations on this marriage with a methodical man who would see to it that Catherine answered her letters. Over this matter, however, all William's efforts were doomed to failure;

31

if Catherine did in fact write an answer she seldom went so far as to post it. Instead, she would throw it on the floor in the confident hope that someone else would pick it up, frank or stamp it, and send it on its way.

One tiny incident which has to do with this same uncle, Thomas Grenville, is worth recording for the light it throws upon the characters of both William and Catherine. She was rightly anxious that they should pay a call on this influential relative as soon as possible after their engagement had been announced, and he. doubtless for some equally good reason, wished this visit to be postponed. Catherine wrote a letter, charming, devoted, but taking for granted that she had but to state her view and William would immediately fall in with her wishes. (All Catherine's requests were written in that form which the Latin Grammar describes as "expecting the answer Yes".) "Let me come and spend one or two quiet hours with you from twelve to two and then leave you to think," she wrote. "I would ride later with you also if possible which would *unaddle* * my poor dear's head. In fact, let me do anything you like. . . . You would not lightly pass over or disregard the feelings of her whose only prayer is that she may add to the happiness both here and hereafter of him to whom she had given her whole heart." When this letter failed of its effect she wrote again, once, twice, and then the correspondence ceased and the visit to Uncle Thomas was postponed as William had wished it to be. From that moment there never seems to have been any doubt as to which of these two strong-willed young creatures should be the master; in fact, the imperious Catherine was not so very wrong when in her love-letters to William she addressed him as the oak tree and referred to herself as the clinging ivy.

The only person who could possibly regret Catherine's impending marriage was Mary Glynne, who would find herself bereft of her lifelong companion. The Pussies had always acted as one, so that nobody was surprised when, nine days after Catherine announced her engagement to William Gladstone, Mary announced her own engagement to William's friend, Lord Lyttelton. The marriage of a sister-in-law is seldom a matter of great moment in a man's life, but the Lyttelton alliance was to be of vital importance to Gladstone both personally and politically, whilst Catherine's relation to Mary's new family was to be something far more affectionate and intimate than her connection with the Gladstone "in-laws". Already, by his marriage to Catherine, William was allying himself with the political clan which centred on the Wyndham and Grenville families, and now through George Lyttelton, whose mother had been Lady Sarah Spencer, he found himself connected with a second and still more influential group of Whig families, Ponsonbys, Lambs, Spencers, Leveson-Gowers, all of them related to the great house of Cavendish. A generation back the bearers of these names had formed an exclusive and all-powerful oligarchy and although by Gladstone's day they had fallen somewhat from this high position, they were still of great importance in the councils of the nation. The fact that he was related by marriage to "the Grand Whiggery" smoothed Gladstone's political path and opened doors which might otherwise have remained closed to the son of a self-made man.

George Lyttelton was only twenty-one, four years younger than his intended bride. In spite of his brilliant scholarship he was in many ways still a boy and boyish he was to remain until aged and saddened by the tragedy of Mary's early death. He sprang from a family that has become celebrated for wit, for intellect, and for a certain saintly eccentricity.

The Lytteltons differed profoundly from the Grand Whiggery with whom they were so closely allied. Essentially they were respectable, caring little for fashion and a very great deal for religion and morals. But conventional they were not nor ever could be. They did not defy conventions, they merely failed to notice that conventions existed, being at once infinitely more simple and more sophisticated than the aristocrats and country gentry who were their neighbours and associates. Their simplicity was the simplicity of the saints; it is easy to sum up the dominant characteristics of this remarkable family in one short adjective—the Lytteltons were good. But, unlike some good people, they were also clever; they observed men and events with a somewhat quizzical gaze and their comments were both pungent and devastating. So intense was their family feeling that unkind outsiders sometimes spoke of them as a mutual admiration society, which was not altogether surprising since they could find so much to admire in one another. The Lyttelton wit was acute, their holiness undoubted, their charm all but irresistible.

Yet, in spite of all this brilliance their attitude towards life was slightly casual; unlike the industrious Scotchman, William Gladstone, the Lytteltons were incurable amateurs. William was a serious-minded genius, in great danger of becoming pompous. Although the Lytteltons believed in taking serious matters very seriously, pompous they never were. They provided exactly the right foil to his earnest spirit; he could share their deep interest in religion, in literature, in all things "of good repute", and they could teach him how to laugh. At first some of the family found him slightly pedantic, not to say "pernicketty"; Sarah, Lady Lyttelton, writing of some small domestic problem, remarked, "The case seems to me to lie in a nutshell or cherry-stone, and the doubt remaining, to afford fresh proof to me of Mr. Gladstone being less practically sensible than profoundly clever," but she soon learnt to value him more correctly. "I had five minutes of Mr. Gladstone's quite unique conversation," she wrote a year or two later; "living with him ought to make anyone wise and good." And when crisis came upon the family it was the "profoundly clever" William Gladstone who proved to be the most "practically sensible" one of them all.

The Pussies were to share a wedding as they had shared almost everything else in life. A few weeks before the double ceremony was due to take place Catherine went down to Leamington with her mother, perhaps for reasons of health, since she refers to herself in her letters to William as "your poor thin thing". As all lovers must, they found even temporary separation a hardship. "You may fancy me sitting at an open window," wrote Catherine, "inhaling the pure country breeze, but somehow there is something wanting. I no longer look round eagerly when the door opens for it cannot bring you to me." Some days before the wedding the two bridegrooms went down to stay at Hawarden. William Gladstone was a singularly handsome man whilst George Lyttelton's unkempt appearance belied his aristocratic birth, so that the Hardeners would nod their heads towards William with the comment, "It is easy to see which of them is the lord."

On the morning of July 25th the whole place was in a pleasant uproar. Bells pealed, cannon boomed, bands blared as the long bridal procession made its way to Hawarden church. In the rear came a pony carriage containing the butler and housekeeper, that same Mr. Whittingham and Mrs. Hands who had cared for the pheasants and ferrets that so delighted the five-year-old Pussy. The sister brides, dressed alike in white satin, were escorted by brides-maids in "mulled muslin trimmed with peach-coloured blonde". The local paper described the church as "crammed to suffocation with females" and inevitably many tears were shed. Like all happy weddings, this one was grave and gay, sad and delightful, all at the same time, and touched in the middle of all the laughter and jollification "with the spirit of the great mystery of Christian mar-riage", to use Gladstone's own phrase. He wrote those words in his diary the day after the wedding as he looked back on all the emotion and excitement, and a few days later he added a phrase descriptive of Catherine, "the brightness of my treasure, her pure, enduring brightness". That brightness was to shine on him un-dimmed for nearly sixty years.

Chapter Three

So they were married; and now came the far more difficult business of living happily ever after. Catherine and William were so much at one in fundamental matters that the success of their marriage could never for a moment be in doubt, but on the surface there were inevitably small difficulties and differences demanding time and patience for their adjustment. Even the golden days of the honeymoon were productive of slight shocks. As a beautiful and much-courted girl Catherine had always taken for granted that other people, especially other people of the male sex, would always be only too glad to entertain and amuse her in idle moments. Now, however, she was to discover that William was not the man to waste any particle of his time, however small. At any enforced wait, on a railway platform for instance or by the roadside, out of his pocket would come the inevitable little volume of Greek or Latin and the young wife would be left to her own thoughts. On comparing notes with Mary, Catherine discovered that George Lyttelton was also addicted to this tiresome habit; he had even been seen to glance at Homer between the overs of a cricket match, and if cricket, which was to all Lytteltons the really serious stuff of life, could not hold George from his books there was no hope that a mere wife would prove more beguiling.

William too must have had his moments of discomfiture when he discovered how supremely unmethodical and untidy was the woman he had married. Even the period of their engagement had been productive of trouble in this respect when he had found private letters left about for all the world to read. In a letter dated July 10th, 1839, Catherine had ruefully owned up to this and to worse offences: "You suspicious thing, to think that *your* letters and *that letter*, a *private one*, would be left about for other eyes to see but mine! I will not scold you for this sting for I am too conscious that I deserve it after all the carelessness you have witnessed. You shall see what wonders will be affected for your sake and not in this particular only, I hope, but in *many, many* others in which I shall look to my dear old Oak for support." Apparently William remained unconvinced that marriage had wrought a permanent cure, for six months later Catherine is still fervently declaring "I *promise* not to leave your letters about".

Of all men William was the most likely to be offended by such casual behaviour. "Order and method were in his blood", wrote C. F. Masterman, "and were the means by which he was able to fill his life so full with multitudinous interests and activities." Order and method were qualities to Catherine unknown. Her life was to be crammed hardly less full than his, yet she conducted it on a system of inspired improvisation calculated to drive any orderly man crazy. That William never allowed himself to be driven crazy speaks volumes for his self-control and also for his sense of humour, a quality with which he is seldom credited. He did in fact learn to enjoy "her unlimited capacity for the unexpected" and to find amusement in the odd situations into which she sometimes precipitated them both. "My wife has a marvellous faculty for getting into scrapes and an almost more marvellous one for getting out of them," he was once heard to remark, and when the occasional catastrophe occurred he was always ready to extricate her with a smile instead of the rebuke which she had often richly deserved.

Over one vitally important matter Catherine was neither careless nor casual. Very early in their married life William gave her the choice between knowing none of his political secrets and knowing them all but preserving absolute secrecy. Rather naturally she chose the latter alternative, and her indiscretions were so few as to be practically non-existent. One of the most moving of the many letters preserved at Hawarden was written after one of her rare slips of the tongue. It is a single sheet of paper, undated, and addressed on one side simply to "Mrs. Gladstone". On the other side are three brief sentences: "Do not be vexed. I am not. It is the first time you ever made a little mistake. W. E. G."

In these early days, however, before time had taught him tolerance, William must have been much irritated by his wife's incurable and incredible untidiness. His drawers were always immaculately neat; hers were a byword in the family for their lack of order. In the Glynnese language two words, offal and groutal, stood for different degrees of rubbish, defined as follows: "*Offal:* All Mrs. Gladstone's drawers. *Groutal:* All Lady Lyttelton's drawers." Again, William's letters were invariably dated and headed correctly and written in a legible hand with few or no erasures, whilst Catherine's, seldom headed or dated and sometimes unsigned, were scribbled on any scrap of paper that came to hand, often on the back or round the edges of somebody else's letters to her. The handwriting is such that it is impossible not to suppose that Morley had her in mind when, after working through the great mass of Gladstone papers, he permitted himself the comment, "It is borne in upon us how grievously the burden of man's lot is aggravated by slovenly dates, illegible signatures, and forgetfulness that writing is something meant to be read."

In other matters also Catherine's carelessness knew no limits. A story is told of a grand occasion, staying away from home, when for some reason or other she was without the services of a ladies' maid, and had in consequence to dress herself for dinner. Nowhere could she find the "body" of the evening frock she was intending to wear. Nothing daunted, she wrapped a shawl around her to conceal the absence of bodice, and sailed majestically downstairs, completely oblivious of the fact that the missing "body" was trailing behind her, securely pinned to the flounces of her skirt. The story would seem to be apocryphal, but it is by no means improbable; she had a splendid disregard for dress or appearance, yet her beauty was such that all clothes became her and jewels sparkled for her with a special brilliance.

Not only were there these differences in temperament to be adjusted but each one had to learn to be at home in the other's family circle. For William this was an easy matter; he had been at school and college with Catherine's brothers and he was a member of her world by education, if not by birth. She on the other hand had never met the Gladstone family, although they had for so long lived in the same neighbourhood. Now, however, the Gladstone house at Seaforth outside Liverpool had been exchanged for a mansion at Fasque in Kincardineshire and there both couples had been bidden to spend part of their honeymoon, which, like the wedding itself, was to be a joint affair. The ever-courteous John Gladstone had written a special letter to Mary assuring her that her own welcome would be no less warm than the one in preparation for her sister.

The couples did indeed separate for a few days, the Gladstones going to Acton Park, lent to them by Sir Richard Brooke, father to Harriet Brabazon, and the Lytteltons to the great house at Hagley in Worcestershire which was now to be Mary's home, but at the end of a week or so they met again to start off together on a tour of the Highlands of Scotland. In 1839 this was something of an adventure; Queen Victoria had not as yet made Highland holidays the fashion and the sisters had been rather dubious as to what they would find in the way of food and accommodation. The inns, however, proved to be surprisingly good and the young people thoroughly enjoyed their unconventional honeymoon. The sight of their happy calvacade as it made its way along mountain tracks delighted the eyes of the infrequent passers-by and gave rise to some speculation as to the identity of the two handsome young men tramping beside the ponies and the two pretty riders wearing the Lennox tartan, to which, of course, Catherine and Mary could lay no sort of claim. All his life William was to be an enthusiastic mountain climber and he was much amused when his brother-in-law, with typical Lyttelton casualness, persisted in walking the whole way up Ben Aburd in his slippers.

At length the party reached Fasque. With her remarkable and kindly father-in-law Catherine seems always to have been on the best of terms, but her letters to Lady Glynne say nothing at all about her reactions to him or indeed to any of her new relations, being merely the reassuring affectionate letters which any dutiful daughter would write to a semi-invalid mother.

In later years her favourite brother-in-law was the sailor, John, whose arrival is always described as "a break", which in Glynnese signifies something "agreable and rousing". Tom, the eldest of the brothers, was much less congenial, and Robertson, who carried on the family business in Liverpool, is invariably characterised by some such adjective as "loyal" or "faithful". Robertson was that invaluable type of relative who is always ready to run errands or to perform some small kindness; he would, for instance, lend his carriage to Catherine for a shopping expedition or meet

William on a wet and windy quayside with the proffer of a much-needed umbrella.

About Helen, the family black sheep, Catherine preserved a wise silence, only occasionally commenting with what passed in Glynnese for extreme discretion "Helen was very X". By the time of William's marriage Helen may have already started to take drugs, although she had not yet committed the crowning enormity of joining the Roman Catholic Church. "Her somewhat peculiar nature", to use Morley's tactful phrase, did not fit her to be any adequate companion to Catherine, who confessed that Mary's departure early in September left her feeling "very blue", but, nevertheless, she was supremely happy with her William. Every day they studied the Bible together, and like all earnest young people of their generation, they read and re-read Keble's *Christian Year*. "William's book is now *the take* *", Catherine wrote on October 10th, referring to *The State in its Relations with the Church*. "There is a very interesting review by Keble." For more mundane reading William had chosen *Nicholas Nickleby* and some of Scott's novels. Of an evening there would be billiards, or "a deadly conflict" over the chess-board, or perhaps singing. This was a special treat, for William had a fine baritone voice and both of them delighted in music. In November they left Fasque for a round of country house visits, reaching Hawarden on Christmas Eve in time for a happy reunion with Mary and George Lyttelton.

In January husband and wife parted for the first time, Catherine going on a visit to Hagley and William of necessity returning to London. "The parting stings", she wrote, and the sting of parting was one that did not lose its sharpness with the years. Twenty-five years later she writes, "I feel so incomplete without you", and later again, "Whenever you are away the sunshine seems gone." William had promised to join her at Hagley and much as she enjoyed her visit to George and Mary—"there they sit at the head of their table like two old married people as sedate as possible"—she was counting the days till his arrival and "listening in vain for the joyous sound of your wheels". The rapture of reunion with Mary was somewhat spoiled by the presence of Mary's mother-in-law, although Catherine was quick to acknowledge that Lady Lyttelton was "charming" and had "tact almost unrivalled". She was ready too to profit by the older woman's experience; "I have been study-

ing Lady Lyttelton's book of instruction regarding household
accounts and taking a leaf out of it," she writes to William, "do
not despair, you will yet, I think and hope, find me a good
manager and a good accountant." A good manager Catherine
certainly became and, after much tribulation, a good accountant,
but as late as 1849 she was still writing to William, "You tidy old
thing, can you tell me without inconvenience what money I have
had out?"

Gladstones, Lytteltons, and Glynnes now counted themselves
one big family and a warm affection was to spring up between
Catherine and the Dowager Lady Lyttelton, a wise and witty
woman whose conversation retained some of the flavour of an
earlier and more robust generation. Her letter of congratulation to
Mary on the expected arrival of a baby is wonderfully lacking in
sentimentality: "I must congratulate you in the lengthening of
your sash; you may not enjoy the symptoms when the sash is very
long indeed but perhaps George will admire it." Both sisters were
expecting babies in June.

Back again in London William and Catherine set about the
pleasant task of furnishing their own home, a house in Carlton
House Terrace given them by John Gladstone. Furnishings had
to be chosen; "Beauty is beauty, even in furniture," said William,
who had something of the connoisseur's eye, and who had already
started collecting pictures, ivories and china. Servants too had to
be interviewed. "Engaged a cook", runs a note in Catherine's
diary, "after a long talk on religious affairs, chiefly between her
and William." William was in fact rather too apt to interfere in
domestic matters, perhaps because he still had to discover how
great a gift for organisation lay hidden beneath his Catherine's
haphazard manner.

The house was rather large for a young couple but both the
Lytteltons and Lady Glynne made it their London headquarters,
and moreover, in G. W. E. Russell's phrase, "the blessing of the
man who hath his quiver full of them was not long withheld". A
son was born on June 3rd, 1840, a fortnight before the birth of the
Lyttelton's daughter, Meriel. He was christened William Henry,
his godfathers being Gladstone's friend James Hope [1] and, to
Catherine's great pleasure, Henry Manning. Maybe her warm

[1] Later Hope-Scott.

heart grieved for him as a childless widower, or maybe she appreciated his trenchant wit, a quality in which Glynnes abounded and Gladstones were a little deficient; whatever the reason she had a special liking for Manning, although at times she found him alarming. "Messrs. Hope and Rogers and Archdeacon Manning dined", ran one entry in her diary. "Rather awed and felt a ph.* at dinner." She need have had no qualms where Samuel Rogers was concerned because he had long been her devoted admirer. "As for Her, I have loved her dearly ever since I knew her," he had written when congratulating William Gladstone on his engagement, "and you must forgive me if I continue to do so." Unlike Catherine, William preferred Hope to Manning, whom he never found wholly congenial; as Manning himself wickedly remarked, "Mr. Gladstone is a substantive and likes to be attended by adjectives, and I am not exactly an adjective."

The summer following Willy's birth was spent on a round of visits, the Gladstones travelling by the new-fangled railroad and taking their own carriage with them. With his usual passion for detail William held very definite views as to the right type of carriage to take and the way in which it should be secured to the railway truck. The baby came with them and proved himself a good traveller except on occasions when, as Catherine phrased it, "he had no room to expand".

The winter brought them back again to London and to political life, but politics at that particular moment were of very little interest. The Whig Government was clearly nearing the end of its tether and parliamentary debates lacked realism or enthusiasm. It must be confessed that neither now nor at any other time did Catherine succeed in taking an intelligent interest in abstract political problems. In later life a friend spoke of "her unashamed boredom with politics in general". She saw politics in terms of persons, and usually in terms of one person only, whose name was William Gladstone. But although she had little understanding of the topics under discussion no one was more assiduous than she in attendance at the House of Commons. If William was to speak, no matter how tired or busy she might be she would find time and energy to climb the long staircase to the uncomfortable, inconvenient Ladies' Gallery, and there she would sit for hours, in her especial corner. In after years, visitors to the House would remark on the small patch of brass railing that had been polished bright and shining by the gentle friction of her gloved hand. Rather than miss any part of the debate if going on to a party, she would change her dress in a cramped little room behind the Ladies' Gallery, much to the amusement of her more conventional friends.

So the first year of marriage drew to a close, occupied chiefly with happy home affairs. Both William's and Catherine's friends considered them a model couple. One of the cousins at Escrick wrote Mary a glowing description of the impression William had made on her family: "We all, individually, collectively, are perfectly *enchanted* with Mr. Gladstone; he is so winning, so gentle, and continues to impart the manifold information he possesses in so very agreable a manner that we all admire him beyond measure. It is indeed a delight to discover that everyone of the many panegyrics we have so universally heard pronounced upon him are so fully merited and that her prospects of permanent happiness are as secure as any earthly ones can be." William's friends were as favourably impressed by his wife as Catherine's were by her husband, and one of them, by name Blakesley, wrote a letter which showed that the process of humanising William Gladstone was progressing in a most satisfactory manner: "The Gladstones have been here. I like her much, and think marriage has improved him very materially. His manner is not so ascetic as it was; he really seems to enjoy life independent of the consideration that it is a sphere for the exercise of duties. He is another instance of superior men selecting superior women, which is generally considered an impossibility."

In May Melbourne's government tottered to its fall, and the Election which followed brought William a pleasing if incongruous colleague in his constituency in Newark in the person of Lord John Manners who was to become a leading spirit in the political extravaganza known as "the Young England Party". "Let wealth and commerce, law and learning die, But leave us still our old nobility", sang this attractive young aristocrat, sentiments not calculated to appeal to his Liverpudlian colleague; yet nevertheless Catherine wrote, "William is charmed with Lord John Manners". His own fight at Newark successfully over, William joined Catherine at Hawarden and canvassed hard in support of Stephen Glynne who was standing for Flintshire, but in spite of all their efforts Stephen was defeated, much to the disappointment of the Hardeners. "I am a great woman for thinking of the Lord," one old dame cried out to Catherine, "but oh, my dear lady, this has put Him clean out of my head." "The flatness of our return to Hawarden was indescribable," wrote Catherine, "the poor dear Hardeners, some shutting their doors from good taste, some hurrying out in tears to proclaim their sorrow, the coachman crying *chaudes larmes*." This same summer of 1841, when Catherine and William were staying at Nuneham Courtenay, they took the opportunity to visit Newman's famous church at Littlemore, which was regarded by alarmed Protestants as a hotbed of popery. "Nothing there to make one jump", was Catherine's sensible verdict.

The Election resulted in a Tory victory and Peel took office as Prime Minister, inviting Gladstone to become Vice-President of the Board of Trade. "*Peel était en quelque sort un Manchesterien de naissance,*" says Halévy, and as such he was quick to recognise the Liverpool merchant's son hidden beneath an Etonian façade, and to discern Gladstone's hitherto unsuspected business talent, a gift which was entirely lacking in Lord Ripon, the titular head of the department. This innocuous old gentleman, better known as "Goody Goderich", showed great kindness to the Gladstones, and Lady Ripon was in the habit of inviting Catherine down to her house at Putney to enjoy a little country air. Catherine was grateful for this kindness, for she was feeling a little ill and not a little lonely.

William's appointment to the Board of Trade had in fact placed him in a key position and made him Peel's right-hand man in the great task of fiscal reform. In practice this meant days, hours, weeks of hard work concerned with such prosaic matters as the duties on muscatels, boot uppers or straw bonnets, or the grievances of lathe-turners, coopers or coal-whippers. There were innumerable deputations to receive, including one from Lancashire, when William noticed among the delegates a young man in Quaker dress who sat forward eagerly on the edge of his chair and intervened "rather fiercely" in the discussion. The young man's name was John Bright.

Catherine was delighted to hear good reports of William's

success with such delegations. "The only interesting part of my dinner", she wrote in her diary, "was some conversation respecting William's giving such satisfaction to the various deputations he receives, that his manner is so straightforward, and his proofs so clear and well made out." This was one of the occasions when she "dined out alone, which I detest". The Vice-President of the Board of Trade was usually too busy for such frivolities. In November husband and wife did indeed snatch a week's holiday together which they spent with her uncle George Neville-Grenville at Cambridge, where he was now Master of Magdalene College. According to Catherine "William appeared to be made very much of and considered almost a lion", whilst she herself enjoyed a series of grand dinner-parties given in their honour and attended "a lecture from Professor Willis upon the Steam Carriage".

At home William had no time either to entertain or be entertained. "The devotion of my time to public purposes", he wrote to Catherine on December 10th, 1841, "will render it imperative on me to be more than heretofore a recluse in my own house," adding in kindlier tone, "I am anxious that *you* should not suffer loneliness because of my absorption." Strange words, these, from a devoted husband to a young wife who had just written to him during an enforced absence at Hawarden, "How *funny* that I should have been so happy here once on a time without either you or Boy!"

"Boy" was Catherine's great consolation when parted of necessity from her husband. She especially enjoyed watching the two baby cousins, Willy and Meriel, playing happily together, and she noted with pride that Willy was "obstreperous and a proper boy". Her other solace was Mary Lyttelton. The two sisters still spent as much time as possible together and when separated they wrote to each other every day. On the basis of these letters, which are nearly all extant, it would be possible to build up a detailed, day-to-day account of their lives. Had she given more time and attention to her correspondence Catherine might have been a brilliant letter-writer. She had the art of making small happenings appear to be immensely important; a party, a child's illness, a picnic, are recorded in her letters side by side with news of politics and the affairs of nations, and all, great or small, are equally absorbing. But she was always in a hurry, with no time to spare for such matters as spelling, verbs or punctuation, nor had she any sense of sequence or of logical construction. Her letters may be lively but they are not literature and much of what she wrote was too ephemeral to be of more than passing interest. And personal and intimate as the letters are the intimacy is all on the surface.

The letters to her husband are also preserved and these are no more revealing than the letters to Mary. It may be that Catherine had no need to write of the deeper things of the heart. After years of happy marriage the conversation of husband and wife often seems trivial, not because they are no longer interested in serious matters but because they are so entirely at one on these things that words are unnecessary or even obtrusive.

So perhaps between Catherine and Mary, and Catherine and William, an intimacy had grown up so deep that the thoughts of each one's heart lay open to the other. Or it may be that Catherine was so extroverted, so turned outward in love and sympathy towards other people that she never turned inwards upon herself to explore the recesses of her own character. She had time and attention for everyone in the world except for Catherine Gladstone. Or it may be that of the really vital matters which touched her to the quick, threatening to upset her admirable balance of mind, she could not and would not write. In later and more sorrowful years she could not bear to speak of her dead nor to have their pictures about her room. Whatever the reason, these letters give us no clue at all as to the deeper labyrinths of thought and character.

Letters, however frequent, were but poor consolation to Catherine, who was now learning that elementary lesson for the wife of a man of genius, the realisation that although she might have first claim on his heart she could never have first claim on his attention. Nothing in her previous life had prepared her for long hours spent entirely in her own company. It is almost literally true to say that before marriage the Pussies had never been parted. "How desolate we used to be", she wrote to Mary, "when one of us was out of the room for a little time even!" Rather naturally she rebelled against her loneliness. "It is a little dreary", she notes, and in her diary she complains, "I have had very little of William this week and felt unduly vexed", but as usual Mary is the chief recipient of her woes. "Oh, dear," she writes to that ever sym-

pathetic sister, "it is mournful work. Here am I and William gone
off at eight o'clock, just having swallowed his dinner. I now seldom
get any sort of talk and even at breakfast he is reading the newspaper."

In the summer of 1842 Catherine could not even accompany
William on their annual holiday to Fasque because she was within
three months of the birth of her second child. When he rejoined
her at Hawarden in September an accident occurred which might
well have proved fatal. Catherine's diary gives an account of the
misfortune:

"What a day I might have had to record but God has been so
merciful to us! I drove in the car with Stephen and my boy,
William, Henry and Mr. Phillimore having gone out shooting.
Little did I think of what had been taking place. Upon getting
near the new school we found Henry awaiting us. His pale face
too soon aroused my fears. What had happened to William?
How can I express what I felt before he could answer? O
gracious God, was all earthly happiness to be dashed away or
was he yet to be spared to me? Thanks be to Him that the dreadful shot which shattered the forefinger of the left hand had left
every other part untouched. I found my precious one at the
Rectory, calm and cheerful, thankful for his escape and thinking
how to make the best of it for me."

The finger had to be amputated but so great was Catherine's
relief at the escape that her letter to Manning describing the
accident is almost joyful in tone and full of praise of William's
bearing: "To you, who know him so well, I need scarcely dwell
upon the way he bore the very agonising operation and upon his
whole Christian behaviour from the moment of the accident—to
have had the privilege of witnessing it—to have had his precious
life so mercifully spared—I would only ask for your prayers to
join in thanksgiving with ours to Almighty God. I feel indeed
unable to look on it in the light of a misfortune."

Until the hand healed William was forced to take life a little more
easily, and Catherine revelled in peaceful evenings when "we play
at chess and are very snug and quiet". (It may be worth noticing
that Catherine quite often makes use of the supposed Ameri-
canism, "as snug as a bug in a rug".) One evening Lord Ripon

proposed himself to a homely dinner in their tiny sitting-room and Catherine was surprised to find him "very light in hand". A month later it was William's turn to write to Manning to announce the birth of a daughter, who was christened Agnes. A letter went also to Mary giving a happy description of Agnes' mother: "I wish you could see her as she is now, looking so fresh and beautiful, her heart overflowing with happiness, and let me add, her appetite by no means to be despised, but, as she calls it, ravenous."

This domestic peace came to an end all too soon and again William was back working sometimes for twelve or fourteen hours a day with little or no time to spare for wife or babies. Catherine was unhappy at home because she could not see enough of her husband, and she was still more unhappy when he must stay in London whilst she went down to Hagley or Hawarden. On one of these occasions he wrote to give her a sketch of his day when the House of Commons was not sitting: "You ask me for my daily life—I will give it you. Up, about half-past eight; nothing wonderful so far. Prayers and breakfast at the usual time—read, write or see people till quarter to twelve—then half-an-hour or so seeing my father—at my office till quarter or half-past six—dine with my father and stay till about half-past eight—back home to read—goggo [cocoa] at nine, and bed about half-past twelve, i.e. in it." By modern standards this account does not suggest an over-strenuous day, but Catherine fretted because it did not allow any time for fresh air and exercise.

In 1843, when Gladstone took Lord Ripon's place as President of the Board of Trade, her anxiety increased. "May the increase of responsibility not injure his precious health!" prayed this over-careful wife, and then in characteristic manner coming down at once to practical issues, "I wish he would have a horse; one ride a week would be better than nothing." Catherine herself, keen horsewoman that she was, had only once had the opportunity to ride in the whole of the four years which had passed since her marriage. Fanciful though they might seem, her fears for William's health were echoed by that supremely sensible woman, Sarah Lady Lyttelton. "Now do take care Mr. Gladstone does not sacrifice his health to his business," she wrote to Catherine, "I hope he will make time every day to play with the boy and to sing

The Battle of the Baltic, beside air and exercise in plenty, or he will never be able to do his hard work. So ends my prescription."

Catherine's own days were growing more and more full of occupation. First of all, of course, came the care of her children. Willy was not quite four years old and Agnes still under two when Stephen Edward put in his appearance on April 4th, 1844. In defiance of prevailing custom Catherine nursed all her babies, which in itself meant that her time and occupations must be planned very carefully. Nannies and nursery-maids she had in plenty, but she herself was arbiter in all nursery questions and she was jealous for her authority. Catherine was a good mistress, careful of her servants' interests—for example, she took care never to dismiss anyone at what she describes as "the fag end of the season" —and her complaints against them are few, but when she finds fault with nurse or governess it is invariably because they take too much upon themselves. She is the responsible person and nothing is to be done without her knowledge, not even the administration of a dose of medicine. It must be admitted that far too much dosing went on in the Gladstone nursery; Catherine fancied herself very much as an amateur doctor and there were times when the children seem to have lived on a diet of blue pills and grey powders. She tried her skill on William himself and her letters record the exact doses administered to the future Prime Minister.

Catherine liked to have the children with her as much as possible and in especial young Willy. This eldest child was always to be particularly dear to her and admiration of Willy was a sure passport to her affection. Of Lady Canning, who was to become a close friend, Catherine wrote, "she won my heart by her intense admiration of Willikins", and she describes Lady Ripon as being "worthy of the boy". Though not to be found in the *Glynnese Glossary*, this idiom was a favourite phrase with Catherine. It implies that a person proves their own worthiness by admiring some particularly worthy object; even Queen Victoria rose in Catherine's estimation because she showed herself "worthy" of Willy.

Sarah Lady Lyttelton was Governess to the Royal Family, and she formed a natural link between the two young women whose marriages had taken place within six months of one another, and whose children were so nearly of an age. Catherine was frequently bidden to Windsor or to Buckingham Palace so that Willy and Agnes might play with their Royal contemporaries, and although beforehand she might suffer from bathing-feel * and "dazzles", once in the Royal presence she was as easily at home with the Queen as with everyone else with whom she came in contact. On one occasion Victoria unbent so far as to exclaim, "Oh, wait a moment; I must just run away and get my gown fastened", whilst Agnes' sturdy independence caused her to fall into "fits of unrestrained laughter". The Princess Royal Catherine considered "particularly engaging", whilst Princess Alice was pronounced "a nice, fat, good-natured clean-looking baby", but the poor Prince of Wales was dressed so oddly as to look "quite a quiz".

Next in importance after nursery affairs came the necessary round of social events and entertainments. This handsome, intelligent young couple were much sought after in London society, and Catherine's diary is full of grand names and grand occasions. There were dinner-parties with the Archbishop of York and Monsieur Guizot, and with the Duke and Duchess of Cambridge —"the Duke of Cambridge very loquacious, came and sat by me, and I was not a little relieved at his soon fastening on William instead". At one dinner she sits next the Duke of Wellington which thrills her intensely, though unfortunately she has his deaf ear; at another, she meets Sir Robert Peel and talks with Lord Stanley, who makes her laugh with his mimicry of famous speakers. He tells her too his prescription for dispelling the fatigues of official life—"a gossamer meal of cold chicken eaten late at night with his feet in a basin of hot water", and afterwards "a stupid novel to compose his mind for slumber".

Doubtless these famous and middle-aged gentlemen enjoyed their conversation with a young and beautiful woman, but she liked them best of all when they sang the praises of her William. A few months before Agnes' birth, when she suffered agonies of bilious sickness at a particularly dreary dinner-party, the occasion was redeemed by Lord Lyndhurst's prophetic remark as to Gladstone's future, "I see plainly his destination but his first step will be Chancellor of the Exchequer." As she proudly records this statement for Mary's benefit she cannot resist a dig at one of the feminine guests who had not been over-sympathetic with her sickness, "Lady M's diamonds were perhaps paste".

The Gladstones' favourite method of returning hospitality was a breakfast party, entailing a real breakfast at ten o'clock and not the evening entertainment which in those days went by the curious name of "breakfast", or sometimes Catherine would give "a little singing soirée" which would be particularly enjoyable to William with his fine voice and excellent ear for music.

Not content with her social round and with her interest in her three small children, Catherine had already started on that course of charitable activities which was to be one of the most remarkable features of her long life. No matter how busy she was, wherever she saw want or distress there she must go to help and comfort. The years were "the Hungry Forties" and foremost among the problems of the day was "the Condition-of-England question". William met it face to face when starving coal-whippers came clamouring into the very offices of the Board of Trade, Catherine found it next door to her at Hawarden during the summer of 1842 when the "Plug Plot" strike raged throughout industrial Lancashire. "You do not seem to be much troubled by the neighbourhood of this turn-out", William wrote from Fasque, adding the typical observation, "This is the time when we may reflect on the rottenness of the system which gathers together huge masses of the population having no tie to the classes above them."

To reflect on the rottenness of this or any other system was an idea entirely foreign to Catherine's mind; she was concerned with people, not systems, and it was not in her nature to argue from the particular to the general. Catherine did not grasp a principle and then work towards its attainment, rather, she saw suffering individuals and in her limitless efforts to help them she sometimes found that she had established a system or a principle as it were by accident. Long years afterwards her daughter was to describe her as having "the genius of charity". At present charity could only take the most simple and direct forms. She did indeed attempt to establish some form of organisation in her London parish—"I am rather full of getting up a Visiting Lady Society", she wrote to Mary—but her multitudinous good works, convalescent homes, orphanages, refuges and the like, were to be the business of later years when there were fewer babies in the nursery. However, there were always sick people to nurse, old people to visit, hungry people to feed.

In the nineteenth century the lady of "the big house" could not be unaware of the truth that the poor we have always with us. It is easy enough to smile at the titbit purloined from the Hawarden dinner-table and left cooling on the mantelpiece in the hall until Catherine could find time and opportunity to slip down to the village on a visit to some needy cottager, but this somewhat primitive type of charity meant personal effort and personal contact, and the Hardeners delighted in the warmth of Catherine's sympathy even if the dinner she brought with her might be a little chilly.

An extract from her diary shows Catherine's firm belief in the personal touch and her dislike of the coldness of professional charity, however well administered: "Lord De Tabley drove me in his cab to the Mendicity Society. We spent more than an hour there going into the details of the whole thing. It was very interesting to hear the examination of the numberless cases and to see the quickness and the knowledge of the interrogators. I could have wished to see less asperity and suspicion in their manner." Asperity and suspicion were never to characterise Catherine's administration of charity, although she could be firm enough when firmness was needed as her letters to erring young women show clearly.

But however busy she might be, Catherine was still less than content because she saw so little of William. She grieved that he could not accompany her when she took the children on short holidays from London to breathe a little sea air—"the thought of seeing the most precious face on earth to me in six more days is too delightful and I live upon the thought", she wrote during one visit to Brighton—and she was especially desolate when, in January 1844, he was obliged to go to London and leave her behind at Hawarden. "I lay awake reflecting upon your last words," she wrote to him, "till I felt ashamed of my weakness, fell asleep, and woke again and then you were gone! There stood the uncomfy sofa, the remains of tea, the fire, but no dear old man! I felt very desolate wishing I had seen you." A week later she wrote in much distress: "I wish I could tell you that I read your intimation as to the impossibility of your spending a week here with the composure I ought perhaps to have done. . . . There is so much to make me desire your dear presence. Well, I have made a clean breast to you; I will however try to be contented, and to acquire what is right and therefore what you would wish. God help me to become in fact better regulated. What I desire so much to obtain is a conquering of the will, and to be able to feel a pleasure even in self-denial just as you, my own darling, do. Indeed I feel very ill satisfied with myself.''

William's reply, although it has been printed several times, is worth quoting again almost in full:

"I am going to end this day of peace by a few words to shew that what you said did not lightly pass away from my mind. There is a beautiful little sentence in the works of Charles Lamb concerning one who has been afflicted: 'He gave his heart to the Purifier, his will to the Will that governs the Universe.' But there is a speech in the third canto of the Paradiso of Dante, spoken by a certain Piccarda, which is a rare gem. I will only quote this one line:

In la sua voluntate e nostra pace.

The words are few and simple yet they appear to me to have an inexpressible majesty of truth about them as if they were spoken from the very mouth of God. . . . The final state which we are to contemplate with hope and to seek by discipline is that in which our will shall be one with the will of God; not merely shall submit to it, not merely shall follow after it, but shall live and move with it even as the pulse of the blood in the extremities acts with the central movement of the heart. And this is to be obtained through a double process; the first, that of checking, repressing, quelling, the inclination of the will to act with reference to self as a centre—that is, to mortify it; the second, to cherish, exercise and expand, its new and heavenly power of acting according to the will of God, first, perhaps, by painful effort in great feebleness and with many inconsistencies, but with continually augmenting regularity and force until obedience become a necessity of second nature.

"And these two processes are carried on together. Your abundant overflowing affection as a wife leads you to wish we were together, while duty keeps us apart. You check that affection, school and subdue it—that is mortifying the individual

E   53

will. That of itself is much more than the whole of what is contemplated by popular opinion as a Christian duty, for resignation is too often conceived to be merely a submission not unattended with complaint to what we have no power to avoid; but it is less than the whole of the work of a Christian. Your full triumph, as far as that particular occasion of duty is concerned, will be to find that you not merely repress outward complaint—nay, not merely repress inward tendencies to murmur—but that you would not if you could alter what in any manner God has plainly willed; that you have a satisfaction and a comfort in it because it is His will, although from its own native taste you would have revolted. Here is the great work of religion; here is the path through which sanctity is attained, the highest sanctity. And yet it is a path evidently to be traced in the course of our daily duties; for it is clear that the occasions of every day are numberless amidst the diversities of events upon which a true spiritual discrimination may find employment in discerning the will of God, and in which also the law of love and self-denial may be applied in the effort to conform to it both inwardly and outwardly so soon as it shall have been discerned. And thus the high attainments that have their crown and their reward in heaven do not require, in order that we may learn them, that we should depart from our common duties, but they lie by the wayside of life; and every pilgrim of this world may, if he have grace, become an adept in them.

"When we are thwarted in the exercise of some innocent, laudable and almost sacred affection, as in the case, though its scale be small, out of which all this has grown, Satan has us at an advantage; because when the obstacle occurs we have a sentiment that the feeling baffled is a right one, and in indulging a rebellious temper we flatter ourselves that we are merely, as it were indignant on behalf, not of ourselves, but of a duty which we have been interrupted in performing. But our duties can take care of themselves when God calls us away from any of them, and when He interrupts the discharge of one it is to ascertain, by the manner of bearing the interruption, whether we are growing fit for another which is higher. To be able to relinquish a duty upon command shows a higher grace than to be able to give up a mere pleasure for a duty; it shows a more practical discernment of the Divine will to distinguish between two things differing only in measure than between one which has a manifest stamp of God upon it and another which is but remotely related to Him, or what is commonly (and hazardously) called indifferent."

"Such a beautiful letter this morning to thank it for," ran Catherine's reply, "a letter which I shall love to read again. What advantages I have in such a dear old man who is always showing me the right way in which to walk; indeed I am frightened to think what I ought to be." To the casual or frivolous reader Gladstone's letter inevitably appears pompous and stilted, a curious document for a husband to write to a wife. It is indeed a curious letter, not because it shows so little affection or understanding but because it presupposes so much of both these qualities. Very few husbands, and certainly very few husbands as busy as William Gladstone, pay their wives the compliment of treating their complaints with complete seriousness. It would have been far easier to write a few loving phrases, hinting gently that after all Catherine had not so very much to grumble at but praising rather than blaming the devotion that could not bear even a temporary parting. Far easier, but it would have given no lasting answer to a question that was bound to grow in importance with the years as the pressure of public business on the one hand and the cares of a growing family on the other combined to make their enforced separations more and more frequent.

Instead, William Gladstone presented Catherine with the key to a philosophy by which to rule her whole life; and he answered it by reference to "the foundation of all mental thoughts and acts, and the measure to which the whole experience of life inward and outward is referred". To complain that he preached instead of comforting is to miss the whole point; he respected her too much to treat her grievance lightly. *Cor ad Cor Loquitur*—Newman's motto—is curiously appropriate to the mysterious relationship of marriage, but it is too often interpreted as meaning that on any and every occasion husband and wife may speak to each other with complete informality, forgetting that where serious matters are concerned heart speaks with heart in a tone of high seriousness. A letter such as Gladstone's would rightly be called pompous if written to an acquaintance, even to a friend; not so, when written to a wife. And it is softened and humanised by the post-script added the next morning, "Thus far last night. Today I only add that what preceded is with me speculation, not practice."

The lesson was a hard one for Catherine to learn. She could do anything for William except do without him. After twenty-one years of marriage, to a letter describing the summer beauty of Hawarden she adds the cry, "Oh, come down! Not even this loveliness does without you, my darling." However, she did at least learn to endure the inevitable separations with a more or less good grace, although it must be admitted that she never reached the stage when she found it possible completely "to repress outward complaint", to say nothing of "inward tendencies to murmur".

Now, however, in unexpected and somewhat untoward fashion a day was rapidly approaching when she might reasonably expect to enjoy much more of her husband's company. Today the question of the Maynooth grant is chiefly interesting for its connection with Gladstone; sufficient to say that on this issue he decided that he could not honourably remain a member of a government which proposed to give additional financial support to a Roman Catholic college, and that he must resign office. To many people his action appeared to be over-scrupulous and almost incomprehensible. Sitting in William's room at the Board of Trade, Catherine wrote to explain his position to George and Mary Lyttleton:

"I fear that what I have now to tell you will rather take it out* of you. Remember it is strictly a secret until I give you leave to tell. In fact it is neither more nor less than that William is virtually no longer a member of the government. The cause (which likewise must continue to be a secret until the meeting of Parliament) is that he is not able with a due regard for character to go along with the Government, at least, to be as it were one of the framers in a part of the measure which they will probably propose with regard to education in Ireland. I am happy to say, for it is relief to poor William, who of course has been sadly harassed for some time, that the best feelings subsist between him and his friends. I am glad we have got leave to tell you

both what has been on my mind so much. Indeed it has been a
trying time to William, and I must say he has gone through it
all as I should have most wished. You may fancy how trying at
the Cabinet meetings to break to them his feelings time after
time. You understand the cause of his retirement, i.e. that he
can't be a *framer* of the proposition about Irish education. I
don't say he disapproves exactly under existing conditions of
the measure but he could not propose it. His feelings towards
the Government remain unchanged. Peel told him that no one
could have acted more candidly or considerately, and was very
kind and open in his manner towards him."

It is to be doubted whether this letter made matters very clear
to the bewildered George and Mary. One of the people most inconvenienced by William's action was Catherine herself whose
domestic plans were of necessity upset by the indecision and delay
inevitable upon resignation. "I am sorry", he wrote penitently,
"that a part of the inconvenience falls on your innocent head."
William's action left her saddened but acquiescent. She was
touched by the kindly concern shown by his colleagues and under-
lings alike: "Canning has written a beautiful letter to give one
quite a lump in one's throat, indeed I have been living all day with
glistening eyes. That kind, hearty Mr. Lefevre, he was turned
quite sick. Then William's good little secretary, Mr. Northcote,
could not help breaking down." The good little secretary was one
day to become Lord Iddesleigh and a convinced opponent of his
one-time chief. Young Willy was taken for a last look at Papa's
office: "He read the words 'Board of Trade' on the door, and I
made him look well at the room and at what he calls Papa being
at his lessons, for I should wish him to remember visiting him
there hereafter." William himself found the severance of personal
ties unexpectedly hard. "Do you know", he wrote to Catherine,
"that daily intercourse and co-operation with men upon matters
of great anxiety and moment interweaves much of one's being
with theirs and parting with them feels much like dying?" However, he remained adamant: "My heart does not waver; pray for
me that I may do right."

Before his resignation was made public Gladstone received a
Royal invitation to Windsor. Lady Lyttelton was delighted to

have him as her partner at dinner and reported that she had been
an object of envy to the other ladies of the Court, who were
tumbling over themselves in their eagerness to have a word with
him. Nearly all women found this serious-minded young man
very attractive; the Queen herself liked him well and during his
stay at Windsor he reported himself to be "very kindly used". A
fortnight later he saw the Queen again in a farewell audience. He
expressed his sorrow at leaving her service and she replied in
tones of courteous regret, ending up with an enquiry after
Catherine. She had no reason to suppose that this personable and
promising young statesman would be long out of office; in spite
of his inconvenient idealism over Maynooth he had remained firm
friends with Sir Robert Peel and before long Peel would surely call
him back from his self-inflicted banishment. Had either Victoria
or Gladstone guessed that when he left the Royal presence he
went out to years of wandering in the political wilderness they
might both have felt slightly aghast. And, for all her jealousy of
his political preoccupations, so too would Catherine.

Chapter Four

CATHERINE may well have thought that when her husband was free of the cares of office he would have more time to devote to his home and family. Six months after his resignation another daughter was born, a plump, healthy baby who was christened Catherine Jessy. But even now William did not find time hanging heavily on his hands. When the House rose he proposed that James Hope and Doctor Pusey's son, Philip, should join him in a tour of Ireland, a country that was even now drawing him like a magnet. "Ireland, Ireland, that cloud in the west, that coming storm"—the famous phrase occurs in a letter to Catherine written this same summer of 1845. However, Hope-Scott and Pusey changed their minds, and Gladstone went off alone to Germany on a journey with a very different aim.

The story of Gladstone's sister Helen is now common knowledge, her drug-taking, her reception into the Roman Catholic Church, and the dubious miracle which cured her nervous ailments. In 1845 she was living in Munich and at his family's request William went out there to endeavour to bring her home or at least to make her see reason. Catherine had but a poor opinion of her sister-in-law, particularly resenting Helen's cavalier treatment of William and her total lack of interest in her small nephews and nieces. Like many healthy-minded people Catherine found it hard to understand that a mental illness can be as real as a physical one and in her heart of hearts she suspected Helen of play-acting. It must be admitted that Helen took great pleasure in dramatising herself. In an undated letter of this period Catherine describes her as coming down to greet them, "dressed as a sort of tragedy queen or *sœur-de-charité*, with gold crosses dangling at her side, full of her little dog, 'a new one'—her first sentence to William!" To make the enormity of this even more obvious, Catherine adds that "William is now with Peel", presumably discussing Protection not puppies, a remark which implied that other and more important people than Helen valued William more seriously.

Now, however, she was too wise to protest against William's departure, although she was convinced that Helen was past persuasion. "It was like you to give me the unexpected treat of a letter this morning," she wrote, wishing him Godspeed. "You have more than you can get through and I will not add to it by scribbling at length. Only take with you my blessing and prayers, such as they are; would they came from someone more worthy to offer them! It seems more like a dream than reality that you are going so far. Your children are all well and I hope to do my duty with them, please God, especially in your absence. When I look at the four it seems an awful responsibility. God bless you, own, own, your poor old wife, C. G."

Gladstone's mission was, of course, a failure, but it did at least result in the formation of a lasting friendship with Doctor Döllinger, whom he described to Catherine as "one of the most liberal and Catholic in mind of all the persons of his communion whom I have known". The question of the Roman Catholic claims was uppermost in his mind at this moment. No abstract argument meant very much to Catherine. Her Christianity was of an extremely concrete kind based on church-going and the performance of practical duties, but she was troubled, as William was troubled, by the drift which was setting in towards Rome. A few months earlier she had written to him enclosing a letter from Newman:

"The enclosed is deeply interesting and has only lived in my bosom until packed off to you. One can plainly see that your note was a soother; 'I prize it very much' are big words from Newman. Does not the rest rather convey to your mind the feeling that his mind is in a very unhealthy state, I mean, more than morbid? I gather from it that there is *no move* in prospect. Does he mean by laying down his arms that he would wish to be quite passive under the idea that he cannot with his views teach, yet leaving one to infer that he would *not* think it right to place himself in the position to do so by going over to Rome?"

From the more than morbid state of mind of poor Doctor Newman, wavering so unhappily between Anglicanism and Rome, Catherine turns immediately to the uncomplicated faith of five-year-old Willy: "he remarked after saying his hymn, 'Now this will make me good all day because it is about God' ".

Catherine's letters were always a wonderful hotch-potch of subjects, thrown together just as the thoughts came into her head, with hardly a comma to separate the serious and the trivial, so that Newman and nursery matters are several times found jostling each other in incongruous proximity. "William is *wild* about the Newman affair," she writes, "and we had nothing but bevys of big-wigged men in the shape of Roundell Palmer, Hope, Manning and so forth", then, without pause, she rushes into a detailed description of Willy's smart new hat, feather-trimmed and bound with velvet. The theological problems which were of absorbing interest to her husband meant nothing at all to Catherine; she is much more concerned with "the beautifully large congregation at Brighton church", or Sabbath observance at Windsor Castle where "the day is spent in a Sunday-like way with the exception of the possibility of Ivory Letters" (a reference, this, to an innocuous round game which more sophisticated visitors regarded as a sad bore) or with that most popular occupation of pious Victorians, the building of churches. Here George and Mary were also involved, and George at least was not altogether happy about his commitments in that direction. "I should say he is a bit puzzled about his power of lugging out £200 for Oak Farm Church," Mary wrote in 1844, "but he made no sort of complaint and I heard him mutter, 'I must manage out of any money that falls in from Oak Farm'."

George displayed even more than his usual optimism if he expected any money at all to fall in from Oak Farm. The name is ominous of trouble. When William returned from Germany in the autumn of 1845 he found the family's financial position looking black indeed. The cause of the trouble was a small farm which was part of the Staffordshire estates owned by Stephen Glynne. By evil chance under the hundred acres of Oak Farm lay both coal and iron. With charming and characteristic generosity Stephen had presented both his sisters with shares in the Oak Farm concern by way of a wedding present, and with equally characteristic laziness he allowed the management of the business to fall into the hands of an agent who was something of a knave and much more of a fool. The credit of the whole Hawarden estate became involved and a crash was inevitable. For two years matters dragged on and then in 1847 came catastrophe. Oak Farm, and the Hawarden estate with it, went bankrupt.

As one man the whole family turned to William to deal with the situation. Stephen, who was the person most immediately concerned, simply handed over everything to his brother-in-law and betook himself abroad. This was probably the wisest thing that Stephen could have done, and Gladstone never reproached him for the folly which had landed them all in such trouble, but other members of the family were less forgiving. Lord Braybrooke had always regarded himself as especially responsible for his fatherless nephews and nieces and he now wrote Stephen a stiff rebuke: "Without mincing matters I must say you are mainly in fault and that most of these grievances arise from your apathy and want of firmness in not managing your own affairs as other persons do. And I must say that large estates were not given us to be wasted."

Catherine's heart swelled with pride to see how everyone relied on William. In a note addressed "For Henry, Stephen and Mary especially", she bemoaned the complicated muddle which her husband was now endeavouring to reduce to order:

"It is melancholy to see the miserable way everything has been carried on without system or judgement, and to feel that nobody knows what is most important to know; in fact, it is a chaos, much of it, so many links being lost. It is like working at a tangled web to come at anything. William is now employed in making notes and writing heads to put us in a way to come at facts, then to seek law advice. I have felt for some time keen pleasure at having a husband who can help so materially. I do feel without him Hawarden must have been sold and now here again is a fresh and important subject which his good old head and wits are hard at work upon."

The fact that William had saved Hawarden gave Catherine peculiar pleasure. To sell was the obvious course, and the one advocated by John Gladstone, that able man of business. But Hawarden was Catherine's home and her husband was learning to count it as his home also and to love it with the same intense and conscious love that she gave to every nook and cranny in house and garden. When Catherine married she had never really left home. William had no country house of his own, Fasque was too far distant to be of much practical use, and neither of them could ever feel at home in London. On one occasion, when she was finding town life particularly unattractive, Catherine dashed off a letter to Mary, undated, unsigned, with no formal opening, beginning simply with the heart-felt cry, "Oh, London, with its turmoil, its clack, its fog, its cold, all so uncongenial but for William's dear face and the children's—no words can express what I feel!"

Catherine flitted easily from one London house to another, for Hawarden alone held any sense of permanency. The place belonged nominally to Stephen, but the house required a hostess and Stephen was only too pleased that Catherine should continue to fill the position which had been hers ever since her mother's illness. He was delighted to have the responsibility for house and stables taken off his shoulders, and he much enjoyed the company of a brother-in-law who shared his own interest in music, art and Church affairs. In his own way Stephen was very attached to his home and he was prepared to forgo most of his income and even to make the appalling sacrifice of doing without the services of a valet if by any means he could help to save Hawarden.

After Stephen, Henry was the person most nearly concerned, but of them all Henry took the least interest in the fate of his family home. He was now Rector of Hawarden parish, enjoying a stipend of £4000 a year and living with his wife Lavinia, George Lyttelton's sister, in a Rectory as large as a sizeable country mansion. A new baby was born to them every year but the only boy had died a few hours after birth. As a parson of "the high-and-dry school" Henry preached the requisite number of slightly dull sermons and visited conscientiously in his parish; he kept a carriage and pair and some excellent riding horses, enjoyed a bottle of good port, and delighted in witty conversation. Admirable and amusing Henry might be but no one could call him energetic, and although he was the next heir to Hawarden his interest in the place was really rather remote. There was only a year's difference in age between the brothers and it might well be that Stephen would outlive him. The title could not pass to a daughter and the family seem to have agreed that neither ought the property to do so. Now that the Castle must be, if possible, let, or temporarily closed if no tenant were forthcoming, Henry welcomed Catherine and her family to the Rectory, taking it for granted that they would treat it as their home (Catherine's sixth child was actually born there in 1849), but this seems to have been his chief contribution to the solution of the financial problem.

Catherine, however, was urgent that Hawarden should be saved, and she backed up William's efforts by every means in her power. She was not an extravagant woman, but her incorrigibly disorderly nature did not easily lend itself to the practice of rigid economy. Now she set herself to keep careful accounts, to watch small expenditure, and to train herself in order and method. Although she had never been very conscious of fashion she had at least a little of the ordinary feminine interest in clothes, confessing to Mary that she found it difficult to resist the lure of the London shops. From now onwards, however, she cut personal expenditure to the minimum. Fortunately she had a natural feeling for colour and texture, and she wore her home-made clothes with such an air that no one stopped to consider whether she were indeed well-dressed. For her daughters, however, dress was a different matter, and when they grew up they suffered.

At the time of the Oak Farm crash, however, even Agnes was only five, and Catherine's letters are full of drawings and descriptions of the clothes she was planning for them, including some curiously shaped garments described as "moon-frocks". Some of her ideas on economy would make the modern housewife smile, as when she protests that no London household can be called extravagant that dispenses with the services of a second footman, but her letters show the time and thought she gave to the question of expenditure even in the smallest matters. Her petty cash account is meticulously kept, including such items as "1/- sandwiches, 3d. milk for baby, 1/3 for two cups of tea, in all 3/- with bun and biscuit", and it is a little strange to find a woman in her position hesitating over the price of a ticket to Brighton, or borrowing flowers and feathers from her sister because her own were too shabby to wear for great occasions.

Her natural exuberance turned economy into an adventure; to

travel second-class, for instance, is the greatest joke in the world, and never once, not even in her private letters to Mary, does she complain or grumble at the change in their financial position. The cheerful determination with which she accepted the inevitable must have been the greatest help she could have given to her husband in his fight to restore the finances of Hawarden to something like solvency.

Other members of the family did not share her single-minded zeal for economy. Lady Glynne had taken a dislike to Hawarden, and she was now established at Hagley, where she lived apart in her own rooms, an object of awe and alarm to the Lyttelton children. Although she still made the Gladstone house her London headquarters the relationship between her and Catherine was slightly strained. As in the case of Helen Gladstone, Catherine found it difficult to understand and sympathise with a sufferer from nervous illness or depression; she was too quick, too overflowing with energy to bear quite patiently enough with her mother's slow, sad complaining, and Lady Glynne had come to lean more upon the gentle Mary than upon the elder daughter who had once been her especial prop and stay. When it came to the question of selling any part of the estate Lady Glynne had of necessity to be consulted, and she was all too apt to raise difficulties. One of the few angry letters that William Gladstone ever penned is a complaint to Mary Lyttelton about her mother's obstructionist tactics. It is written just before the final crash of Oak Farm:

> "I have read what you say about Lady Glynne and the money resulting from the sale of the house, and I must just state plainly how matters stand. We are engaged, Stephen over head and ears, George and I to a lesser extent, in a most wild and extravagant and, in my view, immoral speculation, namely, in conducting an ironworks without either the knowledge or the means for doing this with safety. . . . Under these circumstances I find myself charged with the care of Stephen's concerns, for his they are in the main, and very few indeed have been the weeks of the present year which have not brought me new and serious anxieties about the Oak Farm. Only my exclusion from office and from Parliament has enabled me to meet them. I have

hitherto proceeded on the supposition that Lady Glynne would prefer making every effort rather than that Hawarden should be sold, but please tell her that *that* alternative is open to her. If she is unwilling to embrace that alternative then I must ask either to be relieved altogether of my task, as if I alone had been interested I should probably have been long ago, or else to have all the means which she, or Stephen, or George, can make available at my disposal as occasion may arise. That sale of the house, of which Lady Glynne seems to complain, has, I believe, been the means of preventing a break-up of the nature to which I have adverted. But I know not what new exigencies may arise —all I can do is to state the absolute necessity that we should strain every nerve to avert the evil, as thank God it has hitherto been averted. I am sensible that the demands I make must bear a strange aspect to Lady Glynne and perhaps to you; I am only stating, or desirous to state, strong factors in strong language. I say little of these occasions when they arise because it is impossible to convey fully and accurately all that passes in the communications I hold with Boydell,[1] Freshfield, the bankers, and my father, secondly, because knowing the taste of the subject myself, I do not want to administer it to others beyond what is absolutely necessary. I must add that the ruinous pecuniary loss which would be incurred would also in my view be attended with some personal discredit to us."

This letter shows plainly that in the Oak Farm affair William Gladstone had come into collision with a code of ethics and a standard of values that was strange to him. The land-owning Glynnes considered it a paramount duty to keep the estate as far as possible intact whilst the mercantile Gladstones were horrified by the "immorality" of running a speculative business in an incompetent manner, and stood aghast at the dishonourable prospect of bankruptcy.

This same difference of outlook made for an occasional misunderstanding even with the beloved George and Mary Lyttelton. Where her brothers and sister were concerned no other word can describe Catherine but "bossy". She was by far the most competent member of the family and her interference was not merely

---

[1] The Oak Farm agent.

tolerated but welcomed, especially by Mary, provided that it involved no sort of criticism of George. The question of economy, however, involved George and George's management of the Lyttelton finances. George and Catherine were genuinely fond of each other and a letter from Catherine to William, dated January 30th, 1849, shows the friendly nature of their relationship: "Conceive your old wife going a regular buck to Exeter Hall with George last night. I certainly now feel I have heard Jenny Lind. We sat in the gallery places looking down upon our grander friends."

George, however, was naturally intolerant of government by a sister-in-law, and although William and he were old friends their temperaments were so different that an occasional clash was inevitable. William had a genius for politics and finance, subjects which George found dull in comparison with pure scholarship, cricket and the colonisation of New Zealand. He did indeed attempt to interest himself in politics and rose as high as Under-Secretary for the Colonies, but it was an effort which went against the grain.

Where William and George were concerned Catherine displayed less tact than might have been expected. She was forever pointing out to Mary, in tones that can only be called patronising, how very promising William considered George's speech, although a few small criticisms might not come amiss, or what a successful beginning William considered George to have made at the Colonial Office, and how admirable a Minister George might become, given a little more experience and application. Application—there lay the rub. William considered, and with some reason, that George was slightly desultory, not to say idle. In moments of real exasperation Catherine went so far as to remark that if George chose to exert himself he could earn an income large enough to rid the Lytteltons of all financial embarrassment, adding that in similar circumstances she was convinced that William could and would make a fortune.

Gladstonian caution occasionally collided with Lytteltonian optimism, and once or twice George was moved to protest. A long letter to Catherine begins "It is not fair to accuse us of extravagance in our general style of living". It finishes as follows: "Here endeth the Humble Apology and Defence of George William, Baron Lyttelton of Frankley, Lord Lieutenant of Worcestershire, High Sheriff of Bewdley, Ex-Under-Secretary for the

Colonies, Against the Fierce Onslaught and Grievous Charges of
Extravagance and Moral Poltroonery Brought Against Him by
His Sister-in-Law, Late She-Secretary for the Same, Prime
Ministress in Embryo, Mistress Ewart Gladstone." All disagree-
ments between Gladstones and Lytteltons inevitably tended to
dissolve in delighted laughter.

Nothing, not even financial disaster, could long distract Gladstone from the Church matters which were the deepest concern of
his life. Newman's secession left him comparatively unmoved;
"Manning is the one to take the lead," he wrote to Catherine. "I
think he has looked before and after and knows his own mind
which Newman it seems did not." How mistaken he was in this
opinion the next few years were to show, but meanwhile Catherine
was delighted that they should see much of "dear Archdeacon
Manning looking like himself, his cheerful manner and quick
eye". Some other ecclesiastics were not so much to her liking and
she wrote a pungent account of a meeting with the Archbishop of
York at Escrick: "I gaze upon this *un*earnest flat specimen of an
Archbishop in despair. I tried to speak of York Minster—'I never
go there, it is much too cold', stopped my mouth. Alas, the wife
seems to have still less *in* her but *upon* her plenty of pretty lace
capes, caps and gowns."

Gladstone was naturally much concerned about the proceedings
of the Oxford University authorities against W. G. Ward and
Catherine gave Mary an amusing description of this *enfant terrible*
of the Oxford Movement:

> "Who do you think came yesterday, suddenly announced?
> Could you but have seen William's face! Ward himself as large
> as life, so rapid his movements that he nearly ran into the room,
> and his speech as rapid, everything about him so characteristic,
> extraordinary openness and candour, an honesty quite remark-
> able, and a lack of judgement—oh, that one can see with an eye!
> He came high gee * about this mess Oakeley [1] has got himself
> into by the extraordinary folly of his letter in the paper; as Wil-
> liam says, to write it now when they are all in high hopes of
> Ward's matter being upset legally is beyond * foolish, whatever

[1] Incumbent of the Margaret Street Chapel (now All Saints', Margaret
Street).

he might wish to do afterwards. Well, this he showed Ward, who not only agreed but said he saw it was a wrong step, but that it would not be fair in him not to confess that he had been an adviser in it; this he repeated three or four times for fear William had not taken it in. He is a regular instance of honesty, certainly. William and I could have laughed when it came out, he having prophesied it beforehand."

Ward's affair was of peculiar interest to William because it concerned the University of Oxford, and Oxford was a place very near his heart. His pleasure was great when in 1847 he was asked to stand as parliamentary candidate for the University. Although he succeeded in convincing himself that his heart was not in politics it is to be doubted whether he was speaking the truth when he wrote to Catherine, "How joyfully would I retire from the barren exhausting strife of merely political contention", and certainly he displayed crass blindness when he added the comment "I do not think you would be very sorrowful". If William had retired from "merely political contention" Catherine would indeed have been sorrowful. She knew his mind better than he did, and when in all seriousness he declared himself free from temptation to ambition she must have smiled. She herself was avowedly ambitious for him and her anxiety over the Oxford election was intense. "Poor Cathie is hard pressed by Oxford," he wrote, "and her mind turns upon it." She was in bad health, being with child for the fifth time in seven years, so that it was no wonder she fretted, left behind at Fasque whilst William went off to the fray. Helen was as trying as ever; one night the whole house was suddenly in an uproar and Catherine was relieved to discover that the reason for it all was merely that Helen was having a fit—"that, as you will say," she wrote to Mary, "does not make it much better".

There were difficulties too with brother Tom, and even with old John Gladstone, who, devoted as he was to William, disapproved strongly of his son's support of Free Trade: "He poured a torrent of his feelings on that subject into my ear all mixed up with the hope that you would see the madness of Peel's course and be led to take up an independent and different one. He went on till I was aghast and partly overpowered by his vehemence. I think I had better tell him how completely your mind is made up; he forgets, or perhaps it is his extraordinary power of persuading himself of a thing he wishes." However, affection for his son and anxiety over that son's success soon swept away all trace of bitterness and in a few days' time Catherine was writing, "he is in great force and the Corn Law talk has subsided again".

In spite of an occasional storm Catherine was on the whole content to be at Fasque if she could not be with her husband. She had her children with her and she thoroughly enjoyed acting as holiday governess, taking Willy for French and Bible study, and giving a few first lessons to little Agnes and Stephen. To her surprise, remembering her own quicksilver temperament as a child, she found Willy slow but sure, and she had the wisdom to allow him to go his own pace—"by *thinking* the thing generally comes, so unlike what I was, always in a hurry to say it the moment I had read it over". She loved the company of children, her own in particular, and although she sadly missed William she made the best of their enforced separation:

"The sad blank which your absence occasions, precious thing, is indescribable, but I try to dwell upon this, that one ought to be doing what is most useful, and that it is good for one not to have all that is pleasantest. . . . Ought it not to be a pleasure to help to amuse your father and to teach and take care of your children, and then cannot I roam midst sweet flowers and beautiful trees and pray and think of you? Oh, it makes one ashamed to own that with such rich blessings any feelings of discontent can creep in! I am so thankful you have had so little rain; about half-past-three I peeped out of the window and the dry air and calmness make me think you had a genial night for travelling."

Her heart, however, was with her husband in his election fight. She wrote to tell him of friends and acquaintances who had promised their votes, and, with the partiality of a devoted wife, she was convinced that if the Oxford electors should be so benighted as to choose someone else the loss would not be on William's side: "God bless you, dearest, take care of yourself and try and let the bathing-feel* be lessened by the remembrance that all is for the best, whatever happens, besides, I really think, with

70

others, that a defeat will by no means injure you, though, alas, it must injure the poor University."

Before the results were announced William returned to Fasque, where Catherine was laid up with a threatened miscarriage. As the fateful day approached she found it more and more difficult to keep calm. On July 31st, lying flat on her back, she scribbled a note to Mary, concerned chiefly with her own health and with the matrimonial affairs of various friends, then "near half-past twelve", she added an excited postscript: "Picture me to yourself, love, writing the above to *try* to keep myself calm *en attendant* the well-known pony's trot, which would bring the probable Oxford result. First came trot—then a few awful moments when writing ceased to calm me and I tried my Prayer Book—then William's footsteps followed by the sound of 'good, good!' Another instant and the numbers were in my hand, Gladstone 104 ahead of Round! Dear creature! His excitement, his bright, thankful face were very moving."

Those days of late summer at Fasque were a golden time, with Catherine and William radiantly happy over his success and John Gladstone aglow with pride in his son. All seemed well when suddenly little Agnes, the beauty of the family and her grandfather's especial darling, developed erysipelas. Catherine's nursing skill was put to a severe test and for some days anxiety was intense, but soon she was writing to Stephen from an overflowing heart, "Thank God for his goodness; it really seems as if she were given back to us again."

During Agnes' illness Catherine had referred to William as "the best helper anyone was blest with". The two parents had nursed their child together, the father taking equal part with the mother. Speaking of his father, Viscount Gladstone wrote: "In household affairs, so long as I can remember, he took no part beyond keeping exact knowledge of general cost; my mother managed everything." Matters were very different in these early days. The Gladstone marriage was a partnership in which the senior partner did his fair share, or rather more than his fair share, of work. Catherine, as junior partner, consulted William over all manner of things great and small, and, more surprisingly, she followed his advice. For instance, she wishes young Willy to remain at Hagley but his father wishes him to come to London, so to London Willy comes.

Catherine might argue, but in the end she gave in with a very good grace.

It might almost be said that she relied too much on her husband and burdened him with what was really her own business. A whole sheaf of letters deals with the trying problem of Miss Brown, a governess whose temper was not of the best. William is adjured to speak severely to this lady, and it is typical of Catherine that she begs him to do this not on account of the children but for Miss Brown's own sake—"She is worth moulding, beside it being right to try to help her, so, my own, you will I know do it." When William, after the usual manner of husbands, dealt far too lightly with the tiresome Miss Brown, Catherine refrained from even the mildest rebuke, and wrote instead in penitent strain: "I deeply regret all the worry you have had about what was my province, my love! And Oak Farm, and Free Trade and so on all overwhelming you!"

Oak Farm and Free Trade were indeed such overwhelming problems that it appears almost miraculous that Gladstone should have found any time at all for the moulding of governesses. Now that he was back in the House of Commons he was one of the most notable supporters of Peel's Free Trade policy. In June 1848 Catherine's letters to Mary were suddenly full of politics. She had been to a grand dinner where all the talk was of "Lord John Russell's and Lord George Bentinck's *words*, as the maids say", and she had some rare praise to give to a speech by d'Israeli, as she invariably spelt the name of William's rival. So might a determined Royalist have persisted in writing "Buonaparte".

Next she turned to the ever-engrossing subject of William's own speeches: "You will have taken in that William has been trotted out on both occasions, first, navigation, second West Indian question. I *did* succeed in hearing him, but oh, it was sweltering! My neighbours canvassed William—'My brother Tom was at college with Mr. Gladstone and there he was called the Young Prime Minister, which is likely to turn out true; his eldest brother is a very odd person!' I sat so amused. They listened with great respect to William; at first one could hear a pin drop." In another letter of this summer she referred to a sudden crisis which did not in fact produce the results she predicted: "I rather need some counteraction to the whirl and excitement at the top of which is the West Indian question. William just going to Peel, n.b. no one knows how he will vote. William is firm to his opinion, and he has with him Goulburn, Sidney Herbert, Cardwell, and others, but they have been very quiet, not wanting in the least to whip for votes. It is a very serious question, the turning Ministers out now; William only votes against them because he could not in conscience do otherwise, but is awed at the possible consequences of turning them out."

In the summer of 1849 William was off abroad again on another wild-goose chase, more hopeless even than his efforts to reclaim his sister Helen. Lord Lincoln had been a close friend ever since William's undergraduate days at Oxford, and an equally warm friendship had grown up between Catherine and Lady Lincoln. But now "Suzie" Lincoln had disappeared to Italy, and as Morley tactfully put it, "rumours reached England of movements that might be no more than indiscreet, but might be worse". In plain English, Suzie was living in adultery with Lord Walpole.

Gladstone, in the simplicity of his heart, offered to seek out the erring wife and try to persuade her to return to her husband. Any man less innocent than Gladstone, and certainly any woman less unworldly than Catherine, would have seen in an instant that such a quest was both useless and dangerous. Lady Lincoln knew exactly what she was doing when she deliberately decided to run away with her lover. She knew very well that she was abandoning all claim to her children, whom she dearly loved. At the Gladstones' house she had probably met Caroline Norton, who was a frequent guest there, and in any event Caroline Norton's case was a *cause célèbre*. If Mrs. Norton, who had been declared innocent of adultery, could not regain any sort of right over her children, there was no hope at all for the guilty Lady Lincoln. Moreover, Lord Lincoln was the heir to the dukedom of Newcastle, and a woman must be very much infatuated before she abandons the prospect of becoming a duchess. Where neither husband, children, nor ducal coronet could hold her to her duty, why should William Gladstone suppose that his words would be more persuasive? The world was bound to misunderstand his motives and the malicious gossip which would certainly arise might do his reputation irreparable harm.

Gossip, however, meant less than nothing to Catherine. It

73

might be argued that it was her wifely duty to dissuade him from his foolish errand, but Catherine saw duty very differently. Neither she nor William ever looked upon any case as hopeless because they did not believe that the age of miracles was past. Even if no miracle were to occur, they would not consider themselves discharged from the obligation to make every possible effort to help, futile though those efforts would almost certainly prove to be. Catherine in particular was anxious that Suzie should be treated with gentleness and given every possible chance to mend the error of her ways. A hundred years ago the lot of a divorced woman could be very bleak and comfortless, and Catherine's warm heart yearned to rescue her friend from that unhappy fate. She herself would have gone with William had she not been within a month or two of her confinement. Obliged to stay behind, she did her best to fill a mother's place to Lady Lincoln's forsaken children who came daily to play in the nursery at Carlton House Terrace, and later accompanied the Gladstone children to Hawarden Rectory. William was entrusted with a letter which was returned to its writer unopened. Though nothing could have persuaded her to change her mind, had she but glanced at its contents Lady Lincoln must have been moved by this artless expression of Catherine's love:

"My Dearest Suzie, Upon the eve of seeing my precious husband starting for Italy and so near my confinement I am weak enough to feel sorrowful and to give way more than I should do. I hope physical weakness may have something to do with it but in truth, dear, I would not have it otherwise. I am pleased to show you proofs of the reality of our affection for you and our deep interest in your welfare, thankful that my husband can make up his mind to the sacrifice and anxiety of leaving me just now in the anxious hope that God may bless his errand. Oh, may his Christian and tender spirit, the earnest desire which fills his heart, produce an effect upon you, dear Suzie, and lead you to follow his advice and to listen seriously to what he says. He has no motive but your good; it is that, believe me, dear, which actuates him. Listen then to that persuasive voice which you have so often told me that you liked to hear. He cannot leave you in the awful, the dangerous, the discreditable position you are in, but true and real friendship can make sacrifices, and so he sets forth alone, but with many prayers. Had it been possible for me to have gone with him how quickly would I have done so, and much grieved do I feel that I cannot."

After a piteous description of the unhappiness of Lord Lincoln and his children, and a last appeal to Suzie's better nature, the letter ends: "I will not go on; you know my feelings, you can never have doubted my love, but the sending William is, may I not say, a great proof of it. God bless you and guide you and someday send you to us in peace and quiet. William is very anxious to travel as rapidly as he can and thus save time; you will see as much as you can of him and *take care of him for me*. Willy and Agnes don't forget you."

Never did a Saint George set out in aid of a lady more reluctant to be rescued from her dragon. All his efforts were vain, since Suzie was already with child by Lord Walpole, and nothing remained for Catherine but to attempt consolation for failure when she wrote to catch him in Paris on his homeward way: "My own dearest, I have not words to describe the feelings with which I read your letter today, still less shall I attempt to portray the keen sorrow, the *horror*—your description is so vivid I seem to be going through it all with you, you, my poor darling, upon whom the crushing disappointment has fallen so heavily, you who have done everything you could, everything that a Christian and a dear friend could do to save another." She assures him, "you precious of earthly beings", that he has no grounds for self-reproach: "What very good notes you wrote and how wisely and well you acted! What novel comes up to the realities of life? However dark the ending, I can have but one feeling regarding your endeavour to bring back the wanderer."

Some sort of ray of hope that the wanderer might even now return seems to have flashed across Catherine's mind, for in September she wrote to William to express a wish as startling as it was ingenuous: "Oh, for a penitentiary where for say a year she could be with a kind, judicious friend and under *good discipline*! Archdeacon Manning at the head—might she not come out a new woman?" Imagination falters at this vision of a penitentiary for erring peeresses presided over by Manning. Some such fantastic idea did, however, take root in Catherine's mind, and she plucked up her courage to write Suzie another letter: "I do not know whether on your part all that has ever passed between us is cancelled, or more than cancelled, but on mine it is not. I think you have never doubted that my interest in you was deep; you, whom I have once so tenderly loved, you will perhaps see how very deep it is, as even now I must write to you, even now!" She went on to urge repentance in words whose simple sincerity rids them of any touch of sanctimoniousness, then ended: "Now I would end my sad letter and still subscribe myself, if you will receive it, as your friend Catherine Gladstone." The letter was returned with the curt message that if Lady Lincoln had known from whom it came she would never have opened it. Some time afterwards Catherine received news through a mutual friend who had met Lady Lincoln on the Continent. In the course of conversation Lady Lincoln exclaimed, "Do you know Mrs. Gladstone? Will you give her a message from me, a terrible one? She is likely to see a great deal of my children. For most things they could not be better than with her, but tell her that if ever she speaks against their mother my ghost will haunt her. When she is happy with her children let her think of me." "Oh, poor creature," was Catherine's only comment.

Lady Lincoln not unnaturally thought that Gladstone had come to spy upon her and other people were only too ready to take a similar view of his actions. The whole fantastic, foolish episode is interesting as illustrative of the Gladstones' almost catastrophic lack of judgement in ordinary affairs: it is also an example of the lengths to which they were prepared to go in an attempt to save a soul.

Chapter Five

THE tenth anniversary of the Gladstones' marriage occurred whilst William was still abroad, and the thought of their own unbroken happiness made Lord Lincoln's tragedy appear yet more poignant. As 1849 drew to a close Catherine could look back on ten years of married life darkened by nothing more serious than the passing cloud of Agnes' illness. There were now six children in the nursery, all of them healthy and happy, although recently Catherine had begun to entertain vague fears about young Jessy who did not seem quite so lively or so flourishing as she should. Willy was still his mother's darling, a sensitive child whose one fault was a certain indolence. So many hopes and dreams centred on young Willy that perhaps he found their weight a little burdensome. The position of Heir Apparent is never an easy one. Next came the beautiful Agnes, and then Stephen, serious-minded, reliable "Stephy", whom Catherine rather surprisingly described as being at the age of five "a comical character". He was a child who felt deeply: "he treasures things, they sink in and come out after one would think they are forgotten", and later Catherine wrote of her hope that one day Stephy would take Holy Orders. Both Agnes and Stephy lived overshadowed by Willy's abilities, or by what Catherine fondly imagined Willy's abilities to be, and by the precocious cleverness of their cousin, Meriel Lyttelton. Agnes had her mother's beauty without her sparkle, Stephy his father's industry without his genius. The touch of brilliance so characteristic of both parents seemed to have passed these children by.

Perhaps it reappeared in Catherine Jessy, although it is impossible to judge accurately of the character and abilities of so young a child. In looks this little girl resembled her father, but the accounts of her fearlessness, her physical strength, and her passionately affectionate nature call to mind the three-year-old Pussy so lovingly described by Lady Glynne.

In the library at Hawarden there hangs the picture of a plump, dark-haired, jolly little girl, "a merry happy soul, very fat and chubby", who seems born to be the life and soul of any nursery. Jessy's particular gift was the gift of loving. A strange habit of hers, noted down by her father, conjures up more clearly than anything else an image of this passionate, warm-hearted little creature.

William Gladstone always wore a guard to hide what remained of his amputated finger. By instinct all children hate and fear deformity, but Jessy would carefully remove the guard and cover the mutilated stump with her kisses. She was quick above the average, and it seemed as if she would soon pass Stephy at lessons as surely as she was overtopping him in physical growth. One curious lack of perception worried her mother. This quick-witted child would sometimes fail to obey a perfectly simple command, such as a request to shut a door or straighten a rug. She would disobey not from naughtiness, but from a curious inability to understand what was asked of her, and the sequel would be a wholly irrational fit of temper. Catherine was puzzled, but she consoled herself with the fact that the words, "Love me, Jessy", would always bring the little girl out of her tantrums to throw her arms round Papa's or Mama's neck.

After Jessy came Mary, "the mountain bird", who throve best at Fasque in the bracing air of the Scotch Highlands, and then baby Helen, "not a bit the less dear and acceptable", wrote her father, "because she happens to be the fifteenth Miss Gladstone among my father's grandchildren".

The education of children was a subject in which Catherine took a real and serious interest. Years later she wrote a preface to a little book of instruction to parents, entitled *Early Influences*, and her remarks are interesting as showing the principles which she applied to the upbringing of her own family. In those days when children were often left almost entirely to the care of nurse or governess, she stresses the importance of "learning a child's disposition by means of hourly watchfulness". She does not believe in too much carefulness, however: "Children are often overnoticed and over-petted and considered in every way conceivable", and she has a wise caution that might well be taken to heart by many a twentieth-century expert in education: "the very advantage of charming by interesting books may become an actual snare".

The education of the Gladstone family was not entirely left to their mother. William took an active interest in the lives of his children, playing with them, riding with them, supervising their prayers and their lessons. He could always be relied upon to answer childish questions, and the Lyttelton cousins especially delighted in him as a source of entertaining information: "Who wouldn't enjoy a ride with Uncle William, able to answer any question you ask him?" exclaimed Lucy, the second Lyttelton girl.

The six Gladstones all but made one family with the still more numerous Lytteltons. In nine years Catherine bore six children, but Mary outdid her sister, achieving seven without benefit of twins. Catherine delighted in every addition to her own family— "She reminds me of myself in her love of children," she wrote of a friend, "quite looking forward to the next!"—but she was less happy about Mary's ever-increasing brood. "I trust you are safe from any baby", she remarked in one letter, adding in sadly prophetic vein, "Really, it is wrong, people being made ill by having *tant d'enfants*." Few indeed were the moments when Mary was safe from any baby. When William had been staying without her at Hagley, Catherine wrote to Mary: "William tells me you three had such a funny conversation about having children, and that you and George seemed fully to agree that four were enough —I think he thought you and George rather serious about it."

Serious they may well have been but they certainly did not stop short at the desirable number of four, and the size of their family laid an ever-growing strain both on the mother's health and the father's finances. Jokes about the Lytteltons' poverty were many; the Glynnese Glossary, for instance, in explaining the term "false flash", gives this pertinent illustration: "Lady Glynne applied it to her daughter's marriage with Lord Lyttelton, alluding to the combination in that nobleman's circumstances of respectable rank with comparative poverty, 'quite a false flash'."

The Gladstones worried far more over the Lytteltons' finances than ever the Lytteltons did themselves. William would endeavour to help in any way possible, from attempting to find George a lucrative Government post to proffering the loan of the Glad-stonian carriage and pair, whilst Catherine would write Mary long letters of practical advice, questioning, for instance, the necessity of keeping a second laundry-maid, or urging enquiry into the amount of beer consumed in the servants' hall. More serious, however, was the danger to Mary's health. Before the birth of Mary's babies Catherine suffered agonies of apprehension which were only slightly alleviated when William persuaded George to make use of that anxiety-dispelling invention, the electric telegraph. How-ever, once the babies had arrived they were hardly less dear to their aunt than to their mother.

The Pussies still shared everything in common, even their children. Great cavalcades of nurses and babies were for ever travelling between Hagley, Hawarden and London, and this winter of 1849–50, when the Gladstone family were staying at Hagley, the big nursery at the top of the house was crammed to overflowing with children under the age of ten, presided over by the Lyttelton nannie, "Newmany". And there in the very middle of the turmoil would be Catherine, the beloved Auntie Pussy, holding out her arms to welcome as many small creatures as could possibly squeeze themselves into her embrace. She was always ready to laugh, to sing, to invent games or tell stories, whilst Mary would stand in the door and smile benevolently at the tumult inside, remarking with the ellipsis typical of the Glynnese tongue, "Well, children *are*."

In spring and summer Hagley was particularly delightful: "the children high gee* violet hunting and then full of lamb-catching, and the grand treat of seeing the cows milked, the little calves having their dinner and a drink of milk fresh from the cow". Catherine was at heart a countrywoman and even when in London her family was not to be deprived of the country pleasures which were then so easily accessible: "I want the children to drive into the country and play in *fields*; they need not go many miles, indeed, only just beyond the Regent's Park."

The business of Oak Farm and the Hawarden estate was a shadow on all this happiness, but William and Catherine were not the people to allow their lives to be spoilt by financial difficulties. Catherine was chiefly worried by the thought that his connection with her family had brought this burden upon her husband: "My poor darling, I see the Oak Farm has been pressing on you when you wrote; alas, that I should have brought this thorn in the side, but yet should I not be thankful and abundantly so? To a certainty Hawarden would have gone without you." William hastened to reassure her: "No persons who have been in contact with it [Oak Farm] can be so absolutely blameless as you and Mary, nor can our relationship together be rendered in the very smallest degree either more or less a blessing by the addition or subtraction of worldly wealth."

Politically William was still in the wilderness with Peel but no one doubted that his day would come. Catherine chafed a little that it should come so slowly, and she was eager that he should set up as leader of a party of his own. She was always suspicious of Lord John Russell and she very much mistrusted the Russell-Peel alliance of Whig and Tory Free-Traders, which she referred to as "that flat and miserable sham government". Such political predilections as she had were Tory and she longed to see William at the head of a new and glorious Conservative party. "I wish you had a nice party assembled round you," she wrote from Hagley on February 21st, 1850, "surely many, many would joyfully follow *you*! I cannot bear you having no regular number and I cannot stand d'Israeli as a leader. I could almost like you to stand up grandly and rally your numbers about you! Colonial matters would be the stand and I see numbers flocking in under your standard. Away with d'Israeli and the combination of Peel and Russell!" William replied that she did "indeed rise to very daring heights", declaring, with rather unconvincing modesty, that if a new leader were required the choice should fall not on him but on Lord Lincoln or Sidney Herbert, a suggestion which provoked the indignant rejoinder, "How can Lincoln or Herbert be named in the same breath as my old man?"

Catherine was right; her William was a great man. If he had not been she could not have borne so patiently with a temperament entirely different to her own. "Explanations, wordiness, prosiness bored and bothered her," says her daughter. "She wanted to get without delay to the point; always she preferred short cuts, leaving things to the imagination." William Gladstone's genius was of the spoken rather than the written word; his contemporaries could enjoy the magic of his voice and he did not appear so prosy to them as he does to posterity, who know him only through the vast bulk of his writings and reported speeches. Nevertheless, he was undoubtedly given to wordiness, and sometimes Catherine's impatience broke through. "Oh, William dear, if you weren't such a great man you would be a terrible bore," she was once heard to exclaim, and on another occasion at a lunch party, when he was holding forth at some length on the subject of child welfare, she astonished the assembled guests by remarking tartly, "You know nothing whatsoever about the matter." This outburst cost her a subsequent agony of remorse, but for the most part she had herself well under control. He trod majestically down the middle of the road whilst she leaped and bounded to conclusions, but nevertheless their way together through life was curiously free from disagreements. She accepted his "trolls", as the Glynnese speaker would describe his long dissertations, as an inseparable part of his greatness, although there must have been times when she was sorely tempted to cry, "I could throw my shoe at him", a Glynnese expression "denoting a state of great irritation in the presence of an eminent bore".

Their first ten years of married life had been so happy that Catherine was minded to cry "Touch wood!" "How often one sees after long prosperity a long train of sorrow," she had once written and she was always afraid lest they should take happiness for granted: "perhaps the very prosperity we have been blessed with makes me more on the look-out for a reverse". And with the spring of 1850 the reverse came; Jessy fell ill of meningitis.

All the past winter the child had been ailing and curiously torpid, but in the same letter in which she had recounted her dream of William as a party leader Catherine had noted cheerfully, "I no longer fret about Jessy now." Six weeks later Jessy was dead. The child suffered so severely that the week of her illness was a peculiarly agonising time to the two parents, who shared all the nursing between them. When the end came it was the father and not the mother who broke down in paroxysms of grief; Catherine was chiefly aware of a sensation of relief and thankfulness that at last her child was free from pain. Even in the very middle of her own troubles she could not forget the needs of other people. At the time of Jessy's illness Caroline Lyttelton, George's sister, chanced to be in London in some sort of difficulty and as a matter of course she turned to Catherine. "Dear Pussy quite toiled for us," Caroline wrote to Mary. "You know her powers of cheering and helping, it was genial, the very look of her."

Jessy died in London, but, acting on an odd impulse, William decided that she should be buried at Fasque. Catherine could not accompany him to Scotland for the funeral because the needs of her other children kept her in the south. Agnes and Stephy were both ailing and little Mary was suffering from eye-trouble so, taking one of her lightning decisions, Catherine swept the family off to Brighton, from whence she wrote to William on the day after the funeral: "Oh, if I but knew *you* were pretty well, dearest —it seems a sad silence, now more than ever when my heart if it were possible clings even more to you, clings doubly. Our feelings, our hopes and fears have been so entirely one."

William found comfort in writing a brief memoir of Jessy, striving, as bereaved parents strive the world over, to save at least some memory of his child from oblivion, but although the account was written under stress of great emotion no trace of that emotion communicates itself to the reader. William could move crowds by his spoken words, but all his writings, even the most personal of them, strangely fail to touch the heart. The most curious part of this memoir is an account of Jessy's illness, based on a diary which he kept at the time and giving all medical details, symptoms, food taken, medicines, and so forth with as much accuracy as a nurse's report sheet. Even in the face of death William Gladstone could not be otherwise than businesslike. Catherine's epitaph for her own Jessy was at once more brief and more human, "She was a darling baby."

On his return from Fasque William joined his family at Brighton where Caroline Lyttelton was also staying. A letter from her to her mother gives an interesting picture of Catherine and William: "Dear Pussy looks much worn and sits very silent when there is general conversation going on, else she seems well and says that this time seems to be a great calm after the storms before. As to him, it is very remarkable what a simplicity there is about him. At one time he dwells on their sorrow and on the blessed and elevating thoughts belonging to it, with bursts of tears often; at another, laughs so with the children, and quite enjoys shopping with Catherine, choosing their own tea-cake and the like." William had

perforce to go back to London without Catherine. In the middle of
their mourning he was doubtful of the propriety of appearing
even at official entertainments; "I have made this too much of a
pleasure day", he wrote ruefully to Catherine on the occasion of
his appearance at an Academy dinner. Catherine herself took up a
very much more sensible and realistic attitude. "Oh, no, dearest,
you are not wrong," she counselled him, "it is nearly a month
since our sweet Jessy left us, therefore you are doing nothing unusual, and as to feeling, I have no creep or misgiving; yours lies
deeper and is not to be touched by such things."

Gladstone need not have feared that he was becoming unduly
lighthearted and frivolous, even when indulging in "the incredible
gaiety of a concert at Lansdowne House". Troubles pressed hard
upon him and looking back afterwards on this year of 1850 he
described it as being "a terrible time". Amongst other things he
was much perturbed by the business of "the Gorham Judgement",
a complicated and exacerbated controversy concerned with the
doctrine of baptismal regeneration. The dust of a hundred years
lies thick upon this issue, and it is salutary to remember that not
one in a thousand of devout Anglicans has ever so much as heard
of this judgement, which William described to Catherine as "going
to the very root of all life and all teaching in the Church of
England". Whilst Catherine remained at Brighton she wrote
William a typical letter in which affairs ecclesiastical and affairs
domestic jostle each other in inextricable confusion: "Here is
your dear letter with much more than a crumb of comfort about the
wretched Gorham matter. The Bishop of Bath and Wells is here
and George is going to pump him and get everything out of him
he can. I quite agree with you about Taylor's bill and shall tell
Mary. Our huge Sunday beef fed us all till Thursday came! I trust
from what you say that Archdeacon Manning's spirits are revived
by the move of the twenty bishops."

This year Catherine and William had for the first time together
tasted the bitterness of personal loss. On top of that grief came
religious distress, to be followed by political tragedy. On June
29th Peel was thrown from his horse and died three days later
as a result of his injuries. To Gladstone this meant the loss of a
leader to whom he was bound not only by political affinity but
by personal affection. Catherine's comments on Peel's death are,

however, curiously impersonal, and concerned chiefly with Lady Peel's state of mind. Perhaps for once she was too much absorbed in her own affairs to spare much attention for troubles outside the home circle. The loss of Jessy had made her doubly fearful for the children remaining to her and now with alarm she saw that little Mary's eyesight was seriously threatened. For the sake of this sick child she left William to pay his annual visit to Fasque alone whilst she took the children to the seaside at Rhyl. From there she wrote more cheerfully, giving a better account of young Mary, whom she believed to be greatly benefited by her favourite panacea of sea-bathing.

Then came the last, and in some ways the most tragic blow of all. Of recent years Catherine had spent much of her time at Hawarden Rectory with Henry and his wife Lavinia, to whom she was particularly attached. "Long may the Rectory remain the little earthly paradise that it now seems to be", she had written long ago in her first flush of pleasure at Henry's marriage, and a happy place the Rectory had remained in spite of the non-appearance of the longed-for son and heir. Now all this was to be changed. A few days after Catherine had written so happily to William about little Mary's improved health Lavinia Glynne gave birth to a fourth daughter and a fortnight later, in spite of Catherine's devoted nursing, the young mother died.

Catherine had risen above her own personal tragedy of Jessy's death but she could not be brave in another's distress. Henry was her favourite brother and the sight of his grief and the picture of his little girls left forlorn cut her to the heart. She grieved bitterly for Lavinia, so young, so attractive, so loving and so deeply loved. Catherine herself was in no physical state to withstand the shock of another sorrow. She was once again with child, and whilst she had been sitting up night after night nursing Lavinia she had felt so sick and ill that the dying woman had guessed her secret and the shared knowledge of her coming child had formed an added bond between them. Now with Henry disconsolate, his children left motherless, and her own heart sore for her lost Jessy, Catherine felt her buoyancy forsake her. When the doctors declared that little Mary's health demanded a warm climate and suggested a winter in Naples she could feel no enthusiasm for the idea except in so far as William would benefit by

G

the enforced rest and absence of all business. Of the children it was decided that only Agnes and Mary should accompany their parents abroad; Willy had recently gone to boarding-school and Stephy, with baby "Lena", so called to distinguish her from the other Helen, could be left behind at Hagley. Parting with so small a creature as Lena was a sad business but most of all Catherine grieved over the separation from young Willy.

After a long and uncomfortable Channel crossing the little party arrived at Paris, Catherine sad and unwell, but striving to hide her feelings lest they should cast a cloud over William's well-earned holiday. They travelled on by way of Turin and Genoa and thence by sea to Naples. Three times had William Gladstone visited that city, and each of those occasions had marked an epoch in his life. On his first visit he had suddenly experienced the conviction that the Catholic Church existed as a God-given society and that the Church of England was an integral part of that Church. And just as his first visit to Naples had been a turning-point in his religious life so his second one had proved all-important to his personal happiness, for it was in Naples that his attachment to Catherine had ripened into love. Now once again he found himself in Naples, and this third visit was to prove decisive for his political future.

In the autumn of 1850 Gladstone had gone to Naples hoping for a rest from politics, a quiet holiday which would allow him opportunity to indulge in his taste for Italian art and give him time to pursue his classical studies. Instead he found himself involved in a struggle against an apparently impregnable citadel of evil, "the negation of God erected into a system of government". With his new friend Lacaita, legal secretary to the British Embassy, he attended the trial of Poerio and his fellow Liberals and heard them condemned by a travesty of justice to the living death of the Neapolitan prisons. Later, he succeeded in visiting these ghastly places and talking with the political prisoners. What he saw and heard determined for ever the nature of his political creed; Naples turned Gladstone into a Liberal.

To all this Catherine remained almost entirely indifferent. She cannot have been unaware of the revelation that had burst upon her husband but she was curiously unmoved by it. She is usually supposed to have been in everything subservient to him, making his interests and his enthusiasms the only objects of her thought, yet here he was, engrossed by the sufferings of the Neapolitan Liberals and the iniquity of the government which had condemned them to such a fate, whilst she remained wholly preoccupied with her own concerns. The fact that her letters to Mary Lyttelton are almost completely devoid of reference to the prisoners can perhaps be explained by her fear of possible censorship. This caution was probably justified; to one of her letters William adds the note, "Only think, I am watched by the police", and when he later left Naples his correspondence with Catherine was opened and intercepted.

On one of the very rare occasions when she makes any reference to the situation she first mentions Lacaita by name, then scores the name through. Clearly William had reproached her for her lack of caution, and she had scratched out the name in her usual careless manner, leaving it still legible to the eye of any interested person. (When William himself blacked out a word he did it with most tiresome thoroughness.) No thought of censorship, however, could affect the entries in her private diary, and here there is no mention at all of the subject which William found so absorbing until, nearly two months after their arrival at Naples, the arrest of Lacaita himself shocks her into awareness of the position. Even then her interest seems to have been very short-lived.

Catherine was in fact too tired to make the effort necessary to see beyond her own sorrow and preoccupation. Yearning after England and the children she had left behind, she was in that homesick frame of mind when the arrival or non-arrival of the mail becomes the most important event of the day. "Really, the pleasure is too great", she wrote after receiving her first letter from young Willy. And the remembrance of Lavinia never left her. At the most incongruous moments, when buying wine, for instance, in a *trattoria*, the memory of that deathbed would flash across her mind so vividly that she might almost suppose she saw a vision. Perversely, she clung to her grief, finding in it a sort of pleasure—"How one does like one's mourning!" She longed to be able to talk with some sympathetic person, to dwell again and again on the events of that sad fortnight of Lavinia's illness, but she had the wisdom to realise that she must not sadden or worry William too frequently and where casual acquaintances were concerned she shrank from any mention of her loss.

Both William and Catherine hankered after English news, and William was especially perturbed by the uproar following the publication of Cardinal Wiseman's ill-advised letter "From out the Flaminian Gate" establishing the Roman Catholic hierarchy in England, and Lord John Russell's equally ill-advised reply addressed to the Bishop of Durham, "not such a letter as a Prime Minister should write and positively insulting to the Pope". The Gladstones had fallen in with Lord and Lady Shrewsbury, some of the most influential of English Roman Catholics, and with them they discussed Lord John's "most *ungentlemanlike, aggressive, unstatesmanlike* conduct". On this point they were all agreed, but Catherine was a little suspicious of the Shrewsburys' motives: "He was high gee* about converts or what I call perverts. They even invited us, children and all, to their villa in Sicily. What they expected to make of us I know not." She was hoping that Manning might be able to join them for Christmas. Had he done so William must have become aware of his friend's change of opinion so that the shock of his reception into the Roman Catholic Church might have been lessened and the bitter rift between the two men avoided.

Though Manning failed to appear, the Gladstones did not lack for society: "The foreigners are all very anxious to have William and he has had some interesting conversations with various Ministers, Neapolitan princes, etc. Many say 'Is that *le célèbre Monsieur Gladstone?*' They beg for introductions. You know how this always pleases me, to see him appreciated." Catherine herself came in for her own share of appreciation: "They say I am like a Spaniard and not like an Englishwoman", she reported, a remark which was assuredly meant as a high compliment. Catherine always fought shy of compliments; when the painter Richmond, in most flattering manner, pressed to be allowed to do more drawings of her face, she wrote to Mary, "He did not take it in until he saw me at home in white muslin and blue wreath. How egotistical! Only to you."

Apart from the Neapolitans themselves, society in Naples consisted of a small and intimate group of mixed nationalities, mostly English but including a few pretty Russian girls who much admired William's baritone voice and often invited him to join them in impromptu concerts. Among the English visitors the Gladstones made especial friends with Lord and Lady Holland, and with a Mrs. Monsell, the wife of an invalid parson who had been ordered to Naples in the hope that his health might benefit by the climate. Readers of Miss Yonge will find an admirable portrait of Mrs. Monsell disguised under the name of Sister Constance in *The Castle Builders* and *The Pillars of the House.* She was a remarkable woman, and the friendship with her and with her saintly husband, with whom William frequently enjoyed a game of chess, formed one of the Gladstones' greatest pleasures during this Naples visit.

Monsell's ill-health prevented his wife from joining in those excursions to Vesuvius or Capo di Monte which the Gladstones so much enjoyed. Catherine delighted too in shopping expeditions, when William would hunt for pictures and ivories whilst she indulged her love of giving presents by buying a silk gown for the governess at home or a set of tortoiseshell pins to adorn Mary Lyttelton's hair. The sunlight, the scenery, and the blue skies of Naples were working their own peculiar magic and restoring Catherine to something like her normal strength and spirits.

Little Mary, or "Naples Mary" as she was beginning to be called to distinguish her from her aunt, grew daily more robust and her eyes showed definite improvement, and William had also benefited by the holiday, in spite of the fact that, as Catherine expressed it, "he was dreadfully taken out of by the imprisonments and injustices". She was comforted too by news of Henry Glynne, who was facing his loss with courage and resignation, finding strength in the performance of his parish duties and in the love of his little daughters.

All seemed well, but Catherine's health had not really recovered from the strain of the last eight months, and at the end of November she had a bad miscarriage. It was her first real illness since her marriage and it left her badly shaken in health and spirits, although she was up for Christmas to enjoy a "Christmas Tree" made from an arbutus decked with coloured lanterns. She recorded rather wistfully that, at a New Year's party, "we kissed and wished each other a happy New Year in hot negus; I found it difficult to look merry." A week later she was back in bed with a serious relapse.

Catherine's renewed illness placed William in a quandary. Lord John Russell's ministry was obviously near its end, and at any moment the "Peelites" would be faced with the decision as to whether they would or would not take office under Lord Stanley. Both Lord Canning and Lord Richard Cavendish had written begging Gladstone not to delay his return, yet it was impossible for him to leave Catherine alone and ill in Naples. The problem was solved by the arrival of Stephen Glynne.

Catherine was ruefully aware of the fact that in exchanging her husband for her brother she was getting a bad bargain. In one of her letters she writes an amusing account of Stephen's inability to deal with everyday affairs; instead of Stephen looking after her it is she who must look after Stephen: "I sometimes feel inclined to laugh as I ask him to do something, the very simplest thing such as shutting a window or paying a cab fare; the one he shuts to perhaps without attempting to bolt it and open it flies, the other he pays according to my order but is sure to rush after me to know what is to be done, the man perhaps after him, or, what it ends in, after *me*!"

But she very well knew how important it was that William should return as soon as possible to England, and she was anxious lest people should think he had already lingered too long. Time and again she begged Mary and her other correspondents to make clear to everyone that her illness was a real and serious one, and that, far from making it an excuse to prolong his holiday, William had in fact left her before their friends in Naples considered him justified in doing so. The thought of the coming separation upset her so much that on the day of his departure she fell ill again and had to take once more to her bed, but she said goodbye to him with a good courage. "I was quite anxious William should have as little anxiety as possible," she wrote to Mary, "so I put my best leg foremost, knowing as I did the crying out there was for him." In the event all went well; there was no further delay in her recovery, Stephen proved himself a kind and amusing companion, "Naples Mary's" eyesight was pronounced

greatly benefited by her winter abroad and with the coming of
spring the whole party were on their way to Paris, where William
joined them, a prelude to the joyful reunion with the three
children left behind in England.

Chapter Six

EXCITEMENT ended in anti-climax. William was duly invited to join Lord Stanley's government, but declined, Catherine acquiescing in the wisdom of his decision. This year of 1851 was notable for the opening of the Great Exhibition in the Crystal Palace, which was in great part organised by William's friend, Lord Granville. William himself did not attend the opening ceremony, but Catherine was present and wrote him an account of the scene: "It would be absurd to attempt to describe the sight, one's very idea of Arabian Nights and fairy scenes, and as glittering and lovely as anything of the kind could be. You will be amused that I and Lady Granville kept a place for Lady Stanley, by whom I sat"—the amusement was presumably due to the remembrance of political differences between the husbands of the three ladies. "The Queen looked her very best and the two children quite particularly nice. The sun shone brightly, the fountains played, the [illegible] glittered. The dear old Duke of Wellington [was] so cheered on his birthday; I got a nice shake of his hand, which did me good."

In Gladstone and Lyttelton circles the year was notable for the publication of *The Glynnese Glossary*, compiled by George Lyttelton. Glynnese is one of the wittiest systems of private slang, and many of its expressions have now passed into general use, among them being "over the moon", "killing", "old maidish" and "trapesing". Referring to the words "criersome" and "twarly", meaning peevish or inclined to cry, the *Glossary* says, "the chief authorities are Mrs. Gladstone and Lady Lyttelton, principally the former, as indeed she must be understood to be for all the terms noted in this Glossary where not otherwise expressed". In the words of the compiler Catherine was "the great Queen of

Glynnese" and some of its expressions were peculiar to her, as, for instance, "human" and "not human". "The chimneys are more human", she somewhat surprisingly remarked about her London house, meaning that they had ceased to smoke.

Although William Gladstone was admittedly no expert in the use of Glynnese, the *Glossary* gives him credit for being "the first and hitherto the only person who has succeeded in introducing a variation of his own devising into this jealous and mysterious language".

"To be in an addle", the author of the *Glossary* continues, "is believed to be an importation of that eminent Ex-Minister, and it is frequently used by him in letters both on public and domestic matters to his wife. For about two days before the delivery of a great speech he is, or believes that he is, in a universal *addle* on all possible subjects; and during that time Mrs. Gladstone will, with a wink and a nod, advise her friends to keep at a respectful distance from that Right Hon. Person; and especially to eschew bringing dirt upon the carpet from their boots, which in all cases he will straightaway shovel up and fling into the fire in the very eye of the offender."

The *Glossary* pokes sly fun at many of the great man's idiosyncrasies, his horror of anything spilt on the table-cloth, his habit of making a list of his coats when setting out on a journey, his pleasingly childish greed for sugar and sweets.

Catherine's own letters are so full of Glynnese as to be almost incomprehensible to anyone unversed in this peculiar language. Take, for instance, her description of the scene after some grand party: "As we went away done up in our cloaks I heard nobody more or less than d'Izzy call out to William 'Take care of yourself'. I made a note of this and asked myself who's who and what's what*." Or again: "Judge of the blow not to be met! Was I not gaunt*? Two flies waiting for mawkins*." Or again, "Your secret to be sure is issimus*." Ellipsis was the very essence of Glynnese, as witness the expressions "than which" and "beyond" and the curious use of the verb "to be", best shown by Catherine's phrase describing her feelings at saying goodbye to children who must grow up and leave home for boarding-school, "yes, loving them is".

Catherine had her doubts as to the wisdom of allowing the *Glossary* to circulate beyond the family circle: "Oh, don't let everyone have it," she begged of Mary, "I have the cares of that terrible word *rotgut.*" In Glynnese "to have the cares" means to be worried about something; when, for instance, Catherine writes that the Bishop of Oxford has the cares of the Prince of Wales and Prince Alfred she does not mean that he is in charge of their Royal Highnesses, but that he is perturbed about their upbringing and behaviour. That same bishop, Samuel Wilberforce, was one of the few people who begged successfully for a copy of the *Glossary*; Catherine refused one to Monckton Milnes, but she gave way before the Bishop's plea, presumably supposing him to be shockproof against such words as rotgut.

Such an extensive and complicated language as Glynnese could only grow up in a very self-contained family group. Fond as they were of their innumerable friends, Glynnes, Lytteltons and Gladstones lived very much in a world of their own, and no outsiders ever quite succeeded in penetrating into that magic circle. There was, however, one exception to this rule.

Some time after her return from Naples Catherine made friends with a Mr. and Mrs. John Talbot. The Talbots were rich, aristocratic and unworldly, and John Talbot was much interested in Church affairs, especially the building of new churches. When Catherine was collecting for a new church at Harrow Weald he sent her fifty pounds, enclosing the money in a charming letter which began, "I have never seen Harrow Weald but I have seen *you.*" Under the shadow of grief the friendship was to ripen into deep intimacy.

During the spring of 1852 Catherine was staying at Brighton with various Gladstone children convalescent after some infectious illness. The Talbots had also come to Brighton for reasons of health since John Talbot was consumptive and it was thought that his lungs might benefit from the sea air. Whilst he was there death came to him suddenly, almost unexpectedly, and Catherine was filled with sympathy for the newly-made widow, and deeply impressed by her courage and resignation. A warm and deep affection grew up between them in which Mary Lyttelton shared. The Talbot boys, John and Edward, were made free of Hagley and Hawarden, whilst Lytteltons and Gladstones soon learnt to treat the Talbot house in London as an annexe to their own home. John, the elder son, was nearly grown-up when his father died, Edward, ten years his junior, went with Albert Lyttelton and Stephy Gladstone to a small school at Geddington, and in the holidays Talbots, Lytteltons and Gladstones made one huge family.

"My best love to dear Mrs. Talbot," Catherine wrote to Mary, "I often think of her trials. It is a privilege that we can comfort her a little; how much she returns the comfort I could not attempt to describe." It is typical of her age and upbringing that Catherine, who loved her with an almost sisterly love, always referred to her friend as "Mrs. Talbot", "darling Mrs. Talbot" on occasions, but never "Caroline". Mrs. Talbot was not, in fact, a person to encourage any sort of familiarity; she had few social graces, and her son Edward described her as "a woman of very great reserve and of concentrated rather than expansive affections". Catherine, however, was perspicacious enough to appreciate the fine intelligence and entire sincerity underlying this somewhat formidable exterior, and, above all, she recognised in Mrs. Talbot someone who understood and shared the fundamental principles which governed her own life.

To Caroline Talbot, as to Catherine Gladstone, it was no effort at all to put first things first; religion was to them of such supreme importance that it would have been an impossibility to accord it any secondary place in their lives. Unlike her husband, Catherine wrote or spoke very little about religious matters; she simply took religion for granted, like air or food or sleep. The actual practices of religion gave her acute pleasure. Many years afterwards someone said of her niece Lucy, "Church is Lucy's public house and it is impossible to keep her out of it." So it was with Catherine herself. "Give me credit for not going to evening church", she wrote triumphantly to William, certain that she had acquired great merit by denying herself the pleasure of attending evensong for the duty of a drive in the fresh air.

Just as it seemed a natural and delightful thing to Catherine to love and worship God, so did it seem natural and delightful to her to love and serve her fellow men. The hardest thing in the world for her would have been to emulate the Priest and Levite and pass by on the other side. The early eighteen-fifties saw the beginning of that remarkable work of mercy which husband and wife undertook together on behalf of London prostitutes. They did not merely found shelters and sit on committees, though these things they did as well; night after night Gladstone roamed the dark and dangerous streets, speaking to women and persuading them to come back with him to the shelter of his home. The physical danger was real enough but far more important was the risk to his reputation and of this Catherine was at least as well aware as he was. If his work was heroic her part in it was no less courageous. One night, walking back from the House of Commons with his Private Secretary, Gladstone stopped to speak to a prostitute, whom he persuaded to accompany them. The Private Secretary not unnaturally protested. "What will your wife say if you bring this woman home with you?" he asked. Gladstone looked at him with unfeigned surprise, "Why, it is to my wife that I am bringing her."

By a polite fiction Victorian ladies were supposed to be ignorant of the very existence of prostitutes, yet here was William bringing these women into his own house and handing them over to Catherine with implicit confidence in her kindness and judgement. Even today, when women are expected to take a more realistic attitude, few wives would wish to find themselves faced with so delicate and difficult a situation. The domestic problem alone, must have given rise to thorny complications. What, for instance, did the servants think of these strange guests? How were they housed and where did they have their meals? Surely not with the governess, or with the faithful Hamptons, butler and house-keeper of many years' standing. And did the children never suspect that anything unusual was going on, never ask questions? If so, what was Catherine's answer? Such trivial, even ridiculous difficulties must have been very hard to face, harder, perhaps, than the more heroic anxiety over the risk to William's good name. Indeed, where that was concerned Catherine seems to have troubled herself as little as he did.

In her letters references to his nightly excursions of rescue are very few, and those that exist are entirely concerned with the physical danger involved—"Take care of yourself and don't walk at night to look after people." Pages, however, are devoted to the various women whom they were endeavouring to help back to a respectable way of life, and Catherine herself corresponded at length with some of these girls, using very forcible language when they showed signs of backsliding. To her way of thinking it was the duty of a wife to support her husband in such a work as this rather than to warn him to take heed of tittle-tattle.

In this particular instance Catherine's scorn of worldly wisdom may have been well justified, but often she was inclined to push her disregard of other people's opinions and her disdain of social convention beyond the limits of what was wise or right.

All through Queen Victoria's reign politics remained inextricably entangled with Society with a capital S; the London Season, for instance, was timed to coincide with the session of Parliament, and political fortunes could be seriously affected by drawing-room gossip. To all this side of life Catherine remained supremely, and rather foolishly, indifferent. She could not separate herself from it—indeed, she went about as much as anyone else to balls and parties, and "brought out" daughters and nieces in approved style—but she gave it the smallest possible share of her time and attention, with the result that she was extremely slipshod in her discharge of social obligations.

Invitations would be sent out late or not at all (on one occasion a number were found slipped down the side of a couch some days after the date of the party in question), guests would arrive, only to find their hostess had forgotten all about them, trains would not be met, calls would not be returned. "Called on the injured Mrs. Egerton and loved her momentarily for being out", so runs an early entry in Catherine's diary, which reflects very accurately her attitude towards the dull but necessary business of calling. She never paused to reflect that if Mrs. Egerton were injured— and Catherine's carelessness in returning calls was to raise up a host of injured females complaining to high heaven of her neglect and indifference—it would have been as well to make an effort to find that lady at home and to exercise a little tact in smoothing down her ruffled feelings. The rescue of a prostitute was doubtless a more meritorious action than the dropping of a card upon Mrs. Egerton and her like, but Catherine was the wife of a politician, and one, moreover, who was notoriously careless of the small change of polite society, and it was her duty to see that her charitable concerns did not interfere with her social obligations.

97

With William it was a case of "could not"; it was not in him to cajole or conciliate people with those little attentions which have so small a meaning and yet so great an influence. His short sight made it difficult for him to recognise faces and even in the lobbies of the House of Commons he would walk past people without giving them a word or sign of greeting. This might seem a trivial failing and one for which he could hardly be held to blame, yet it was a serious handicap to his efficiency as a party leader. It should have been Catherine's part to cover up her husband's lapses, and it was a part for which she was ideally fitted by her easy spontaneous manner and her natural sympathy with all sorts and conditions of men. When she chose to exert it her charm was powerful enough to capture anyone, from Queen Victoria downwards. Unfortunately, where William could not Catherine would not. Dull parties, dull people, and in especial dull politicians both teased and bored her, so that she was far too apt to make a necessity of virtue and plead her family ties or her innumerable charitable occupations as an excuse. No one could grudge the time and attention devoted to her children but she would have been a better wife to William and a greater help to him in his career had she given less of her energy to good works and more to the business of entertaining and being entertained.

At the end of 1851 old John Gladstone died, full of years and honour. Catherine mourned a father-in-law who had always shown her great kindness and courtesy, mourned too for the change of régime at Fasque. She described Tom, the new head of the family, as being "so grey, so short, so narrow-minded", and though admitting that he meant well she bemoaned to Mary "that such an ungenial son should succeed so genial a father, whose charm and simplicity were so great and joined to so grand and large a heart".

In the winter of 1852 it was found possible to reopen Hawarden Castle. At Catherine's suggestion a definite arrangement was made with Stephen as to the sharing of expenses, and although nothing had as yet been settled about the question of accession in her own mind Catherine already looked upon young Willy as the heir to the estate. It is typical of Catherine that even whilst the Castle remained shut she had been full of plans for the improvement of Hawarden Church, and for the provision of a reading-room and model lodging house in the village, all to be paid for out of the family's depleted finances.

Hawarden was the place she loved most on earth, but it was haunted by many memories: "Sometimes when we are all assembled snug in the dear old library with a blazing fire and children's merry faces I feel how little I can enjoy it really." When Gladstones, Glynnes and Lytteltons gathered in one immense family party to celebrate the first Christmas back again in their family home it went to Catherine's heart to see the gap in their ranks: "Last night we placed all our children of a row, babies standing even, such a goodly array, but I felt all the time that one was not, dear little Jessy."

However, she had the greatest of all comforts in baby Harry, born the spring of this same year, and very soon the spell of Hawarden reasserted itself so that she was able to join wholeheartedly in all the merry-making. Schoolchildren, farmers and villagers were invited to a great party with a glittering Christmas tree in the library, high-tea in the drawing-room, and ale in the servants' hall. On this sort of occasion Catherine was in her glory, but nothing could be complete for her without William and he was kept in London by a political crisis. Catherine yearned to be with her husband at this exciting moment and begged impatiently for news: "Anything you tell me is quite safe, and if you have anything more to do with Lord Aberdeen do write me word; remember, you can do almost anything with him."

Lord Derby had appointed Disraeli Chancellor of the Exchequer, one of the few parts in which that versatile genius found himself seriously miscast. On December 3rd Disraeli presented his Budget proposals in the House of Commons, and at one o'clock on the morning of December 17th Gladstone rose and demolished that Budget in a speech which ranked as his greatest parliamentary triumph so far. Catherine chanced to be travelling between Hagley and Hawarden on the morning after his speech, and at Stafford station she rushed to "claw" a copy of *The Times* containing a report of the scene in the House. "Oh, that I could have been with you there and afterwards", was her heart-felt cry. She thrilled over the long letter he wrote to her describing the occasion, and one little homely touch went straight to her heart. In the midst of the press of great affairs he had remembered to tell

99

her that before making his speech he had snatched a brief nap
wrapped up in a fur cloak that had been her present to him: "Oh,
your sleep in the fur was such a treat to me!"

Sidney Herbert's wife, Elizabeth or "Liz", also wrote Catherine
an account of the speech, telling of "the deep, hearty 'Hear Hears'
from the whole body of English gentlemen of age and standing
on both sides of the House" and going on to describe Gladstone
as "terrible in his wrath". "We held our breath," wrote Liz, "for
fear not of what he would say, but of how his physical strength
would bear the conflict between his righteous, honest indignation,
and the immense calmness and dignity necessary to his position.
He did it nobly." On reading the reports of the speech Catherine,
who was still something of a Tory at heart, rejoiced, "especially
in the *Conservative* winding up, magnificent, beautifully done, and
with such heart—surely the opposing party must be gratified at
the same time as they must be vexed".

After such a personal triumph as Gladstone's had been Catherine went so far as to suppose that he might become Prime
Minister on the fall of Derby's government. In fact he became
Chancellor of the Exchequer in a coalition government headed by
Lord Aberdeen, for whom both Catherine and William had a deep
affection and respect. William was busier now than ever before
and Catherine bemoaned that he could not spare a moment to
Hawarden in its spring glory, "the woods resplendent with blue
bells, it broke my heart you did not see it". He did however find
time to visit his friend, Samuel Rogers the poet, now a very old
man, and wrote to Catherine to pass on Rogers' message, "Give
my love to your wife; if there is anyone I *worship* it is her." On
top of all the normal Exchequer business and the preparation of
his great Budgets came the Oxford University Bill which he was
to pilot through the House of Commons in the face of the most
violent opposition. A long and interesting letter from Catherine
to Mrs. Talbot begins with a comment on this same Oxford
question and goes on to discuss Palmerston's character. It is
dated January 5th, 1854:

"William is much taken up by Oxford Reform matters and
in spirits at Lord John Russell's concurrence. This is a great
moment for working for Oxford and it takes William's mind

up very much indeed. He wrote a very long Church letter to
the Bishop of Oxford on Sunday, pages and pages. I could not
help rather glorying as I was reading it that such a one should
come from the Chancellor of the Exchequer—so much for what
people speculated upon. This brings my mind to your thoughts
regarding Lord Palmerston. There is a certain degree of truth
in what you say which also strikes me but I can't go the whole
way. Lord Palmerston is certainly very important to keep but
after all it is only up to a certain mark. Lord Palmerston has
no amount of following and to a certain degree he is more
dangerous in opposition. I much agree with you that there is
very much to lower one's spirits touching party spirit and
politics and principles, still I do think character and principle
tell upon the long run. England can appreciate integrity of
purpose, high worth and truth even politically. We are not sunk
so low yet, thank God, that it should not win the day in the
end, and much as I see there is in Lord Palmerston to be very
important I am also struck to see how much is felt to be wanting.
When you take into consideration the man's ability, his courting
of popularity, agreable manners, temper, experience, position
and so on—But I really must stop myself. We have been
signally guarded and protected. I call to mind the family's
horror at William speaking out his Church sentiments before
he could be said to have gained a position—again the meetings
in his houses upon Gorham matters, and Oh, how dark did
earthly prospects then seem to be!—his own particular friends
going over to Rome, his very sister long before paving the way
—I should be the very last not to feel that a special Providence
had guarded him and that truth has prevailed so far in the long
run. I must not forget that a reverse may come, only most
certainly it would not be for me to be little trustful from
experience alone."

This sense of a special Providence watching over her husband's
career was to grow stronger and stronger, leading Catherine to
regard political opponents as not merely mistaken but wicked.
She delighted in "the calm, triumphant facility with which you
demolished d'Izzy" but far worse than the declared enemy was
the wolf within the fold, the two statesmen whom she described

as "the violent Palm and the shuffling J. R.". Lord John Russell was Leader of the House of Commons, and "Johnnie" was Catherine's especial *bête noir*, "the clog which will one day drag you all down", as she described him. "Such a sham as it makes it all, to be sure, with your leader," she wrote indignantly, *"what is what, who is who?* Unearthly, not human,* words in fact are too weak to express it." One of her letters gives an interesting account of an interview between the Peelite Sidney Herbert and the Whig leaders in the House of Lords:

> "December 18th, 1854. Mrs. Herbert writes that Sidney had a curious interview with Lord Lansdowne loudly declaiming against Johnny and asking Sidney in his own name and that of Lord Clarendon to undertake to be his bear-leader, to advise him and keep him straight, adding that Johnny was very penitent, had expressed great affection and admiration for Sidney and was willing to be guided by him! I answer I am amused but not surprised and not flattered for of course the Whigs' game is to keep the said Johnny as leader. Because he is penitent (for he must see he would cut his own throat were he not) we are to forgive and swallow everything! ! !"

Although January brought great joy with the birth of Herbert John, Catherine's last and dearly-loved child, 1854 was a sad year for the whole family. It saw the deaths of Lady Glynne and of a small niece, another Catherine, at Hawarden Rectory. In March war had been declared against Russia and no less than four of Catherine's cousins were with the British army in the Crimea. Two of these young men, Grey and Henry Neville, the sons of "Uncle Braybrooke", were not to return; Henry died in battle and Grey in hospital at Scutari. Catherine was constantly writing letters, knitting "muffettees" and sending parcels from Fortnum and Mason's to her cousins in the trenches before Sebastopol and these young men wrote back letters similar to those written by other young men in other trenches, cheerfully making light of danger and discomfort—"the Russians did me the honour to send three bullets at me"— rejoicing in the luxury of a proper bed and clean sheets when on sick leave at Constantinople, and, of course, complaining of the ways of politicians at home—"The facts as stated in Parliament are almost invariably untrue." The facts as stated by young Neville himself were sufficiently startling; out of a total of 53,000 troops the effective strength was only 15,200 and one regiment was reduced to 152 men. "I don't tell you all this as a croaker", writes the young officer, adding with the apparently baseless optimism typical of the British soldier, "I am sure we shall get out of this business all right."

All her life Catherine loved to be in the centre of affairs, especially when great events such as the Crimean War were going forward. Just before Christmas 1854 she wrote from Hawarden: "It feels very odd here, so quiet. I don't think I like it for in London one could feel to be of some use in the war troubles, whilst it seems unnatural to hear the twaddle remarks and croaking of country friends with no reliable information and no hope of details. But the children are—oh, in such nice order, so sweet and so good, and so healthy. Agnes, whom I set to work in the schools about shirts, works herself at one, whilst Lucy collects pence for the Crimea."

Catherine's efforts "to be of some use in the war troubles" all but brought her into most unfortunate collision with Florence Nightingale. Sidney Herbert was Miss Nightingale's great prop and support and it was only natural that Liz Herbert should take a share in the work in which her husband was so greatly interested. Catherine could never find Liz a wholly congenial person. She did her best to love her because William and Sidney were such devoted friends, but there was a curious instability about Liz to which she could never quite reconcile herself. Nevertheless Catherine threw herself heart and soul with Liz into the good work of providing nurses for the military hospitals in Turkey. Unfortunately these efforts took the form least likely to commend itself to Miss Nightingale, who was already established at Scutari. Foolishly, but in good faith, the Herberts fell in with the schemes of Mary Stanley, an ambitious and unscrupulous woman who was secretly anxious to steal some of the limelight from "dear Flo". Mary Stanley was to be the leader of a second party of nurses, a reinforcement neither demanded nor desired by Miss Nightingale, and it was with the selection and equipment of these nurses that Catherine was so much occupied, together with Liz Herbert, Mrs. Talbot and Lady Canning. When at length everything was ready for departure Catherine attended a farewell service and bade goodbye to the party at the railway station, presenting each nurse with the parting gift of a shawl.

All too soon she found herself caught up in the quarrels and recriminations that broke out as soon as the nurses landed at Constantinople. Florence Nightingale had right on her side, and she treated Mary Stanley exactly as that lady deserved, but although there was little to be said for Miss Stanley herself some of her nurses were honest, well-meaning women who had come out in perfect good faith to do what they conceived to be their duty. Two or three of them wrote bewildered letters back to Catherine, pouring into her ever-sympathetic ears their complaints against Miss Nightingale's behaviour and bewailing their enforced inaction.

Mary Stanley herself wrote Catherine a long and most disingenuous letter, setting out her side of the question, and broadly hinting that Miss Nightingale was bent only on her own aggrandisement and that she was in consequence most unpopular with the authorities. "I came out loving and admiring Flo," she wrote, "and I was long and loath to believe she was not as great as I had believed her to be. If you knew what it was to me to hear everyone complaining of her—!" Could this pious wish have been realised Catherine would have discovered that to Mary Stanley any such complaints were as balm in Gilead. The letter goes on to praise the egregious Lady Stratford de Redcliffe, adding the comment, "I grieve to see that Florence considers her exertions as interfering and that what ought to be such a support is thrown away." According to Mary Stanley Lady Stratford de Redcliffe was not the only person whose help was despised and rejected: "I was so disturbed at the hard view Florence took of the Herberts, coming fresh as I did from them and their untiring efforts to serve her." Further complaint against Miss Nightingale ends with the exclamation, "How often have I longed for Mrs. Monsell or someone like her!"

Since her husband's death Mrs. Monsell had become the Superior of an Anglican Order of nuns and she would therefore seem to be the very last person whose presence would have commended itself to Mary Stanley. This second nursing party had been organised by her with the definite though secret intention of enabling the Roman Catholic Church to share in the glory attaching to the name of Florence Nightingale, and for that reason the party included a large number of Irish nuns together with two priests. Nevertheless, Mary Stanley's letter continues with the lament that an Army chaplain had "preached against one of her nurses for lending a soldier a copy of *The Christian Year*". This assumption of Tractarian orthodoxy ill became someone who was at the time of writing actually under instruction preparatory to her reception into the Church of Rome.

Fortunately Catherine soon heard the other side of the question. "A long letter from Miss Nightingale, very interesting but annoying," she wrote to Mary. "After all the trouble and all the care here it seems that Miss N. had managed the doctors with enormous tact and had even got over all their jealousy, *but she had promised that no more nurses should be sent*! Forty-three arrived, and her breath was taken away." It is to be hoped that Florence Nightingale forgave Catherine for her innocent participation in Mary Stanley's scheme and that she accepted as a peace-offering the kindly present of a warm dressing-gown that Catherine was at pains to have delivered to her.

Throughout 1855 the political situation of Gladstone and the other Peelites grew ever more difficult and obscure. Catherine had a great admiration for the Peelite leader, Lord Aberdeen, and when the threat of war had first appeared on the horizon she had comforted herself with the thought that they had such a Prime Minister, "peaceful and just". On January 30th, 1855, the peaceful and just Aberdeen resigned and Gladstone took office under Lord Palmerston, a step which pleased Catherine's brothers more than it did Catherine herself: "Well, Lord Palmerston has been here with William. You may form your own conclusions. We are just writing it to Henry and Stephen. Won't it be *nuts* to them?" She herself had little belief in "that $\left\{\begin{array}{l}\text{sham}\\\text{unearthly}\\\text{not human}\end{array}\right\}$ Cabinet" as she described Palmerston's ministry, and she positively welcomed William's resignation after less than three weeks in office, although she found the suspense and the excitement very agitating as a letter to Mary clearly shows:

"The Cabinet are now sitting and then comes the House of Commons, where things will be decided (I mean as to us). If

you could but imagine the sort of suspense———! William walked
to St. James' Church with us and came away before the sermon
for the Cabinet. Now I have just been sniffing in William's
room and find Prince Albert has sent a box. I also smelt out
letters with 'Immediate' on them from Graham and Sidney
Herbert. More I know not and I can only wait. Argyll I fancy
will remain with the rest of the Whigs. Henry and I are sitting
tight* in my boudoir from whence we can see when the cabinet
breaks up. Then we shall rush to the House of Commons. I
feel that I go on talking to pass the anxious time but oh, I am
not really to be pitied because whatever William decides will
be right."

Catherine might be convinced that William was right now and
always but other people were for the most part puzzled and dis-
approving. On this question Catherine came near to quarrelling
with Mrs. Talbot for even from her dearest friend she could brook
no criticism of her husband. "To doubt William's sense and judgement, seems to me altogether extraordinary", she wrote, ruffling
up her feathers, and then proceeded to quote a thought-provoking
dictum of William Gladstone on the subject of William Gladstone;
"He says that if he is wrong he must be extremely wrong; there is
no medium." Her protest ended with the defiant exclamation, "If
WILLIAM has not sense and judgement I don't know who has!"
Sense and judgement he may have possessed but it was going to
be very difficult for him to give a comprehensible explanation of
his reasons for resigning so quickly: "William has just been in to
see me, so dear, looking so white and handsome, and breaking to
me that his statement on Monday will be nearly as great an effort
as last year's Budget, but he added 'I am in good heart' and the very
greatness of the undertaking is inspiration. Bless him! may he be
helped through!"

Once the excitement was over Catherine found life something
of an anti-climax and she was worried as to the repercussions of
William's resignation on the Lyttelton fortunes:

"Have you been sitting tight* for Lord John Russell sending
for George to be Under-Secretary of State?" she wrote to Mary
on February 27th. "What an ebb* it all is! After the excitement
of feeling how grand our speeches were, how fine and bold

the line which William had taken, the reality and bother of packing up comes upon one, the selling Budget[1] perhaps and getting rid of the dear pony, the cares* of finding ourselves at Hawarden and William often obliged to leave me there, the anxiety about the wretched Government and the Church, all gather round and it is not very pleasant but I am more thankful than ever that we took the line we did take. I am afraid Palmerston is a wretched Prime Minister."

On the issue of resignation Sidney Herbert and Gladstone acted in unison, but although the two remained firm friends the stress of the hour and the trying, indefinite position in which the Peelites now found themselves worked upon their nerves and later in the year a quarrel flared up between them which threatened to become serious. The issue was small, merely a question as to the right parliamentary procedure to adopt when criticising some Government measure, but tempers were strained and, very unwisely, their womenfolk rushed into the fray. At length peace was restored, both sides deciding to put the blame on Lord Aberdeen's amiable but tiresome habit of agreeing with everybody. As Catherine put it, not very grammatically, "two people may go to him with opposite views upon any subject and each come away satisfied that Lord Aberdeen agrees with himself".

The war dragged on through a weary winter. "The snow is falling—bread riots have begun—the Ministry find it very difficult to go on but will try—Cardwell has refused to be Chancellor of the Exchequer—this is said to be a sad blow to Palmerston—is it not plucky of him? I hope it is not unpatriotic to be glad, for Cardwell would perhaps have been better for the country than elderly Sir F. Baring, and William would have been too glad to have lent any helping hand he could. I fear Lord Palmerston is more weak and inefficient even than William expected, which says much!" So Catherine wrote in the spring of 1855 to Mary Lyttelton, who was at that moment devoured by anxiety over the serious illness of her eldest child Meriel. Catherine's own anxiety centred on Mary herself.

In June Mary fell slightly ill and Catherine hurried to Hagley where she found her sister nervous and despondent, much

[1] A horse.

107

dreading the ordeal of her eleventh confinement, which was due to take place in July. To find the level-headed and courageous Mary in such a state of mind disturbed Catherine, but she petted and soothed her sister, arranging for her to come up to the Gladstone house in London where on July 23rd a seventh son duly made his appearance. The doctors, however, were not satisfied with the mother's condition and they warned Catherine—it would have been more sensible to have warned George Lyttelton—that the birth of another child would almost certainly cost Mary her life. Catherine was no prude, and she wrote to her sister in very plain language telling her that her duty to the eleven children she had already borne forbade her to run any such risk. There could have been no mistaking the seriousness of the danger, yet in the autumn of 1856 Catherine was writing in alarm to William, "Alas, there is a secret at Hagley which has come upon me quite as a blow; what think you of Number Twelve upon the way?"

All that winter and spring Catherine carried a heavy burden. She knew that Mary was under sentence of probable death, knew too that Mary herself was very well aware of the position. It was her own hard task to keep up an appearance of cheerfulness. In the autumn she was again at Hagley nursing Mary through a bad bout of illness, making light of disquieting symptoms, and dealing with a household where the mistress was in bed ill, the nurse had collapsed, and the cook and kitchenmaid were laid low with suspected smallpox. Matters were not helped by "poor George's nursing and unearthly manners* in sickness" nor by the fact that Catherine herself was extremely exhausted and unwell. Somehow or other she overcame all these troubles and succeeded in nursing Mary back to a semblance of health. It was typical that in the midst of all these preoccupations she remembered that Naples Mary and Lena would be missing their daily Scripture lesson, and wrote to William urging him to give ten minutes daily of his valuable time to the business of teaching Bible stories to the two little girls.

In spite of the threat hanging over Mary the Christmas holidays were particularly gay and cheerful. In the New Year the Gladstone family descended on Hagley in full force, and the mob of excited happy children busied themselves with the production of private theatricals, the eldest actor being Willy, now aged sixteen, the youngest Herbert, aged three. A properly printed playbill was produced which read as follows: "Royal Lilliputian Theatre. On Wednesday Evening, January 7th, 1857, will be Performed, for the First Time on any Stage, the Highly Attractive Melodrama, entitled, Marina, or the Truant Heart." Endless rehearsals took the place of lessons, and as Lucy Lyttelton recorded in her diary "the excitement becomes dangerous and boundless". Catherine, who always delighted in theatricals, threw herself enthusiastically into all the bustle of preparation and Mary Lyttelton too took her full share, although some of those who saw her during those happy festivities commented sadly on her changed appearance. As George Lyttleton remarked more truly than he perhaps realised, this twelfth baby was like the last effort of a gallant, high-mettled racehorse. Catherine was the only person, except Mary herself (and possibly William), who knew what that effort must inevitably cost, but it seemed as if her fears had been groundless when on February 7th Mary gave birth to a son without any undue difficulty. The relief was too much for Catherine's composure; crying out, "The baby's born", she rushed into the Hagley schoolroom and there, with her nieces Meriel and Lucy, indulged in the rare luxury of "a quiet cry".

George Lyttelton took Mary to Brighton for her convalescence, where Catherine joined them, and together the three enjoyed a last spell of happiness. Comic but prophetic invitations were sent to William—"Lord and Lady Lyttelton and Mrs. Gladstone request the honour of the Prime Minister's company at dinner on Saturday and Sunday, to remain two nights, plain fare but excellent Southdown mutton, fish, and claret"—and plans made for Mary which looked as far ahead as the next September.

Although everything was not quite well with her Mary felt strong enough to move to Mrs. Talbot's home at Falconhurst in time for Lucy's confirmation, which took place in the little church that was John Talbot's memorial. When Mary returned to Hagley William insisted on lending her his own horse, which rejoiced in the topical name of Budget, so that she might enjoy the luxury of a daily drive, as the Lyttelton finances did not permit them to keep carriage horses. But Mary's journeyings were at an end. In July she took to her bed and Catherine came down to be in charge of the nursing. New doctors, new remedies were tried, and all proved useless. When Mary was told she must die her cheerfulness never failed. Her outlook was refreshingly robust. Death did not come quite as soon as the doctors had expected. "Don't let's sit tight* waiting for it to happen," she exclaimed in the Glynnese idiom, and again, when discussing the future, "I can't think of anything poorer* than Sunday at Hagley without me." She firmly admonished her mother-in-law, with more sense than tact, not to "fash herself" over the children because "you are too old for that". Only twice did her control break down; once, when lying gazing at Meriel she cried out that the parting with a first-born child had a bitterness all its own, and again, when bidding goodbye to William, she begged him with tears to be especially tender towards Catherine, "for it will make a great change and after a time she will feel it more and more".

Catherine's burden was the heavier because William could not be there to share it with her; the parliamentary debates on the Divorce Bill, a measure to which he offered strenuous but unavailing opposition, kept him in London all through the weeks when Mary's life was slowly ebbing away. Conscience forbade Catherine to call him to come to her: "I should not wish you to leave your duty, that would do me no good." In letter after letter she strove gallantly to appear resigned, but after all her brave and pious words came the despairing cry, "And yet I do feel at moments that my heart would break when I look at her." The sisters seemed to grow yet more united, more dear to each other as the inevitable parting approached. When her own strength failed Mary turned instinctively to Catherine's ardent vitality— "so warm", she would say, "so life-giving". Except for one paroxysm of suffering, when she struggled in her sister's restraining arms, crying out, "Let me go, let me go!", Mary died as she had lived, quietly, without fuss, and with a gentle humour all her own. "There, can't you be quiet?" she would say, laying her hand on her fluttering heart. "There's nothing the matter, nothing to frighten you; why are you so silly?"

On August 16th William, escaping for a day from the House of Commons, came down to Hagley to bid her goodbye, and on August 17th Mary smiled at her husband, lay back in Catherine's arms, and died.

Chapter Seven

MARY was dead and a light had gone out of Catherine's life. Whilst William still lived no greater tragedy could have befallen her. Jessy's death had been bitter grief, but the loss of Mary shook the very foundations of her being. She could not remember a time when that beloved sister had not been there to listen, to sympathise, and to understand. With Mary something of her own self died too; no grief could rob her of her gaiety, but she was never again quite the laughing light-hearted Pussy of old.

Characteristically she found her best comfort in the task of comforting others, especially George Lyttelton and his twelve motherless children. Catherine could hardly bear any reference to Mary and she shrank painfully from the memories attaching to Hagley, but almost at once she faced the ordeal of a visit there and faced it alone, since William was not free to accompany her. She put a brave face on it, writing to her young nieces, "You must not fear I shall not like being at Hagley; it will feel like doing something for your darling mother."

From now onwards a great part of the responsibility for the Lyttelton children was to rest on Catherine's shoulders, for no matter how full of courage and good sense Meriel might be she was as yet only a girl in the schoolroom. When Auntie Pussy paid one of her frequent visits to Hagley the twelve motherless creatures did not feel themselves to be so entirely bereft, and she on her side found comfort in their touching love and care for her and in their evident delight in her presence. But nevertheless this first winter after Mary's death was a weary time for Catherine, and it was not surprising that early in 1858 she fell ill with no very definite symptoms beyond what she described as "a few tiresome antics*". The doctors ordered complete quiet, and it was whilst she was resting at Hawarden that the Palmerston government was defeated on the Conspiracy to Murder Bill. On hearing the news she wrote William a characteristically rapturous letter:

"My own, Yes, I was 'cold', for this news is as unexpected as it is joyful. Thank God that our dear England's honour should thus far be preserved and how thankful I am that *you* should have nobly borne your part! That dear note of yours, oh, how valued it was, a kind thought and precious to me, it makes up so much for our bodily separation. You were with me in spirit as I am now with you. Dear old thing, I was especially thinking of you when I was going to bed that Friday night—you must about that very time have been very near rising—it is nice for me to think of that. Poor old England! The House of Commons can do its duty, and surely with such a Palmerstonian House that is doubly glorious. You will smile at my eagerness, but I could not help suggesting to Henry to send over his fat horse, that has nothing to do, for a *Times* yesterday, and at half-past four the great news therefore became known. And you might have seen me lying upon a couch in the snug Rectory library, where we dined at seven, Henry reading your speech whilst the cheers of self and children resounded. How can you say you had nothing to do with the division? Such a statesmanlike, fine and calm speech, all full of matter—why, you were the only speaker of any weight or consequence except d'Izzy. However, we won't quarrel about that, I am in too good humour. We shot* poor Palm's rabbid [*sic*] state, so unlike his usual way, and the excitement of the House for the result and the hats waving. Poor Palm, I am sorry for him, for he is hit in every way. Surely he cannot do otherwise than to resign."

Whilst negotiations were proceeding for the formation of a new government under Lord Derby Catherine was sent to Brighton to recuperate. The visit did her more harm than good for the place was over-full of memories of Mary as she had seen her only a year ago in her little bath-chair "drawn by a donkey instead of a Christian". It would indeed have been hard to find any place that did not speak to her of Mary. Later in the year she drove over from Hawarden to Norton Priory, a house she had not visited since honeymoon days. "Oh, the old place!" she wrote to William;

"Did it not bring such a tide of recollections, all gone, of youthful days and of the vast changes? I was much tried by the combination of feelings. I found Mary was mixed up so nearly in my mind with everything. Even the honeymoon time brought back the strength and depth of love I must have had for her, for instead of thinking of you alone, she was, as it were, in every thought."

It was clear that Catherine's spirits required a more drastic tonic than sea air and quiet. William had refused all blandishments from the Tories, and, lacking a place in the Government, he was free to go where he would. At this juncture Bulwer Lytton, the Colonial Secretary, invited him to undertake a special mission to the Ionian Islands, with the Poohbah-like rank of Lord High Commissioner Extraordinary. Catherine, less trusting and more shrewd than her husband, at once recognised this offer as an attempt in Walpole's famous phrase to kick an inconvenient states-man upstairs, and she saw too exactly how cunningly the trap had been baited. Gladstone's first book of Homeric studies had been published in March of this same year, 1858—"I take great rank* upon Homer", Catherine had written—and the Tory leaders were well aware that a visit to the scenes of the *Iliad* and the *Odyssey* was the strongest enticement they could offer to lure him away from England and English politics. "I shall be glad if you do not under-take the mission," Catherine counselled, "you must take care not to let the poetry of it mislead you."

Not Homer, but Catherine herself, was the deciding factor in Gladstone's acceptance of this mission. In the same letter in which she advised against acceptance she had written a word or two about her own health: "I feel so unhinged as to wish to see Griffiths [a local doctor]; I cannot at all account for these odd, unearthly feelings." The doctors were urging travel, if possible in a warm southern climate, and in these circumstances the invitation to Corfu appeared almost providential, so William, who in his heart of hearts had always hankered after acceptance, decided that to Corfu they would go.

Of all the children only Agnes was to accompany her parents. That same autumn Willy had gone up for his first term at Christ Church, his father's old college. During his time at Eton Willy had been asked to balls and parties at Windsor Castle, and in 1857 he had been chosen to be one of a party of boys who were to accompany the young Prince of Wales on a trip to Germany. Catherine wrote with pride that the Prince was reported to like Willy best of all his travelling companions. Before she left for Corfu she went down to pay Willy a visit at Oxford and there found herself a delighted spectator at a tennis match between her son and the Heir Apparent.

The Gladstone party arrived at Corfu on November 24th, and immediately Catherine fell under the spell of that lovely island. She, who had been forbidden all but the most gentle exercise, soon found herself walking two or three miles without fatigue and even indulging in the half-forgotten joys of riding. She delighted in seeing her husband appreciated—"their quickness in finding out William, so curious the murmuring in these villages of 'Gladstone' "—and she wrote with pleasure that "there are some very clever men among them here and they can appreciate talent and straightforwardness although so few have the latter attribute themselves".

Gladstone's difficulties had been immensely increased by the publication of a despatch stolen from the Colonial Office, but Catherine remained hopeful: "I believe in spite of everything William's mission will be of essential good. You know how he rises with difficulties, and no doubt they have been wonderfully increased by the despatch publication." She enormously enjoyed their trips to the various islands. "You would have delighted in Ithaca," she wrote home to one of her aunts; "of course they appreciate the worshipper of Homer. We always land upon the first arrival at each island with great pomp—the salutes—the manning the yards—the guard of honour which meets us as we get out and the old and dear *God Save the Queen*. William has been well-received except here, Cephalonia, and we think it was a paid cry got up, shouts meeting him for union with Greece."

She wrote an amusing account of the occasion when William had to announce to the Corfu Assembly that no such union would be allowed and to offer in its place the new constitution which he had drawn up:

"It was well to have a fine day yesterday for William's procession from the palace to the House of Assembly. Fancy

114

Arthur Gordon[1] upon a fiery steed with smart trappings in his party dress and Wortley and Strachan in theirs bumping by His Excellency who sat in the state carriage, alone in his glory upon one seat, Lacaita opposite, the rest following in carriages and the General and his staff all splendid with plumes waving. As the procession walked slowly by to be admired Agnes and I and Captain Glasse in full gear trotted by in order to get good places to see the entrance into the House. The speech was long and beautifully delivered, first the Queen's message of refusal about the Union with Greece, then the offer about remodelling the Constitution; they will be mad if they refuse it but if they do William says he will have placed England's honour high and the consequences must be theirs."

As wife to His Excellency Catherine had her own part to play, visiting, receiving and giving parties: "I am trying to make General Buller's wife visit the Greek ladies; they are so much pleased at my having done so and the social intercourse is a thing to be thought of. Lady Young [her predecessor] never even sending her cards had a very bad effect, they feel it is not treating them as ladies. One grateful good lady has presented me with four little silver cups which have been in her family for years." Catherine gives an account of a typical evening party, this particular one held on the island of Ithaca:

"We were entertained at the Residency, first a dinner party for twenty, then a ball. As usual William and the lady of the house, myself and the Count. Music bad and the party so wonderful that it was as much as I could do not to *burst*, William's face over his dancing—and my partner, who had not danced for years! But there was much that was curious and interesting, for instance at the end of the room in a doorway were standing a whole group of villagers, all in their dirty clothes, enjoying the scene, so happy, and the windows crowded outside with faces of wonder. All very primitive. The Bishop was among the guests at dinner eating nasty greens, but drinking champagne."

One official trip took the Gladstones to Corinth and Athens, where Catherine was received by the Queen of Greece, who asked

[1] Lord Aberdeen's son, acting as W. E. G.'s private secretary. C. G. complained that he was "all run away with and distracted by scenery".

her "no end of questions" about Queen Victoria and the Royal Family; whilst another, even more romantic, took them to Albania to visit the "harem of a rich Turk". When on February 19th, 1859, the day came for their return to England William had indeed to count his political mission a failure, but, looking at Catherine restored to something like her old health and spirits, he could feel that in one respect at least his decision to come to Corfu had been amply justified.

Back at home, life which had seemed so dreary and drained of meaning was once again filled with interest and excitement, even pleasure. For Catherine as for William the years between 1857 and 1860 formed as it were a watershed dividing the streams of life. In William's case the shift of direction was political rather than personal. For him the crucial moment had come as early as 1850 with his Naples visit, but not till 1859 did he take the final decision and declare himself a Liberal, thereby cutting himself off from the associations and aspirations of his political youth. For Catherine too the end of the fifties meant the breaking of old ties and the acceptance of middle-age. Jessy, Lavinia, Lavinia's little daughter Katie, her father-in-law, her own mother, her sister Mary—in the course of ten years she had lost all these beloved people and it was not to be expected that this experience of grief could leave her unchanged. The ardent girl whom Gladstone had married was now a wise and mature woman.

In Catherine's estimation one of the greatest joys of travel was the return home, when the children always delighted in concocting some prodigious surprise as a welcome. On one such occasion she had been greeted by an array of dressing-gowns hung out of the windows in place of flags whilst Willy and Stephy pranced round the doorstep waving branches of evergreens and cheering at the top of their voices. The elders were nowadays too grown-up for such behaviour but her welcome was no less warm and at Hagley too her return gave cause for great rejoicing. There had been a horrible moment when it was thought that the Gladstones might be detained in Corfu, a prospect which struck consternation into the hearts of Meriel and Lucy: "Oh! result to shake all plans and politics! We Shall Not Be Able To Come Out!!" Catherine planned that these two should share a London Season with their cousin Agnes, who was now of an age to cause considerable heart-burning among the more susceptible of her father's private secretaries. Meriel Lyttelton was soon to marry her childhood playmate, John Talbot, but Lucy remained to be her aunt's dear friend and companion.

Meriel's marriage took place in 1860, so that at the age of eighteen Lucy found herself in a position of unenviable responsibility. Not merely had she to take the place of a mother towards the army of younger brothers and sisters but she had to act as mistress of the great house at Hagley. In all her cares Auntie Pussy was friend and counsellor so that the bond between aunt and niece grew to be even more close and intimate than that between mother and daughter, and the new relationship with Lucy came in time to be almost as important to Catherine as her old relationship with Lucy's dead mother.

Of necessity the affairs of the Lyttelton children made great inroads upon Catherine's time and attention and she was anxious that William should not find himself in any way inconvenienced or neglected. "I cannot tell you how much I thank you for letting me have Meriel and Lucy," she had written shortly after Mary's death when proposing to invite her nieces to Hawarden, "I hope I shall be able to show you that you won't suffer for it. That shall be my study." Now in April 1859 she wrote to him from Hagley in the same strain, well aware how the presence of a crowd of young people must interfere with the peace and orderliness he found so essential: "Thank you, my darling, for your letter. Your unselfishness makes me wish that I could see my way without putting it upon you, but I feel a great additional duty is thrown upon me now and you, poor dear, must share some of it. I am not as I was when we married. I must keep my promise and do what I can for her darlings. It is a sacred duty." Generously and uncomplainingly did William help her with the discharge of this duty, but it is perhaps significant that about this time he set about the building of his new library at Hawarden, a refuge which he named "the Temple of Peace".

The business of "bringing out" the three girls kept Catherine in London throughout the political crisis which marked the summer of 1859. After the fall of Derby's government it was clear that Gladstone could have what office he wished, the only question being whether he would take office as a Liberal or a Conservative.

It was a question that many people were asking and some people asked it of Catherine. On June 18th Lucy recorded that at a great "breakfast" or evening party, held at Wimbledon, "Auntie Pussy had many political talks with different great guns". It is to be doubted if any of these great guns were very much the wiser for the conversation; those who attempted to extract information out of Catherine were reckoning without her admirable and adamant discretion. William's old friend, Sir Charles Wood, had a discussion with her on May 22nd which left him persuaded that William intended to join Derby but sitting next to her at dinner a week later he found himself equally convinced that William would join Palmerston. On June 20th came the answer to the riddle; it was announced that Mr. William Gladstone had accepted the office of Chancellor of the Exchequer in Lord Palmerston's government.

The appointment was received with very tepid approval by the Lyttelton family. "Why," asked Lucy, "if he can swallow Palmerston, could he not swallow Dizzy and in spite of him go in under Lord Derby?" Lucy underestimated the strength of the antipathy between Gladstone and Disraeli. Distrust of Dizzy was a cardinal article of faith in the Gladstone household. About this time young Naples Mary was playing with another little girl. "Is your father a Whig or a Tory?" asked this child. "I don't know," came the answer, "but Dizzy is a beast."

Catherine had just completed the move into the Chancellor's official residence in Downing Street, a house which met with no approval from the younger members of her family—"It's so dirty", Herbert complained, "and we can't climb any trees"—when she was summoned to Hawarden Rectory to nurse Henry's little daughter, Honora, who had fallen dangerously ill. "I can bear anything but poor Henry's face", Catherine wrote piteously to William. The long hours spent watching and waiting brought back memories of other sick-beds, and she described the night vigils when "all besides was still but that clock patiently and solemnly seemed to strike upon our very hearts". On July 21st Honora died, and Catherine wept for her little niece, wept too for Henry who had once been the most gay and light-hearted of all the brothers and sisters at Hawarden.

Agnes also had been ill and for her sake Catherine spent August at Folkestone, where she fell in with many friends and acquainttances, including Thackeray. Nevertheless, she fretted after William: "God bless you and help me to be more what I would like to be," she wrote, and again, "I have got Tenison [*sic*] but it is not like your reading it to me." Catherine's spelling did not improve with the years. Anyone in need of a "pick-me-up" is described as wanting a "philip", on the voyage to Corfu she and Agnes retire to their "births", and Henry, who is troubled with deafness, consults an "orist". These eccentricities of orthography make her letters strange reading, especially when combined with the more obscure Glynnese idioms. In a letter of 1860, for instance, telling how she drove with Agnes into Chester to present a bouquet to Queen Victoria, she remarks that "the beauty of the nosegay made a great impression upon passing pigmen".* Mixed up with Glynnese were expressions all her own, not to be described as malapropisms because they were so much to the point, remarks such as "Poor piper always has to pay", "Really, he is A.2", or "His life is based on a pinnacle". She had a light and happy hand with mixed metaphors. "What would the nation do without you?" she wrote to William, "you stand as a great *pillar* at the door to ward off desperate blows"; and again, "You work like a dragon, furiously", as if these mythical creatures were believed to be peculiarly industrious.

Lucy's description of her Auntie Pussy as "flying into activity" gives the best possible picture of Catherine at this period. Never again was life to be so full or its conflicting duties so distracting. Later, when the children were all grown up, William's position was such that political duties of necessity came first but now it was difficult to decide between the claims of home, politics and charity. "How is she to do that," asked Lucy, after detailing various new charitable enterprises which Catherine proposed cramming into her already over-full life, "besides all her other innumerable kind deeds, and her season and societyums* and be deep in politics, and be everything to Uncle William—all at once? She looks terrible fagged already."

Terribly fagged or not, somehow or other everything was done, and well done. This is the more surprising when it is remembered how disorderly Catherine was by nature and how strictly limited was her expenditure. The really untidy, unmethodical person can manage well enough if possessed of sufficient means—and sufficient leisure—to repair her errors and omissions. Catherine was an untidy woman with no leisure and little money; she could not afford the small luxuries which make a busy life so much less exhausting. The stables, for instance, were run with strict economy. Contrary to custom, this department was the concern of the wife, not of the husband—"If you will make *me* your Master of the Horse," Catherine wrote to William, "I will save money." If William needed the coachman and horses there was seldom a second carriage available for Catherine. William had a rooted objection to cabs and is stated to have been in one only three times in the course of forty years; not so Catherine, whose method of transport was considered most unconventional by a generation who supposed that its womenfolk would always, as a matter of course, travel first-class. When wife of the Prime Minister of England she wrote cheerfully, "I find the trams very useful but full this week [Easter]. Having sprung on one a rough driver nearly pushed me off as the inside was fullissimus*." A story told by her daughter Mary is worth quoting in full as illustrative of her warm heart, her absentmindedness, and her usual method of travel:

> "One day going to the Convalescent Home at Woodford she was so quickly absorbed in the pitiful tale of a fellow traveller that she forgot to alight at her own station and had to borrow money from the poor lady in order to get back to her destination. That night at a dinner-party she collected sixty or seventy pounds, and having asked the lady to visit her next day, was able to get her a passage to Australia, so saving her a separation from her husband. The said husband was highly sceptical of his wife's story—'Well, you have been taken in—the idea of Mrs. Gladstone travelling third-class and without any money!' "

Catherine's disorderliness, however, was not allowed to disturb or disorganise her extremely orderly husband. By nature the most unpunctual of women she schooled herself never to keep him waiting, to see that a carriage was always at his disposal, and a hot meal ready whenever he should need it. Gladstone was punctual to the minute at mealtimes, and if other members of the household were late he would prowl around singing a mysterious chant which he reserved for these occasions. Once, however, he himself arrived several minutes behind time, excusing himself by saying he had been much absorbed by the problems of his next Budget. "I can't understand Uncle William," exclaimed his irrepressible niece Lucy, "how you can get so excited over all those dull figures." "Figyures, my dear Lucy, figyures?"—it was thus that the great man always pronounced the word—"They mean the happiness of millions."

Never before had Gladstone stood so much in need of all this care and understanding thoughtfulness on Catherine's part. The eighteen-sixties were to him a curiously difficult and trying time. A Cabinet controlled by Palmerston or "Johnny" was a much less friendly assembly than the Cabinets of Aberdeen or Peel, and Gladstone too often found himself playing the part of a lonely *Athanasius contra mundum*. Sidney Herbert was now a peer and in August 1861 he died of cancer at the early age of fifty-one. Of Gladstone's old associates in the House of Commons only Sir James Graham remained, and to him Catherine addressed a touching letter, begging him to speak in support of the 1861 Budget:

"My dear Sir James Graham, You have always been so kind to me and such a warm friend that I have the less scruple in opening my heart to you about my husband.

"Perhaps it may not have struck you how very deeply he would feel the kindness, how much it would please him, if you were to speak upon his Budget.

"He does not know I am telling you this. It is because I know you love him—I know you take a deep interest in his career—that I venture to speak to you, and I know he cherishes the old days, what his veneration is for Sir Robert Peel, and the dear friends with whom it was his pride and his pleasure to act.

"You are now the only one in the House of Commons to whom that special feeling can apply, Lord Herbert being gone. Even a few words thrown in by you would refresh William's spirit and would come with great weight from you. You do not know how he values your approbation, your affection. No one knows but myself what he has gone through in the last two years, but I believe that the fruit will be reaped. He has waited, quietly, patiently, and this I value more than all.

"If I have presumed too far in writing to you your kindness

will at least forgive me. Believe me, dear Sir James, your affectionate and obliged

CATHERINE GLADSTONE."

Sir James Graham answered this letter by speaking at some length in support of the Budget, a speech that was his last considerable effort in the House of Commons. Catherine was right in saying that she alone knew what her husband had gone through because it was to her that he turned in all moments of difficulty. In 1860 there was trouble between Gladstone and the rest of the Cabinet over the supposed threat of war with France. "Why, my own, what work you have on hand!" Catherine wrote anxiously. "I am longing to be with you and look after you . . . I seem to live upon your letters for indeed it is trying to be from you especially in your anxious labours." In January 1861 he wrote to her from a railway carriage to tell her of his quarrel with Lord John Russell over the question of the Morocco Loan. Her reply was characteristic: "My own, indeed it does all come and go railroad pace. I am thankful that the crisis is over—wonderful! —but sadly grudge all the worry on your account before you were at your best. Please do not trifle with your health and beware of fog and unhealthy sort of exercise. I was moved at your turning to me in the railroad to deposit the wonderful anxiety. How well you wrote in the train, poor darling!"

Gladstone was not a character of tough resilient fibre like Palmerston or Disraeli, and he suffered more than most men from the inevitable knocks and blows of political life: "These batterings are sore work but I must go through", he wrote to Catherine. And again: "This sort of controversy keeps the nerves too highly strung, and makes me sensitive, fretful, and impatient. I am not by nature brave, I am always between two fears, and I am more afraid of running away than of holding my ground." He was a man who, for all his force of character, craved the support and sympathy of his fellows, and if his political colleagues were unsympathetic he turned the more eagerly to Catherine.

The happy home life at Hawarden served as a safety-valve. It was not rest that Gladstone craved for or freedom from work as much as the certainty that his own home would be a place free from jarring elements or discord. There he must be able to enjoy the harmony that was so conspicuously lacking in political life. The creation of such a home was Catherine's most vital work. At Hawarden he could relax and enjoy his books, his tree-felling, above all, his children. The two small boys, Harry and Herbert, were an especial joy and delight, her "sugar-plums", as Catherine called them in one letter. She was far too wise a parent to have favourites, but she had a special place in her heart for both her eldest and her youngest child, and Herbert, like Willy, was particularly dear—"About Herbert there is something certainly which seems to go to my soul". Harry and Herbert's early departure to school was a real grief, "I call it a kind of slow poison," she wrote at the end of one holiday, "one going after another, and the little boys' departure hanging over our head." The children in their turn were equally wretched. "Of course we are very miserable, it will last for quite a week I am sure," wrote poor Harry from school. "Oh, it is so very, very horrid!"

This hatred of school was not due to any coddling at home. When at Hawarden the little boys ran wild as young colts, indulging in many hair-raising pranks. On the rare occasions when stern measures were deemed necessary chastisement, very firm but very gentle, was administered by Mamma armed with a Japanese fan. The greatest of crimes was to disturb or distress Papa.

This might seem to suggest that Papa was a distant and awful deity, and in fact Gladstone had neither time nor opportunity to supervise the upbringing of his younger sons as closely as he had supervised that of Willy and Stephy. Mamma was now the active head of the household, sole arbiter in day-to-day matters, and it was understood that Papa's work must not be interrupted by any nursery crisis. Yet these two small boys regarded their father with intense devotion. When the moment came for their visit to his room they would be found waiting on the threshold, "like little dogs who never resent exclusion but are overjoyed when they are let in". Papa was the dispenser of teaspoonfuls of black coffee, the giver of small gifts, the singer of comic songs, a champion player of "Commerce" and a doughty batsman at "Cricket round the Hat".

This exciting and famous parent treated Harry and Herbert exactly as he himself had been treated by his wise father, never talking down to them, encouraging them to think for themselves, to put forward their own opinions, even to contradict. "A lie, a lie," the shout would go round the dining-table. (The expression on John Morley's face beggared description when first he heard the Grand Old Man's opinion treated in this manner.) Papa was tolerant of everything except untruthfulness.

There was the dreadful affair of the Wellingtonia, a choice young specimen of its prickly kind which two small boys coveted for a Christmas tree. "We cut some two or three feet off the top, erected it under a holly tree, and adorned it with tapers stolen from bedrooms. It was quite dark and we made things cheerful with a small bonfire. Suddenly and most unexpectedly we heard the paternal voice out of the darkness—'What are you doing there?' 'Nothing', we shouted, as in absolute panic we bolted." Next morning Harry and Herbert appeared chastened and sub-dued in the Temple of Peace, waiting for justice to be meted out to them. To their surprise, nothing was said of the dangerous bonfire, the stolen candles, even of the damage to one of Papa's most cherished trees. Their fault, it seemed, lay in their craven flight and in the cry of "nothing", a silly and obvious lie when the evidence of crime was all too apparent. Even so, no punish-ment befell them, only a few serious words spoken with a twinkle in the eye which betrayed the fact that their wickedness had some-how appealed to Papa's sense of fun.

Mamma too could be relied upon to show surprising sympathy towards small and naughty boys. One of her great-nephews has recorded a typical story: "Sixty-five years ago she gave me a drum, not because I had been good but characteristically because I had been naughty and she thought that to punish a child of seven by locking him up in a room for several hours was wrong and stupid." It is not surprising that the same nephew wrote of his Auntie Pussy, "She was adored and adorable."

"Home Ties" were now stretched to include Henry's two remaining daughters, Molly and Gertrude, all Lytteltons and Talbots, and in fact any relation who might need Catherine's help. In 1863 her favourite brother-in-law, John Gladstone, who had recently lost his wife, fell ill with a carbuncle or "grievance", to use Catherine's word for any such swelling. As a matter of course she went down to his Wiltshire home, and nursed him devotedly. In spite of all her care—"I feed him on delicate morsels of mutton-

chop"—the "grievance" proved fatal, and Catherine was left to
mother his orphan family, inviting them for seaside holidays and
arranging for the girls to share a governess with Naples Mary.
Albert Lyttelton's abscess, Lucy's scarlet fever, John Talbot's
delicate chest, all these ailments were Catherine's affair, as well as
the frequent illnesses of her own offspring. Stephy suffered from
eye-trouble and Herbert's delicacy was a constant anxiety. Sea air
was Catherine's favourite specific and she was for ever running
off to Brighton or St. Leonards or Folkestone with one or other
of her charges who was temporarily "a lazar". Bournemouth she
particularly enjoyed because there she could indulge in her two
favourite pastimes, sea-bathing and church-going, "I have been
in the ocean and cannot tell you what the waves were like, we have
daily service here, so nice," she wrote breathlessly. In the sixties
Penmaenmawr in North Wales became a favourite haunt of the
Gladstone family and a summer holiday there each year was soon
part of their accepted routine.

All this activity meant that Catherine was separated from
William much more frequently than she liked. She did not grudge
this so much if the necessity arose from reasons of health but she
was in despair if she were obliged to go visiting without him no
matter how pleasant or how exalted the company in which she
found herself—"the Duchesses are so nice and kind but I feel
small without you". Whenever possible she accompanied William
at meetings or political tours. Such excursions were to her a
pleasure rather than a duty; of one such occasion she wrote, "If
my going down does the least good how glad I am and besides in
point of *treat* the hearing you is ever to me like listening to beautiful, sweet music." The woman who wrote so ecstatically of her
husband's voice was fifty-six years old and had been married for
twenty-nine years. She was with Gladstone during his famous
visit to Tyneside in October 1862, delighting in the tremendous
reception he received. Always kind and considerate towards newspaper reporters, during the triumphal voyage down the Tyne she
chanced to exchange a few words with a raw young man who was
"covering" Gladstone's tour as his first important assignment:

"As we were returning to Newcastle in the evening I
happened to be standing near Mrs. Gladstone, and she entered

into conversation with me. It was the first time that I had ever seen her. 'I think this has been the happiest day of my life,' she said to me with that exuberant enthusiasm in the cause of her illustrious husband which was one of the sweetest and noblest traits in her character. Exactly twenty years later, on October 8th, 1882, I sat beside Mrs. Gladstone at dinner at Leeds. I recalled our meeting on the steamboat twenty years before and her face kindled with an expression of delight. 'Oh, I shall never forget that day! It was the first time, you know, that *he* was received as he deserved to be.' "[1]

One place where Catherine could never accompany William was Balmoral, where he was obliged to spend some time every summer as Minister in Attendance on the Queen. After the Prince Consort's death nearly all official entertaining ceased, but the Gladstones were still occasionally invited to parties at Windsor, and Catherine wrote an account of one of these visits in a letter to a cousin at Escrick: "Only think of the dear Queen allowing William and me to dine alone with her and her children one day. I shall never forget the interest of that evening, I like to think of her gleams of happiness with her children. Their ways together are so snug and so pretty. After dinner a large dog came to be petted and succeeded in jumping right into H.M.'s lap. The evening before we had a large dinner and I sat next the Crown Prince of Prussia and was extremely pleased with him; *she* is more charming then ever."

In 1864 it was suggested that the Gladstones might spend their summer holiday at Abergeldie in one of the houses on the Royal estate. The scheme came to nothing but the fact that the suggestion was ever made is proof positive of the friendly feelings existing between the Queen and Gladstone before their relationship was bedevilled by time and by Disraeli. Catherine considered that William was slow to profit by the opportunities presented to him by his visits to Balmoral. On one occasion she urged him to interfere in a matter of considerable delicacy. On October 1st, 1864, she writes from Penrhyn Castle: "I devour your letters eagerly and am shocked about the weight. I wish H.M. would seriously consider about Banting, really her age is nothing and what may not her size become eight or ten years hence?" Another and more important matter that exercised Catherine's mind was Victoria's determination to seclude herself in perpetual mourning for the Prince. So urgent did this question appear to her that she sent William a long and tidily written letter, quite unlike her usual scrawl, dated October 1st, 1863:

"I wonder whether you will have any opportunity of giving advice to the Queen. I believe she would welcome it and be thankful. One of the things Lady Lyttelton has always pointed out is her reverence for the truth being told her. Do not forget the engine of what the Prince's wishes would be and how he would see it as follows:

"1. The enormous consequence to the Prince and Princess of Wales to have her to show them the way.

"2. The bad consequences of not taking a certain share after two years.

"3. The duties need not be what she considers the follies. Again, nothing would tend to keep more in the people's heart their affection for the Prince than to see the Queen making exertions.

"And last but not least to one like the Queen, because it is her duty to take her part.

"If the Queen will open Parliament might not her speech be read for her? Don't forget the Minister's duty is to speak openly. Don't say it is not your place. Her choosing you to be with her at Balmoral places upon you the extra responsibility of advising her more than if you were only called in for audiences. Her extreme simplicity of character should help you. I hope if you dine again in that charming way you will be able to cast off some of the consciousness which takes off from the pure enjoyment. It all comes from your modesty, but you have been called to the post you now occupy; you never sought it, accept it and look upon it as giving you a social position and a right to speak as general adviser. It seems to me in the light of a responsibility, and such an opportunity ought not to be neglected, and I like you to take a lesson and not to feel only Chancellor of the Exchequer. What a long troll! *And that I should lecture you ! ! !* Pam [Palmerston] sends

£20 [for her collection for the blind] and seems to like doing it."

Catherine could never assemble her thoughts in consecutive order but her haphazard reflections are full of sound sense. The suggestions contained in her letter would have been most un-acceptable to Queen Victoria, but it is at least probable that she would have found them more palatable had they been presented to her in Catherine's warm, inconsequent style rather than in William's impeccable but frigid periods. Unfortunately William could never bring himself to obey Catherine's classic command, "Do pet the Queen", and it is one of the minor tragedies of history that in later years the two women were so seldom brought into personal con-tact. Had their earlier intimacy persisted Catherine might have done much to smooth over difficulties and sweeten the bitter-ness that was to poison the relationship between the Queen and Gladstone.

Even in later years, when that bitterness was at its worst, Catherine still remained on terms of almost personal friendship with the Queen, writing to tell her of such intimate matters as the expected birth of a Gladstone grandchild, declaring, "I always feel a desire to go to Your Majesty whether in sorrow or in joy", and signing herself with the familiar "affectionate". Long ago, in her own great grief, the Queen had unburdened her soul to Catherine, who never forgot the experience. "The first time after your awful trial", she wrote on July 20th, 1882, "when your Majesty so kindly talked freely to me I can never forget, the recollection never fades from my mind", and she had the wisdom and sympathy to refer constantly to the Queen's loss. In letters to the Queen on matters of personal interest such as a daughter's engagement she would write quite naturally and without any shadow of embarrassment about the Prince Consort and about Victoria's abiding grief for his death—"There are moments which open the heart".

Chapter Eight

CATHERINE's life would seem to be full to overflowing with all these political, social and domestic interests, yet none of these were ever allowed to interfere with the duty of charity. In Lucy Lyttelton's diary the record of the social and political round is constantly interspersed with such entries as, at Hawarden, "A horse ran away with a boy who was thrown and grievously hurt; Auntie Pussy flew off to nurse him", or in London, "a detachment from St. Martin's school came for tea, games, and little gifts and enjoyed themselves hugely". Such individual acts of kindness were now growing into an organised network of charities, and the eighteen-sixties saw the development of most of the schemes to which Catherine gave so lavishly in time, money and energy. These refuges, soup kitchens, orphanages and the like were not the result of long consideration of social problems, rather, they sprang up spontaneously as one happy person reached out to help other unhappy people. Catherine Gladstone could so easily have pleaded her duty to husband and family and confined herself to the more respectable and less onerous forms of charity. Personal service is not expected of the wife of a Cabinet Minister. Catherine, however, was bored and irritated by the socially presentable charity that stopped short at drawing-room meetings, and she much preferred to take her part in the actual work among the poor and outcast.

The Gladstones' friendship with Mrs. Monsell, now Mother Harriet of the Clewer Sisterhood, had led Catherine to take a great interest in the various works undertaken by that sisterhood. Chief among these was the House of Charity in Soho, a refuge for people "of unblemished character". Although there were only too many of these "unblemished" unfortunates, the proviso

129

excluded all those unhappy creatures who night after night huddled together in chilly misery outside the Workhouse gates, where a board hung bearing the cheerless announcement "Take notice, the Casual Wards are full".

Catherine threw herself into a scheme to provide a refuge for these homeless wanderers. She called together a committee, she wheedled £1200 out of the pockets of her personal friends, she bought a disused slaughterhouse in Newport Market, Seven Dials, a neighbourhood proverbial for poverty and crime, and there she established a refuge which every night provided a hundred men with food, shelter and, in some cases, a new start in life.

A small refuge could not, of course, deal with more than a tiny fraction of the destitute, but when the wife of the Chancellor of the Exchequer went round to her influential friends person- ally begging for the Newport Market Shelter, those friends began to enquire into the conditions that made such a shelter necessary. Although Catherine would never have thought to use so grandilo- quent a phrase, her efforts were instrumental in arousing people's consciences, and helped materially towards the passing of the Houseless Poor Act which provided better accommodation in Casual Wards, thereby lessening the load of misery which nightly haunted the London streets.

The years of the American Civil War saw Lancashire engulfed by the terrible Cotton Famine and here too Catherine played her part in relieving distress. When the crisis was at its height she left husband and family and went down several times to see for herself the state of affairs in the Cotton Towns. There she was welcome not only for the help that she came to bring but because she was a sign that Lancashire's woes had not been forgotten by the higher powers. "Mother," said one small child, "who do you think we have had in the school? The Government's wife." Her letters to Lucy describe the relief work which centred chiefly round the churches:

"It was a stirring life to behold. In the little parsonage at Trinity imagine a kind of open house from morning to night, the kitchen with its one-handed Peggy [1] cooking in the midst of

---

[1] Servant-girl.

poor people waiting, mothers bringing their girls for plans, one
in search of something to lie upon, another for something to
bury her child, or a distressed tailor or dressmaker, and we all
making the little kitchen our headquarters and meeting at our
several points of interest. But the chief time was spent at sewing
classes, industrial classes and kitchens, and oh, Lucy the Irish
stew was excellent! Think of a thousand people fed daily and
think of my delight at seeing the people laden with it, good and
hot."

Not content with starting an industrial school and several
kitchens, Catherine set about more personal forms of charity. She
herself selected ten or twelve girls from the most distressed families
and carried them off to Hawarden where they were housed in an
empty house in the yard and trained as domestic servants in the
Castle itself. Catherine continued this scheme for several years
until prosperity returned to Lancashire, placing the girls in suitable situations as soon as they became proficient. The expense in
actual cash must have been considerable and the cost in trouble
and anxiety to Catherine and her long-suffering domestic staff is
one which only a housewife can properly gauge. Meanwhile a
squad of unemployed men were found work in making roads
through Hawarden park and all these men, like the girls, had to be
fed, clothed and housed. These unfortunate people did their best
to show their gratitude and to cause no difficulty, but problems
were bound to arise and for all these, great or small, Catherine
was ultimately responsible. The Chancellor of the Exchequer too
took his share: "Never mind the tooth-brushes," Catherine
scribbled at the end of a letter, "they were for the factory girls."

After Catherine's efforts on behalf of the distressed cotton
operatives came her work for the victims of the cholera epidemic
in London. Between June and November 1866 nearly 8000 people
died, most of them in the East End. Relief work centred round the
London Hospital where Catherine was already a regular visitor.
Everywhere in hospital and at home people were dying so fast that
the undertakers could not cope with the work of burying the dead
and special hearses had to be improvised capable of carrying a
dozen coffins at a time.

Cholera is not in fact a highly contagious disease but at the beginning of the epidemic the fear of infection amounted almost to panic. Nurses were hard to find and no amount of money would persuade the East End women to enter the hospital and help with essential laundry and housework. It was at this moment that Catherine Gladstone appeared in the wards, not indeed to nurse, but to help and encourage the patients and to organise relief for their dependants. A cholera ward is not a pretty sight nor is it pleasant to witness the agonies of those who die from this disease, yet there Catherine was to be found day after day in the midst of filth and smell and squalor. The child patients were her particular care. She had comforted many a dying parent with the promise that their children would be properly cared for, and in character-istic manner she proceeded to implement her promise.

Doctors and nurses grew accustomed to seeing the wife of the famous Mr. Gladstone hurrying down the hospital corridors, carrying in her arms some small patient wrapped only in a blanket, his own clothes having been burnt for fear of infection. She would carry off these children to be fed, housed and clothed at her own expense, sometimes in her own home—"Should you mind", she wrote to William, "three *clean* little children being taken to Carlton House Terrace?"

Her courage and energy are the more remarkable when it is remembered how full her life was that summer of 1866. She was much engrossed in the political crisis then raging and she was busy nursing Harry and Herbert, who had both been taken ill at Eton, Harry's illness taking a serious form. On August 19th she wrote almost casually to William, "I don't go into the cholera wards now I am tired nursing Harry, and there is plenty of other work and organising."

Organising indeed there was in plenty. Catherine had collected enough money to open a temporary home at Clapton for child convalescents and orphans. At this Home she was a frequent and most welcome visitor. As soon as she stepped inside the door she would be overwhelmed by a mass of excited children, as long ago in the Hagley nursery, boys and girls scrambling over each other in their eagerness to touch and cling to this dearly-loved lady.

Clapton, however, could only be a temporary expedient. What was to be done permanently with the hundreds of orphans who had lost one or both parents in the epidemic? Catherine herself had received applications on behalf of no less than six hundred and twenty-four children. Existing institutions would take the majority but there would not be sufficient accommodation for the whole number. Catherine had made herself responsible for the boys, Mrs. Tait, wife of the Bishop of London, taking the girls. At Hawarden there was an empty house, and at Hawarden there was also the trusty wife of the coachman, who had boys of her own and was quite prepared to take charge of another dozen or so.

So to Hawarden came twelve or fourteen little boys, where they could be under Catherine's watchful eye, and in time, when trade improved and the Lancashire mill-girls could return home, more and more little boys came to fill the larger of the two houses, till in the end there were thirty urchins roaming the Hawarden wood and fields, growing strong on country food and air, and causing an amount of damage and worry that can be well imagined by those who have had experience of "evacuees". Yet, when the original batch grew up and Catherine might feel she had redeemed her pledge to their parents she still kept the home full of needy little creatures to whom she could give care and affection and the chance of a proper start in life.

The orphanage at Hawarden was not the only charity to spring from Catherine's experiences in the cholera epidemic. She had seen hospitals full to overflowing and patients of necessity sent back to their poverty-stricken homes when they were still in obvious need of care and rest. The answer to that problem was a convalescent home, as Catherine was one of the very first people to realise. The few convalescent homes already in existence were so hedged about by conditions of payment and admission as to be almost valueless.

Catherine's successful efforts to establish a free convalescent home show her in the unexpected character of an organiser. It seems natural to find her clothing naked children or kneeling by the bedside of a cholera patient; what is more surprising is to discover this immense capacity for self-giving going hand in hand with business sense. And in this work, as in so much else, she had the backing of her influential husband: "May I just throw in that when you can take up the things I do it makes my poor little work tell doubly?"

In spite of many difficulties a Home was opened at Woodford, under the title, "Mrs. Gladstone's Free Convalescent Home for the Poor". Catherine only permitted this use of her name because it was judged necessary as a guarantee to subscribers who were being asked to give money on terms which were then very novel and to most people very unattractive. Catherine would have no truck with the established system by which a subscriber to a charity acquired rights of nomination; her home was to be open to all, with no closed places, no canvassing for admittance, and no privileges for subscribers. She was never a person to believe very strongly in any form of privilege for the rich except the simple privilege of giving. Her ideas on this subject met with such opposition that at times it seemed as if the scheme must founder on this rock, but in the end it was not her charity that collapsed but other charities which came into line with her principles.

Catherine's habit was always to do things herself. "It does not do to run away", she wrote to William about the Convalescent Home, "and leave all the organisation to the intrepid workers." It was she, or Lucy, her *alter ego*, who visited the hospital and selected the patients to be sent to the Home, it was she who shopped hats and crockery and an endless variety of odds and ends for the Orphanage at Hawarden, it was she who went down to Woodford to visit the patients, talking to them, praying with them, playing country dances on the piano. "My work has become of some consequence", she wrote almost apologetically to William. It is to be doubted, however, if she ever grasped the full consequence of what she had done; whether, for instance, she realised that in opening a Convalescent Home she had been a pioneer of a new development in Hospital services. She thought in terms of individuals rather than causes, but on the strength of her almost unpremeditated achievements it is fair to claim for her a modest place not too far behind such women as Florence Nightingale, Elizabeth Fry and Josephine Butler.

All this activity would have been remarkable enough in a woman who made charitable work the main concern of her life, but it is doubly remarkable when seen against the background of Catherine's circumstances. The year 1865 was a decisive moment in Gladstone's career and an exceptionally busy time for Catherine.

Lucy Lyttelton had married Lord Frederick Cavendish in 1864 and was now installed in a house a stone's throw away from the

Gladstones' in Carlton House Terrace, but Catherine still had two girls under her wing, for Naples Mary was of an age to be launched upon London society. A quick, clever girl, Mary was possessed of her father's intellectual tastes together with her mother's inconsequence. Many years later she was to draw that mother's character in a brief biographical sketch, incoherent, ungrammatical, vividly alive. The desultory schoolroom education provided for young ladies could supply her mind with no sort of mental discipline, as her parents seem to have realised, without, however, making any real attempt to repair the omission. Music was Mary's especial gift and music she treated very seriously, but even here her lack of training in thoroughness and accuracy could produce some startling results. "Oh yes," she would say lightheartedly, *"that's* how Beethoven wrote it but I prefer playing it like *this.*"

The gaieties of Mary's first season were interspersed with much political excitement. Ten years earlier Catherine had noted that Palmerston walked like an old man, and now it was clear that for him the sands were running out. Catherine overcame her antipathy to "Johnnie" sufficiently to pass on to William some wise words from the Duchess of Sutherland urging him to conciliate that gentleman: "The Duchess wishes you would cuddle* a little with Lord John Russell."

A general election was impending and now for the first time Catherine had a son as well as a husband standing for Parliament. She burst in one morning upon Lucy Cavendish and, "her clothes tumbling about her, sat down on the floor and poured out Willy's electionums* which are exciting her as she *can* beexcited". Willy's prospects at Chester were not improved when he fell ill with a carbuncle at the very beginning of the campaign. However, his mother and other supporters worked tirelessly, probably more tirelessly than Willy himself, who was somewhat indolent and devoid of ambition. "Please put in a pin", Catherine begged of William on one occasion when she wished him to urge Willy on to greater effort. Willy won the seat, and his success was some consolation for his father's rejection by the University of Oxford.

This reverse was in reality a political gain but William's heart was naturally sore. Catherine wrote to Lucy describing how he had borne the blow:

"Do you know, my dear Locket, that trying as the whole thing has been I feel the thankful feelings do almost predominate—to see his whole bearing and lovely conduct; not one shade of anger, only increased anxiety and love for his dear University. And the way in which after the first shock he at once wrote that address, so noble and so beautiful. He could not even stop to mourn and though feeling the news a kind of death he had nothing for it but to buckle on his armour and go forth to the battle.[1] I watched him anxiously as the workings of that dear pale face and the pacing the room showed the deep emotion, but thank God he has been helped through all and though a few short hours afterwards he was on his legs facing thousands of people at Manchester and then at Liverpool he seemed almost inspired. You will have read the speeches and you may imagine the effect of such words with the pathos of that voice. He had difficulty in getting through but he did so magnificently."

His election fight successfully over, William planned a trip to Scotland but instead he was summoned to Court Hey, the home of his brother Robertson, whose wife had just died. Catherine was fond enough of these relations but she found the conventionality of Court Hey life a little trying. On one occasion she carried on a long and interesting conversation with Robertson's butler, "a break* for him", was Catherine's comment to her amused companion, "after getting pompous orders and nothing else for so long". Now, instead of going to Court Hey, she set out with Agnes and Mary on a round of Scotch visits, beginning with Inveraray Castle. The weather was pleasant, the company congenial, and for Mary in particular the days passed quickly, filled with such amusements as fishing, riding, otter-hunting and falling in love with Lord Lorne. Catherine, however, was restless and unhappy away from her husband and when the said husband proposed that she should stay on in Scotland without him her despair was complete: "Oh Papa dear, do not expect me to linger on in Scotland without you, which has already become uninteresting to me! Consider how 'life's little sand runs out'! As for me your unexpected letter has made me as low as a cat, and sick." A few days

[1] The election fight in South Lancashire constituency, where W. E. G. had also been nominated as candidate.

later she wrote in somewhat happier mood, "Your letter came as a refreshing shower."

From Inveraray Catherine moved to Fasque where the uncongenial Tom was lying ill with one of those carbuncles which seem to have been the special "grievance" of the Gladstone family. "My note is,*" wrote Catherine, "that were I to stay here long I should have the blue devils." She was the more agitated because old totterton* Palmerston was on his deathbed and with Palmerston gone, Gladstone's path lay clear to the highest position of all. "I have shivered not a little," she wrote to him from that gloomy mansion at Fasque. "Is it wrong that at such a moment I should think of you? The prayer came into my heart and comforted me that if much is before you so strength may increase, fitted for the burden. It always feels a great trial to be away from you in moments like these." On October 18th Palmerston died. "Johnnie" must of course be the immediate choice as Premier, but Catherine knew, and all England knew also, that Gladstone was the man of destiny. Great was her indignation at the mere suggestion that anybody else could fill the key position of Leader of the House of Commons:[1] "I cannot for the life of me take in how General Grey could lead; knowing all about him, and his weak physique too I consider it would be no go."

No go it was and Gladstone duly became Leader of the House and Chancellor of the Exchequer. "I am continually thinking what antics* can be arranged to help you as leader", Catherine wrote, but it was at this moment, when his hands were full with matters of state, that with typical inconsequence she asked him to interview a governess for young Lena. This was not the most incongruous domestic errand that fell to the lot of the Chancellor of the Exchequer; he was often asked to go shopping, even for such articles as sponges or crockery—"mind that the teapot is strong and won't break". Nevertheless, in her own mind Catherine was already seeing him as Prime Minister, and although she was never one to court popularity she was naturally anxious that he should stand well in men's sight.

When the Cattle Plague broke out during the winter of 1865–6 she wrote to him from Hawarden urging him to seize this opportunity to increase his hold on the farming interests:

[1] J. R. had now become Earl Russell.

"The people hereabouts are all eagerly looking out and watching what you will advise! 'Our hope is in Mr. Gladstone, we know he will do what he can', this the poor things all say. It is only right you should take the opportunity of showing to the country the interest you take in agricultural as well as in manufacturing interests. You ever think too little of yourself but now in a great position you must study general popularity; and Providence who send this scourge upon our land has willed that *you* should be in a great position to give scope to the great gifts He has given you, and to minister in the hour of difficulty and distress."

Catherine was always accusing William of under-estimating himself: "Curious, the comment in one of the newspapers about your being too modest. I believe it may be a *fault* sometimes in great positions." She herself stayed at Hawarden during the winter of the cattle plague in order to help the estate agent with schemes of relief. One day she would be discussing the possibility of planting flax, on another buying pigs to give to poor people who had lost their cows, next she would be busy with such practical problems as the swift destruction of infected beasts or the disposal of their carcasses, or she would be carrying off the family of some hard-hit farmer to rest for a while as her guests at the Castle.

Catherine's ambition for William received a sharp check when Russell's government resigned after the defeat of their Reform Bill in 1866. The rebel Whigs who brought about the Government's downfall were known as the Adullamites or the Cave of Adullam, "to which everyone", as the Old Testament had it, "was invited who was distressed and everyone who was discontented". Catherine, with her usual disregard for spelling, invariably referred to them as the Dolomites. The unexpected defeat left her "more miserable and taken out of than I have ever seen her", to use Lucy's words, but her spirits were revived by an extraordinary demonstration. On the evening of June 26th William chanced to be away from home and Catherine was dining alone with her daughters. Startled by a sudden uproar they peeped out of the window and saw the whole of Carlton House Terrace thronged with people shouting "Gladstone for ever!" A message from the police begged Catherine to show herself so that the mob might then be persuaded to disperse. Followed by her three daughters she stepped on to the balcony and bowed right and left to the delighted crowd, who gave one final vociferous cheer and melted peaceably away. The Tory press saw fit to take her to task for this harmless and indeed necessary demonstration, but as Lucy Cavendish remarked, "Who could resist it if they were cheering one's husband and one knew he deserved it?"

This summer which was so full of political excitement had also seen the cholera epidemic, Catherine's work at the London Hospital and at Clapton, and the illness both of Harry and Herbert. It was not remarkable that Catherine and William should both stand in need of a holiday and it was decided to spend some of the winter months in Italy, Catherine insisting that they should travel by the St. Gothard pass although it was really too late in the year for this route to be safe. They did in fact meet with an accident, but although their carriage overturned they escaped with nothing worse than a shaking. Most of their holiday was spent in Rome, where William indulged in his passion for listening to sermons and the two girls, Agnes and Mary, enjoyed a "set to partners" with three attendant young men. Rome, however, did not prove to be all that Catherine remembered and had hoped to find again; the climate was disappointing, William developed a bad sore throat, and twice their rather uncomfortable lodgings caught on fire.

During the summer of 1867 Gladstone suffered a second and worse defeat when he failed to secure the rejection of Disraeli's Reform Bill, "this badissimus* bill", as Lucy described it. "What flesh and blood can stand the wear and tear of Reform?" Catherine wrote to her brother Stephen. "I find convalescent hospital a relief." As a relief from the gloom which over-hung the whole household Catherine organised a party at her temporary Convalescent Home: "A monster Cavalcade got up by Auntie Pussy (who but she?) consisting of nine carriages containing about thirty picked swells were actually induced to travel all through North East London to Snaresbrook where the many-coloured party spread themselves about the gardens of the Home and inspected our convalescents."

In spite of set-backs Catherine was well aware of the intensity of feeling for "the people's William" and she was greatly heartened by the deep interest and anxiety displayed when an accident out tree-felling nearly cost him the sight of one eye. At Christmas Lord Russell formally handed over to him the party leadership, writing "a very interesting, kind letter", and two months later Derby handed over the premiership to Disraeli.

At last the lists were clear for the struggle between the two chief combatants. On March 8th, 1868, Catherine gave a "drum" or evening party at which Disraeli, who was one of the principal guests, spent most of his time in gently teasing the young and pretty Agnes. Catherine and Lucy had spent the afternoon in very different society: "We went down to the East 'by sea' as Auntie Pussy called it, embarking at Hungerford pier and landing at the Tunnel; thence conducted to the Workhouse by a dirty little boy who was enchanted by a bit of bread and butter out of my basket for payment." Exactly a week later Gladstone fired the first shot in the political battle by giving notice of his intention to move a Resolution proposing the Disestablishment of the Irish Church. The Resolution passed the House of Commons and in the General Election which followed the victory went to Gladstone, in spite of Disraeli's delaying tactics, and in spite of a popular rumour which had it that "Mr. Gladstone and his wife are Papists and that one of his daughters is an Abbess".

On December 1st the fateful telegram from Queen Victoria arrived at Hawarden to be received with the famous comment, "My mission is to pacify Ireland", and on a cold December afternoon Catherine drove into Chester to meet General Grey, the Queen's Secretary, insisting in her usual hospitable manner that he should stay the night at Hawarden rather than return by the mail train. As they talked together on the homeward drive Grey was somewhat disconcerted to discover how very much his hostess knew about the secret intricacies of the political situation. Arrived at Hawarden she led him straight into the Temple of Peace where Gladstone was hard at work by the light of two candles. (Economy in candles was one of his foibles and he had once commented unfavourably on the Royal extravagance in that respect.) The two men sat and talked for hours in the flickering firelight, and next morning they travelled together to Windsor. Four days later William Gladstone was Prime Minister of England.

Chapter Nine

WILLIAM had reached the heights, but Catherine's life was little changed, less changed, in fact, than was either right or desirable. The Gladstones did not even move to Downing Street, preferring to use the official residence as an office and to remain themselves in their own home in Carlton House Terrace. The choice of houses was symbolic. Catherine had no intention of blossoming into a political hostess. In spite of her passionate absorption in her husband's career, as a Prime Minister's wife she fell short of complete success because she could not or would not make the necessary social effort. Not that she failed to entertain and be entertained; her engagement book is full of balls, drums, dinner-parties and country-house visits, but the names are still those of personal friends rather than political supporters. Catherine might have argued that William had no desire to entertain politically on a large scale.

Lucy Cavendish records a series of "little Tuesday drums", adding that "Uncle William kicked at the notion of having regular Parliamentary squashes, and these have been far pleasanter, but I should fear many people have had their feelings lacerated". However hard William might kick it was Catherine's wifely duty to see that he did not lacerate the feelings of his Liberal supporters. She, however, chose to entertain for pleasure rather than for political profit. She was always a person who believed in killing at least two birds with every stone and her political parties were often arranged with more than half an eye on the entertainment of her three unmarried daughters.

Catherine never had any qualms as to the strange mixture of people at her parties; she took an almost unholy delight in bringing together the most incongruous and ill-assorted guests, and some of her dinners and "clever breakfasts", as Lucy always called them, must have tried her powers as a hostess to the uttermost. One list reads "Dean Stanley, Lady Augusta Stanley, Bishop Wilberforce, Lord and Lady Spencer, Caroline Norton, Lord Cowper and John Bright", surely an odd collection of celebrities to sit together round the same dinner-table.

Perhaps Catherine was too unconventional ever to fit into the rigid mould of a political hostess. If her parties were not of the type usually expected of a Prime Minister's wife, neither were her clothes nor her conversation. There was an invincible casualness about her way of life which was to some people infinitely attractive but to others merely disconcerting. In London, for instance, if William were not at home there would be no fixed hours for meals and guests would quite frequently arrive to find their hostess asleep upon the sofa or dining frugally off a single peach.

On one occasion during Gladstone's first ministry Arthur Godley, later Lord Kilbracken, was invited to bring his young bride to spend a few days at Hawarden. They were asked to arrive at a small wayside station by a most inconvenient train but not liking to object to arrangements made for them by the Prime Minister's wife they duly did as they were bid, only to find, when they alighted in a snowstorm, that no sort of conveyance awaited them. The stationmaster could suggest nothing better than a hawker's cart, so Godley piled the luggage on to this curious vehicle, sat his wife and her maid on top of the boxes, and himself leading the horse's head, set out through the snow for Hawarden, distant more than two miles. It was a very wet, cold and angry little party that at length drew up by the front door, but Catherine's welcome was so genuine, her dismay so profound, and her apologies so abject, that soon they were all laughing together round the fireside like the oldest of friends and treating the misadventure as the best possible joke, whilst Sir Stephen Glynne stood in front of the fire toasting his coat-tails and remarking whenever there was any pause in the conversation, "I am only too anxious that it should be understood I have nothing whatsoever to do with the affair!"

This complete absence of formality which was so delightful a feature of life at Hawarden could appear odd and exaggerated when seen in the glare of the limelight which beats upon Downing Street. Not, of course, that any of Catherine Gladstone's actions could seem so odd as the behaviour of "that funny old woman", Mary Ann Disraeli; unexpected, fantastic, disconcerting Catherine could be, but never ridiculous. She failed as a hostess because she had no time to take her social duties seriously, being far too busy with her charitable work and, above all, with her family. Although the elder children were grown up and even Herbert was nearing the end of his schooldays their lives still centred on their home and parents.

As member of Parliament first for Chester and then for Whitby Willy perforce spent much of his time in London, but his heart was at Hawarden and not in the House of Commons. He had failed to make a success of his Oxford career and he was totally without ambition. Apart from music, a taste which he had in common with the whole family, his chief hobby was mountaineering, and Catherine wrote nervously of his "mountain escapades". It was a pastime that was just becoming popular with the muscular intelligentsia, and both Willy and Stephy delighted in it. Stephy had been hampered in his studies by bad eyesight, but he had done respectably if not brilliantly at Christ Church and had gone from there to Cuddesdon Theological College, being ordained deacon the same month that saw his father take office as Prime Minister. He was now a hard-working curate in South London, and when she could spare the time Catherine delighted to visit his parish and to help with such matters as church decorating—"Tell the girls, I am trying to decorate Stephy's church," she wrote at Christmas, 1869, "and that I have seen a new antic* making letters in straw and a cross in rice."

Of the three girls, Agnes, the eldest, was something of a thwarted Florence Nightingale. She had been brought up to hospital visiting, so it was not surprising that at the mature age of twenty-nine she should propose to start training as a nurse. Catherine might have been expected to applaud her daughter's decision. She was herself an excellent nurse who took a serious interest in the technique of nursing. When, for instance, at the age of seventy-four she had occasion to help nurse one of her daughters through a serious illness, she wrote to William letters full of medical detail, saying with real interest that she was very glad to have had the opportunity to learn so much from the doctors. She had loudly acclaimed the heroism of those mothers who had watched their daughters set out to join Florence Nightingale in the Crimea, yet when her own daughter proposed taking up similar work her reaction was almost hysterical. She wrote in great agitation to Lucy, begging her to use her influence with Agnes who was "far too young"—at twenty-nine—for hospital life, in fact she behaved exactly as Mrs. Nightingale had behaved thirty years earlier in similar circumstances. Agnes was made of more pliant stuff than Florence Nightingale; she remained at home and in the event married happily though somewhat late in life.

Agnes could the more easily have been spared to a nursing career because Catherine's other two daughters were still at home and unmarried. Clever, inconsequent Mary was fully occupied with her music and her many friends, whilst Helen or "Lena", more quiet and self-effacing than Mary, though no less clever, occasionally acted as secretary to her father. "Will you allow Helen to study the cypher that she may be the more ready when any unearthly* telegram arrives?" Catherine wrote to William, adding, "I think it very wholesome for her to feel herself useful and to master a thing", surely an odd reason to use as justification for making a nineteen-year-old girl free of the secrets of state. Of the two youngest boys Harry was preparing to carry on the Gladstone business tradition and to enter the family firm, whilst Herbert was still at Eton, where his many illnesses had interfered with his scholastic progress, a fact which Catherine had to explain and justify to his over-exacting father.

The affairs of these seven young people were primarily Catherine's concern but she made very sure that they should be William's also. He was now Prime Minister and his time was fully occupied with the affairs of the nation but nevertheless she consulted him almost as freely and as frequently as of old. She wrote to him constantly about such matters as Herbert's health, Stephy's eyesight, or Willy's love affairs, and he was even consulted about the purchase of a horse or the laying of a fence in Hawarden park. And he was expected to concern himself not only with the problems of his own family; he settled the sum to be spent on the trousseau of his orphan niece, Kate Gladstone, he was told the result of a doctor's consultation on Molly Glynne, he was kept up to date with the affairs of innumerable Lytteltons and Talbots.

All these people formed as it were a second stream of consciousness flowing through and around the course of William Gladstone's political life. Morley said of him that his recreation was to turn from work to work, from effort to effort. His home was not a place where everyone conspired to keep him free from work or worry; rather it was the centre of a large circle of people who all, in greater or lesser degree, depended on him and looked to him as their head. Friends and visitors, even the children of the house, who saw Catherine for ever planning ways and means of shepherding her husband's time and strength naturally supposed her to be the effective head of the household. They could not know how often she consulted him in private, how many letters sped between London and Hawarden telling him of the small problems of everyday life. She was the executive power and he the legislative. Even though he might have the cares of the British Empire upon his shoulders she was far too wise a woman to take upon herself that share of family responsibility which rightly belonged to him as husband and father, nor would she ever allow their partnership to develop into that "one-man show" which is a travesty of true marriage.

The first year of Gladstone's premiership passed untroubled by family crisis. For the moment the centre of interest was not Hawarden but Hagley, where no less than three engagements caused Lucy to exclaim, "Oh, dear, dear! political life has quite dropped out amid this excitement." May Lyttelton's romance with Edward Denison ended sadly, but Lavinia's happy marriage to Edward Talbot, this year appointed the first warden of Keble College, was to form a new centre and rallying-point for the younger generation of both Gladstones and Lytteltons. The third romance was George Lyttelton's marriage with Sybella Mildmay. Catherine would not grudge George this late spring of happiness; "I am very much pleased with that arrangement", she wrote, and she welcomed bride and bridegroom with open arms when they came on a visit to Hawarden. The new Lady Lyttelton was indeed a charming person to whom life had previously brought little but unhappiness. She immediately became one of the family circle and it is creditably reported that the only time relations with her step-children became seriously strained was when her artistic conscience impelled her to protest against the time-honoured Hagley custom of playing indoor cricket in the long gallery, to the extreme detriment of priceless seventeenth-century carving.

The relationship between Catherine and Lucy Cavendish continued close as ever—"What a different life it would have been," Catherine wrote, "if I had not had you to soothe sorrow and to share happiness!"—whilst William Gladstone was becoming ever more appreciative of "Freddie" Cavendish's ability and rocklike integrity, qualities hidden from the general public by his deficiency as a speaker, which was made all the more obvious by the hereditary Cavendish lisp. Catherine wrote to Herbert in 1872, "Freddie is a right-hand man and as usual perfect, no words can say his value". Lucy had relinquished the post of lady-in-waiting to the Queen which she had held for a few months before her marriage, but she still kept up a close connection with the Royal Family whose members remained devoted to their one-time governess, Sarah, Lady Lyttelton, known to her pupils as "Laddle". When on a visit to Windsor during 1869 Lucy ventured to protest to Princess Helena against the Queen's lengthy absence from London and the centre of affairs. This was the cloud, still no bigger than a man's hand, which was to overspread the horizon and darken the relationship between Gladstone and his sovereign.

The kindly feeling, however, between Queen and Minister still persisted though Gladstone's Irish Church policy was putting it to considerable strain, and he had already, as he expressed it, told the Queen "some home truths", a course of action which filled his more tactful wife with apprehension. His visit to Balmoral in the autumn of 1869 proved a great success. "Really twenty-eight miles and cranberry pie, it sounds very good but do not take on too much," wrote Catherine even more elliptically than usual in reply to one of his letters, "I love the dear Queen more than ever for taking care of you."

Eighteen seventy was a golden year of private happiness and political achievement. Gladstone's popularity and prestige had never stood higher, and Catherine saw her husband happy and successful, guiding the destinies of a grateful nation. Like all her family she suffered severely from the "dayums", a Glynnese term denoting a passionate addiction to anniversaries great and small, and on September 13th, 1870, she wrote to remind William of that shooting accident which, twenty-eight years earlier, had all but cost him his life. It seemed as if she were indeed justified in saying "God's good providence spared you for great works". In the home circle at Hawarden all was happiness. On an afternoon of early autumn, in this same year of 1870, Catherine sat on the lawn revelling in the unseasonable warmth. She could hear the thud of a ball and an occasional shout from the fives court, where the boys were playing a strenuous game, whilst Mary and Helen busied themselves with preparations for a blackberrying expedition. One thing only was lacking to her contentment and that was the presence of her husband. Her thoughts turned longingly to him as they always did in any moment of special joy or sorrow, and she added a brief sentence to the letter which she was writing to him describing the happy scene, "My heart is with you as it ever is and I am praying God to bless and watch over you."

Happy and prosperous though her family might be Catherine was not, of course, wholly free from anxiety. For some time Herbert's health had been giving trouble, and in April, when the brothers were away in Wales on one of those mountain expeditions in which they all delighted, he was suddenly taken so ill that Catherine had to rush to the rescue. She found the boys living in a very primitive inn near Dolgelley. By night she slept on the floor beside Herbert's bed, by day she helped the old landlady with housework and cooking, a curious but to Catherine not unwelcome change from life at Hawarden or Carlton House Terrace.

Later in the year Catherine was again summoned to Herbert's bedside when he fell seriously ill at Eton. Although she succeeded in moving her patient to London against the doctor's advice, he was not fit to travel to Hawarden and she had perforce to miss the family gathering at Christmas. Her heart was very full when she wrote to greet her husband on his arrival home: "A grim and grubous* day. I hope dear old Hawarden is shining upon you but I am sure it is all bright within at all events and welcomed you with merry voices and loving young smiles abundantly. I am almost oppressed with thoughts—the many blessings and all the mercies poured upon me so long and so bountifully. Your work seems in a degree to earn it, if I may express it thus, but my work is nothing. I know you won't think so, but so it is. One more letter and the dear Hawarden bells will ring in that blessed Christmas. They will sound ever in my mind."

A fortnight later, writing on the day after Catherine's birthday, William expressed his own opinion of that work of hers which she held so cheap: "I found in Dryden yesterday a line *most* suitable to be addressed to you on that day, 'And ever be thou blest, who liv'st to bless'."

Politically the year was over-shadowed by the outbreak of the Franco-Prussian War. "The tints never were more beautiful," Catherine wrote from Hawarden in the month after the battle of Sedan, "and the foliage and all speak of peace here, such a contrast to what is passing outside." The war shocked and distressed her as if she had been personally involved in the tragedy. She grasped eagerly at news suggestive of any "glimmerings of peace" and she assured her husband that he might safely confide in her: "I am carefulissimus* as to peace and over-dull for fear of being quoted."

In the early days of war the Gladstones were staying with Lord Granville at Walmer Castle, and Catherine would sit for hours on the ramparts gazing across the Channel to the coast of France, whilst Gladstone and Granville were busy with the telegrams coming in from the seat of hostilities. Granville was now Foreign Secretary and Gladstone's most trusted friend and ally. His mother had been that wise and witty woman, Harriet, Lady Granville, his grandmother the famous Duchess of Devonshire, and he had inherited the humour and good sense of the one combined with the charm of the other. Granville was the very person to lighten the somewhat ponderous character of Gladstonian administration; he could keep party members happy by the exercise of small politenesses and easily turned, kindly jokes, and his witticisms sweetened the sobriety of official correspondence. He excelled at irreverent, thumbnail sketches of his distinguished colleagues; Argyll, for instance, is "impulsive and fizzing", Clarendon's "normal state is a passion for office", and Bob Lowe must not be omitted from the Irish Land Committee "although he will not be quite a sweetmeat", that same Lowe who, according to Mary Gladstone, "hates eating, loves music, and understands thorough-bass". Even Gladstone himself was provoked to a slight witticism on the subject of this gentleman, whom he described as "so helpless under attack that he was like a beetle on its back".

Gladstone found it easy enough to unbend with "Pussy" Granville and he was very much at home at Walmer, where he could enjoy such unsophisticated delights as rook-shooting. On one occasion he proposed a visit to a neighbouring fair, declaring that his one desire was to ride on a merry-go-round, and he was scarcely to be turned from his purpose by the united appeal of his fellow-guests who considered such an outing beneath the dignity of a Prime Minister. Horses, other than the painted merry-go-round variety, held no appeal for Gladstone, but one year he was actually persuaded to accompany Granville to the Derby. Granville professed himself much perturbed because the sporting world believed the Liberals to be "a pack of muffs" and in order to dispel this idea he challenged the Tory Front Bench to a point-to-point race. The challenge was taken up by one Ward Hunt, a stout gentleman who had long been a well-known figure both in the Northamptonshire hunting field and on the Front Bench in the House of Commons. "I am quite ready to ride on your own conditions, viz., age for age and weight for weight," wrote this massive follower of the Pytchley. "I suppose Bright is the nearest approach to a welter-weight among your colleagues; if he cannot draw twenty-five stone with his saddle I have no objection to Stansfeld putting up behind too." This sporting offer unfortunately came to nothing; "Bright is of no use," Granville replied, "he cannot pronounce the name of your hunt."

Other valued friends were the Tory Lord and Lady Salisbury, of whom Catherine wrote, "Both are true, I believe, as gold." The Gladstones were constant visitors at Hatfield, even in moments of the greatest political tension between host and guest. After a visit in 1870 Catherine wrote to Stephen Glynne to describe the beauty of the newly-restored church and Great Hall lit by the new-fangled invention of gas. The Salisburys and the Gladstones had exactly the same standard of values: "We began the day with an early celebration [of Holy Communion] in the chapel. It is so very nice to see these good people doing so much and so very *un* fine and unselfish." They also had a more mundane bond in their mutual dislike of Disraeli. "The Motleys[1] are to visit d'Izzy's and Chatsworth, Lord Salisbury shocked at the former," Catherine wrote from Hatfield in February 16th, 1870; "Lord Salisbury says this is

[1] J. L. Motley, American Ambassador and historian.

a time when honest and able heads should consult together and put away party."

No one can live for long on the heights of happiness, and although no major disaster marked its course, 1871 was a year full of irritating difficulties. Two letters which Catherine wrote from Eton during the course of Herbert's illness clearly indicate the chief source of trouble. "It is sad", she writes in the first one, "to see how little, nothing, H.M. does to show interest in the boys, not even noticing them as she drives for fear of cheers." In the second she touches directly upon the question which was to wreck the relationship between Victoria and her Prime Minister: "I do hope my letter of yesterday inspired you to detain H.M. here, surely so good for her and wholesome."

Throughout this year Gladstone was engaged in a tussle with the Queen over her determination to seclude herself as much as possible in the vastnesses of Deeside or the Isle of Wight where she was neither accessible to ministers nor visible to her loyal subjects. He was worsted, and the battle cost him Victoria's trust and affection which had once been his in full measure. For a long time Catherine refused to believe that "the dear Queen" could display such ingratitude towards her faithful servant.

Gladstone's visit to Balmoral, usually so pleasant, was this year a very melancholy occasion. "The repellent power which she knows so well how to use has been put into action against me for the first time," he wrote sadly to Granville; "I have found myself on a new and different footing with her." A copy of this letter was sent to Catherine, who replied, "Oh, I can hardly think that H.M. can be changed really after such a thirty years! She must see that it was right what you did, sooner or later!" A few months later, when the Prince of Wales was lying desperately ill, she wrote, "I wish you could see H.M.; nobody could comfort her so much", and as late as 1873 she was still protesting, "I do believe the Queen loves you." Whatever might happen to William, Catherine herself never fell from favour.

In January 1872, when relations between Queen and Prime Minister were extremely strained, the Gladstones were bidden to Osborne. Towards Catherine Victoria was all graciousness, insisting that she should sit next to her, talking without restraint about the Prince and Princess of Wales, and even remembering to enquire after Herbert's health, urging that he should not be allowed to row for fear of over-straining himself. "It is funny," wrote Catherine with pleased surprise, "but we got on capitally and she chatted and talked comfortably."

Though the Queen herself might be changed, other members of the Royal Family remained firm friends with the Gladstones. One of Catherine's more surprising sentences describes an evening party when she herself was feeling rather unwell: "I was not human at the Marlborough party but Papa flirted with Princess Mary", a remark which gives one to suppose that the stout and cheerful Duchess of Teck found Gladstone quite light in hand.

Mary Gladstone's old love, Lord Lorne, had married Princess Louise, and attributed the match partly to the Gladstones: "Lorne writes me a charming letter. He says it is a little owing to our kindness in asking him to our pleasant breakfast that things have fallen out as they have. You know, he says, Princess Louise is one of *somebody's* greatest admirers."

Another firm friend and admirer was Prince Leopold, but most important of all were the Prince and Princess of Wales, whose unfailing support and affection were to be some consolation for the Queen's treatment of Gladstone. At times, however, the Prince's behaviour could cause some embarrassment. Catherine's standards were not exactly those of the "Marlborough House set" and she was not at all happy to find herself entertaining the Heir to the Throne to dinner on the very day when he had appeared in Court as co-respondent in a divorce case.

Visits to Sandringham were a great delight, the Princess treating Catherine with the greatest informality and an almost daughterly solicitude, visiting the older woman in her bedroom to see that she was perfectly comfortable and when commiserated with over her own stiff knee bounding upstairs two steps at a time to demonstrate her powers of locomotion. Catherine delighted in this beautiful creature, and her letters are full of such phrases as "the Princess is as dear as she is lovely".

The Queen was not the only person to cause trouble. The parliamentary atmosphere was stormy, and Catherine wrote to her Eton son a graphic if ungrammatical description of a typical debate, "Fancy, Herbert, how grubous* in the House last night, most of the beasts growling and squabbling." The question of the

Alabama claim, usually referred to by Catherine as "The Alhambra", dragged on throughout the summer of 1872, interfering even with such pleasant engagements as the Fourth of June, when Herbert was to recite at "Speeches". William's zeal for economy was another source of trouble, irritating many of his best friends, including Catherine herself. On October 13th, 1871, she wrote to him: "I will attend to your wishes with regard to not sending letters to you on private matters through the official bag. I have never telegraphed through the Foreign Office at all and I paid 1/- for a wretched government telegram from Downing Street. When I think of us receiving no help as to house-rent or stables, always allowed to a Prime Minister, it does seem funny that when writing to you from Downing Street I must put stamps on all my letters. However, your wish is law though I don't see it."

Both Catherine and William were, in fact, beginning to show signs of strain, and Lucy Cavendish took it upon herself to point out that her aunt was overworking. She suggested that Catherine should not be quite so assiduous in her attendance at the House of Commons, urging that at the end of a long and tiring day it would be better to go home and rest. The reply was a very gentle snub: "I can never take amiss anything you say and I know love prompts it, but I must just observe that the House of Commons is almost my only real relaxation. I don't mean that just the exciting bits may not tire, but on the whole it comforts me. I can look at him and be at peace." The loverlike phrase strikes on the ear with a curious pathos. This elderly woman knew of no greater pleasure or relaxation than to sit quietly watching her husband. Wisely enough Lucy dropped the subject and next time she was moved to protest she addressed herself direct to Uncle William, with, it must be said, no better result. Where overwork was concerned Catherine was incorrigible.

About this time, however, she began to suffer from recurrent attacks of erysipelas which should have warned her that with increasing years there must inevitably come a decline in physical strength. It must be admitted that in her case the decline was surprisingly small; on January 6th, 1875, the anniversary of her birthday, William wrote in his diary, "It is wonderful to me, her power; what a blessing she is and to how many!" A year later he wrote against the same date: "Dearest Catherine's birthday, at sixty-four she has the vigour and freshness of thirty-four."

Though Catherine would never spare herself she was urgent in her insistence that William should find time for rest and recreation. Even during the unhappy Balmoral visit she begged him to do the impossible and "enjoy life in a holiday fashion", and in August 1872, when he was planning a political visit to Willy's new constituency at Whitby, she wrote, "Your life is too precious to be thrown away and such a time as these last three months will tell afterwards unless you obey the dictates of nature and lay yourself by to sleep and repose." A year or two later she made the odd but very typical plea, "Oh, please don't go to early church! Think of me when in doubt and give the prudent one the preference."

The summer of 1872 was a trying time politically and darkened also by personal loss. On July 12th Catherine was summoned to Hawarden by a telegram announcing the sudden death of her brother Henry Glynne. The cause of death was obscure but as he had been out in a thunderstorm and returned home very ill it was supposed that he had been struck by lightning, an incongruously dramatic end for someone so determinedly matter-of-fact as Henry. Catherine mourned sadly for this brother, whose own life had been so full of sorrow, and all Hawarden mourned with her for Henry had been well-liked as Rector. Now the village was determined that Stephy Gladstone must step into his uncle's shoes. The question of a new parson was debated with all the high seriousness appropriate to a Cabinet appointment and Catherine expended as much energy in persuading the over-modest Stephy to accept the living as ever William had done two years earlier in forcing the unwilling Lord Hartington to take the office of Irish Secretary. In the end all went well, and Stephy was duly installed at Hawarden Rectory with his pleasantly eccentric cousin Albert Lyttelton as his curate.

The summer of 1872 ended with a round of Scottish visits, including one to Fasque, where, as usual, "dear Uncle Tom cannot help being grubous* and grim". Catherine did not enjoy great houses "where we have to dress and play company"; what she preferred were intimate parties, "small, spicey, and good talk", so it was natural that she should be happiest at the Balfour shooting

lodge at Strathconan, enjoying "a round table of Balfours, Gladstones, and hot soup".

Both William and Catherine delighted in Arthur Balfour, "that
very pretty quaint boy, tall and funny", and in common with
nearly all the young women in society, Mary Gladstone had fallen
not a little under his spell. The acquaintance had begun in 1870,
when Mary and Arthur Balfour were fellow guests at Hagley.
Mary and her namesake cousin, "May" Lyttelton, spent hours at
the piano and whenever they were making music Arthur Balfour
was there to listen, giving brother Neville cause to complain, "He
seems to do nothing but hang about the girls."

If Balfour could have made up his mind then and there to speak
to the one who was the real object of his devotion he would have
saved himself and other people much heartbreak. May Lyttelton
of the shining hair and wide-apart brown eyes had fallen in love
with Balfour and he with her, and no obstacle lay between them
but his incorrigible indecision. Matters dragged on and on; May
drifted into a short-lived engagement with another man whilst
Balfour appeared to be paying at least as much attention to May's
cousin Mary as to May herself. A visit to the Balfour home at
Whittingeham became almost an annual fixture with the Gladstones and Catherine has a pretty picture of an excursion to a
nearby beach, "all the boys and girls making fortifications on the
sand, just like children in their eagerness and energy".

March 1873 saw the defeat of the Government in the House of
Commons on the Irish University Bill. Catherine was in the House
to witness this catastrophe. She realised that matters were going
badly and although Gladstone made one of the finest speeches of
his life she was too old a parliamentary hand to believe that this
effort could turn the scale. As Gladstone came out of the Chamber
he found wife and niece waiting *"mornes et mélancoliques"* by the
door to the Ladies' Gallery stair and gave Lucy a light, con-
solatory kiss. He was not unduly perturbed by the reverse for his
mind was turning more and more away from politics towards
those controversies between religion and science, and religion and
"the new criticism", that were among the greatest topics of the age.

Lucy described him the previous November as being "high
gee* theology, reading the horrible new atheistic book of Strauss's
to Auntie Pussy's great irritation". With his mind on such matters

it was peculiarly irritating to him to be forced to deal with the sort of personal problems which he found almost intolerably perplexing. Disraeli refused to take office and Gladstone had to continue as Prime Minister, and to deal with the exasperating business of Ayrton's unpopularity at the Ministry of Works and the disclosures of administrative irregularity at the Post Office. It must be confessed that he did not deal well with these matters and even Catherine cocked an enquiring and quizzical eyebrow when the erring Postmaster General found his enforced resignation sweetened with a peerage—"It rather sticks in my throat, Monsell a peer, rewarded for what?"

With these and similar troubles absorbing all his attention it is not surprising that William failed to notice the very broad hints thrown out by Catherine as to an exciting event about to take place at home, and he expressed himself as entirely taken by surprise when Catherine wrote to him at Balmoral to tell him that Agnes wished to marry Edward Wickham, the Headmaster of Wellington. Even the Queen unbent sufficiently to tease him a little about his ignorance. Catherine described a dinner-party which took place at Windsor a month or two later: "H.M. held converse with me as we all stood rather like fools round the remains of dessert, perched one by one at different corners of the dining-room; she expressed herself as a little amused at Papa at Balmoral knowing so few details of Agnes' choice."

Catherine was delighted with the proposed marriage but she was not exempt from the mixed feelings which must fill any mother's heart, "I have yet to learn how to part with a child!" Although Agnes was over thirty her marriage was the first break in the family circle. A letter of Catherine's to Herbert, written this same autumn of 1873, gives a vivid picture of their home life at Hawarden: "It is evening, dinner over, Willy reposing in an armchair, ditto Uncle Stephen, Lucy on a footstool at Albert's feet, Papa, half-reading, half-talking, as Lucy bursts forth in very animated strain." A large and cheerful party assembled for the wedding which took place on December 27th. Ten days afterwards Gladstone wrote to Granville announcing his intention to ask for a Dissolution, and at the same time he informed his family that once the Election was finished, he was resolved to retire from politics.

Chapter Ten

THE blow to Catherine was staggering, although not entirely unexpected. Her distress was the greater because, try as she might, she could not but believe that William's judgement was at fault. It is always a shock to discover that one's own personal pope is after all not entirely infallible. Now for the first time in thirty-five years of married life, husband and wife were at variance on a major issue, and to Catherine a disagreement with William was a novel and most disagreeable experience. William was convinced, or convinced himself that he was convinced, that retirement was the right course; Catherine was equally certain that it was the wrong one. He talked much of his long service to politics, of his longing to serve the cause of religion more directly with his pen, and his desire to devote himself to the exposition of Homer according to his own most unconventional view of that poet, and he even went so far as to plead ill-health, a somewhat specious argument on the part of a man who thought nothing of walking twenty-five miles over a Scotch mountain or rising at six to cut down a tree before attending early service. Catherine would have none of this argument; William might choose to see himself as an ageing man who had earned the right to withdraw from politics and prepare himself in peace against his latter end; she, with less imagination but more accuracy, saw him as a healthy individual of sixty-five, at the very height of his powers, possessing all the energy and twice the stamina of a man twenty years his junior.

Looking at the matter from the standpoint of posterity and knowing how brief Gladstone's retirement was in fact to be, it is easy to belittle the importance of this personal crisis. To Catherine the prospect of retirement felt like a little death. Her distress was increased by the necessity now laid upon her to speak plainly—

"perhaps one great trial has been my feeling it right to tell Uncle William all the disagreeable things". Where politics were concerned William had always confided in her but he had never consulted her, and she on her side had seldom if ever thought to offer advice. She had conceived it her wifely duty to support William's views rather than put before him the arguments on the other side; "my husband right or wrong" might almost have served her for a motto, and in consequence she found it most unpleasant to be impelled to take up the role of Devil's Advocate. At odds with her husband and at war within herself she found it difficult to keep her temper and something of the old passionate Pussy rose again to the surface. She poured out her feelings in a letter to Lucy, dated January 22nd, 1874, quoting rather appositely the verses which Gladstone's friend, Francis Doyle, had written on the occasion of her wedding:

"How can it be that I should not have written a word to you since all these events? Dear old things, you and Freddie! I know what the blow would be to him. It seems as if one had gone through a severe passage, a shock. In truth and in fact I have felt as it were unable to write especially to one so deeply interested as you are. I feel as it were ashamed. No, that is a wrong word, but as one who was not quite in a fit position to condole. I have indeed used arguments the other way to my husband before he left me and gone through a kind of agony in seeming to be just otherwise than

'A star whose light is never dim, A pillar to uphold and guide.'

All the time it was not because I was sure; it was because I spoke as far as I could see and because I wished he should first weigh every obstacle and know what others might say of him. . . . I am now very calm, very proud of him, and though sad for our dear country and friends, I console myself with the thought that if his Queen and country needed him he would be the first to fly to her help and forget all rest and selfish thoughts. He is strong and well. You would not have me try to deaden the solemn feeling that this is a great passage."

Again and again she stressed the note of solemnity. Her innate love of drama found some consolation in the thought of the greatness of the occasion. She could endure and almost enjoy life when it was tragic but she could not bear it to be humdrum. The question of Gladstone's retirement was not to be settled till after the General Election, which resulted in a heavy defeat for the Liberals, Gladstone himself coming in a poor second in his Greenwich constituency. Catherine took defeat badly, perhaps because she had hoped that in the event of victory William would reconsider his decision to retire. She had never made any secret of her dislike of "d'Izzy" but now her remarks take on a tone of strident and rather disagreeable bitterness. "Is it not disgusting," she wrote to Herbert, "after all Papa's labour and patriotism and years of work to think of handing over his nest-egg to that Jew?"

Disraeli took office in March 1874. "Today the new broughams go down to Windsor", wrote Mary Gladstone, lapsing into a malapropism more worthy of her mother. The blow was very slightly softened to Catherine by the election successes of Willy and of Freddie Cavendish. Referring to the determined antagonism of the brewing interest she had written to Lucy during the Election: "Bless you and bring you safe and victorious then we can better afford to see d'Izzy swimming in beer." The business of resignation entailed a visit to Windsor, where Catherine dined resplendent in "blue satin, quite new, and diamonds and lace". Blue was always her favourite colour and on one occasion, when wearing a blue velvet frock, she was surprised and delighted by a compliment from the usually taciturn Hartington—"That's the first bit of blue sky I have seen today."

The Election had found the three Gladstone brothers sadly divided. Tom was of course a Conservative and although shocked Catherine was not surprised that he and his son should think it worth while to make a long journey home to Fasque for the express purpose of voting against William's party and policy. Even the faithful Robertson was loud in denunciation of the Liberals. Robertson was in fact fast breaking up. He would sit for hours silent and unkempt in his comfortless home whilst his business affairs were allowed to go to rack and ruin. Trouble occurred with the Gladstone property at Seaforth and although William tried to take the matter in hand he could salvage little or nothing from the wreck. What chiefly distressed him was not the financial loss, serious though that was, but the fate of the house that had once been his home: "How utterly trumpery is money when it comes into competition with love! Which this affair brings out. What I am really sorry for is the house of my childhood, if it is, as I fear, hopelessly defaced." He was almost equally horrified to discover that Robertson had left the Church of England and now attended a Noncomformist Chapel. It chanced that during this trying spring of 1874 Catherine was away from William at Easter time and on Easter Day she wrote to cheer and comfort him:

"All Easter blessings abundant and full be yours. It is a comfort we can be specially together in church and I can imagine you and our children assembled together good and happy and whilst I picture all this and dwell upon it I seem to gather and enjoy the brightness which is there. It would be wrong to feel any sadness because I am away in body, but it does feel strange and I hope it is not wrong, the feelings as to the past which bring such serious thoughts, so much to be thankful for, and so much to dwell upon, a chapter as it were finished. God bless you, give you peace and comfort. How thankful ought I to be to have had such blessings—and one like you!"

Financial troubles combined with his retirement from the party leadership to decide Gladstone to sell his house in Carlton House Terrace. As a purchaser was not immediately forthcoming the house was shut up and Catherine grieved to think of it shuttered and unused, a house-agent's board disfiguring its elegant Regency façade. Next William broached the subject of selling the bulk of his collection of china, books, pictures and *objets d'art*. Such a step was clearly reasonable; if they were to take another London house it must be a smaller one, and at Hawarden there was not enough room for all his treasures.

William faced the issue with equanimity; he needed money, he could no longer house his valuables, therefore they should be sold. The financial crisis found him commendably calm. He even indulged in very mild jokes on the subject, telling Helen that he felt as if he were selling everything except his skin and entrusting Mary with a letter to Catherine "to save one penny in the distressed circumstances of the family". Catherine could not emulate William in what he described as "the habit of my life which makes me turn my eyes off a disagreeable resolution and go to work on giving it effect as if taking medicine". She had been thrown off her balance by William's decision to retire and all these secondary troubles added to her distress. She regretted the house that had seen so much of joy and sorrow, she regretted William's beautiful treasures, and most of all she regretted his retreat into private life. However, she attempted to appear resigned: "Whatever comes in the way of trial and disappointment I hope you will find me anxious to share and uphold, and trying to follow your beautiful example with double earnestness as trials increase."

William was well aware of Catherine's state of mind and his letters to her during this period are full of a gentle and almost inarticulate tenderness. "Last night I overslept myself and came down at ten (you should do so sometimes)," he writes in half-humorous reference to her refusal to take enough rest, and again, "Take care of yourself for the sake of so many." When she is away from home he ends a letter with two brief lines, "Come as soon as you can—stay as long as you can." He was not given to terms of endearment, but one sad letter begins "My Beloved and Own C.", a letter which speaks of the sudden death of Stephen Glynne on July 10th, 1874. Now of the four brothers and sisters only Catherine remained, and the old home felt desolate to that last survivor of a peculiarly loving and united family.

From Penmaenmawr, where the family were on holiday, Catherine wrote to William pouring out her grief. She received a characteristic reply: "No doubt it is better I should let you say without stint all you feel of unthankfulness. I doubt not you share the common lot. How much, how extraordinarily much, you have had in your sister and your brothers, but as in the base case of money so in this noble matter of love the more we have the more we desire and we become insatiable. And who can wonder that when the river ceases to flow the land should feel parched and thirsty?" Catherine's answer to this letter was equally characteristic:

"Your departure makes a fresh gap. Oh, how one clings to you! I have not half said or shown what I feel we owe to you, and although there may be something in excuse for the absorbing interest about one thing it is by no means enough. I am *very* sorry to have seemed at any moment thankless or wayward.

I know it was [illegible], I felt wrong at the time. I did not half consider the extraordinary blessings, the wonderful time we have been allowed to be a happy family, above all, the having *you*. Forgive me, I will try to be better. I know what short-comings I have, and have had years ago, oh, so much I wish in my heart undone! Do not contradict any of this; one's own heart is alas, the best judge. You do not know how much I need forgiveness. If I thought you such a prize then, oh, how doubly is it now! The last week has shown me more than ever what you are, and what an example."

In death as in life Stephen remained unbusinesslike, and his death gave William yet more work and financial worry. Although he had been urged to make a new will, and had indeed left his brother-in-law under the impression that he had done so, the only will to be found dated from the years before the Oak Farm crash. Echoes of that crash still sounded. On going through Stephen's papers William found that some important valuations were extremely inaccurate, thanks to the agent who had been respon-sible for the bankruptcy—"In truth it bears the mark of Boydell's ravages". Stephen's neglect of his own business had been quiet and relentless. He had asked simply to be left alone to enjoy his hobby of church music and to pursue those archaeological re-searches which earned him that modicum of fame which is repre-sented by an article in the *Dictionary of National Biography*. Perhaps it was fortunate that he had been so passive a character; a more self-assertive man might have found it impossible to share his home with an extremely forceful sister and a brother-in-law who was Prime Minister of England.

On Stephen's death Hawarden became William Gladstone's property, but he immediately made it over to his son Willy. Catherine was now free to carry out a reform on which she had set her heart. During Stephen's lifetime Hawarden Park had remained closed against all comers, although she had begged him time and again to allow at least some rights of restricted entry: "To me it is quite horrid, the entire solitude and the feeling that scarcely anybody may enjoy the innocent pleasures of the lovely park." Pleasure was not pleasure to Catherine unless it were shared.

In September 1874 William set off with Willy and Lena on a tour of Germany, planning to visit both sister Helen and Doctor Döllinger. Much of William's time with his sister was spent in attempts to persuade her to return to the home and the faith of her family; time wasted, said Catherine, who did not believe that Helen could be prevailed on to return to Scotland or to Anglicanism, or ever be cajoled into sanity. In the course of this wild-goose chase of a holiday William was tactless enough to write reproaching Catherine with her own peripatetic habits. "I have some fear lest you should get into perpetual motion," he wrote on hearing of a sudden journey to London ostensibly undertaken for the sake of Stephy's health; "I am afraid our tastes move in opposite directions for I feel an increasing aversion to journeys." Catherine was not at all pleased to receive this letter and William made haste to retract even this very mild censure, but in truth the rebuke was not undeserved. A habit of life dating back to earliest childhood, when the Glynne *berline* had been for ever in motion between the various stately homes of England, made it impossible for Catherine to remain long in one place, even if that place were Hawarden. She must be for ever running down to Oxford for a peep at dear Herbert, rushing to Penmaenmawr for a sniff of sea air, looking in on Aunt "Coque" or Aunt Charlotte to be sure these elderly ladies were well and happy, or visiting her convalescent home at Woodford to see for herself how matters were going there. Never was there a more restless spirit.

William had determined to hand over the party leadership to Lord Granville and Lord Hartington, acting jointly, but the transfer was not yet complete. On January 7th Catherine wrote to Harry in India describing the difficulties in the way: "Papa went off to London with a heavy heart to be badgered and worried respecting him leading. That nasty man Harcourt is a difficulty, unprincipled and ambitious, aiming perhaps to be a second d'Izzy towards Papa [acting] as d'Izzy did towards Peel."

Meanwhile at home the children's love affairs were giving both parents much food for thought. Willy's wooing of various young ladies was conducted in characteristically desultory fashion, whilst Arthur Balfour's attentions to Mary were becoming sufficiently marked to attract the notice of William Gladstone, the most unobservant of fathers where such matters were concerned. "Mr. Balfour breakfasted here," he wrote to Catherine, "I really delight

162

in him, neither more nor less. I thought he rather lingered here, even when I was obliged to show signs of moving, that is all I can say. We were three only." And Catherine, writing from the Balfour home at Whittingeham to describe Mary and Arthur Balfour playing duets on the piano or "the Infernals", the Balfour term for concertinas, had to remind both herself and William very firmly of the many similar scenes they had witnessed during the last three years and the little that had come of them. Mary was a shrewd young woman and she probably knew much more than her parents did about Arthur Balfour's real intentions.

In January 1875, a month or so after the Whittingeham visit that had so roused Catherine's hopes, May Lyttelton went to a house party at Ashridge. Arthur Balfour was among the guests. May came back glowing with happiness; he had made it clear to her that he loved her although even now he had not gone as far as a formal proposal. But he had delayed too long; a week or so later she fell ill of a fever which soon declared itself to be serious, and at once Catherine came down to Hagley to nurse May as long ago she had nursed May's mother.

The inconvenience to Gladstone was enormous, because the question of his retirement was about to be settled and that involved domestic problems in which Catherine's assistance was almost essential. She made one last effort to turn him from his purpose, writing two long letters[1] much more carefully phrased and argued than was customary with her, in itself a considerable effort when all her attention was concentrated upon her patient. She felt herself as much involved in his decision as ever he could be himself, and she spoke of "the great desire, the trembling desire that you should do right". Coming down to practical matters she begged him not to take any definite step until he had again consulted that wise friend, Lord Granville. But Gladstone's mind was made up and on January 13th, 1875, he formally resigned the leadership.

The Carlton House Terrace house had now to be sold and a decision taken as to future plans. "Do you look to permanently residing for part of the year in London as a matter of course with a dwelling of our own?" asked William. "I confess my feelings

[1] These are published more or less in full both by Sir Philip Magnus and Mrs. Drew.

and desires rather turn otherwise." It was decided, however, that a London house was a necessity, and now came the business of finding one. The old house had to be sold and the new one chosen, and all this without Catherine, who dared not leave her patient. William was now arranging for the sale of his collections and of various pieces of furniture, a step which he declared Catherine regarded "with discomfort and reluctance". Like all wives, she was convinced that William would be cheated and accept too low a price, and she wrote hurried illegible remonstrances which provoked him to reply, "You will, I dare say, write me all your first thoughts and *please* as a favour not to put them on corners or crossings or the tips of envelopes." William was in fact not so ill-used as some of Catherine's correspondents; this same year she wrote to Agnes from the train on the wrappings of the egg-sandwiches which had served her for lunch. A certain amount of entertaining had still to be done and Catherine wrote out a delicious menu for one of the famous breakfast parties— "good rolls, muffins, hot toast, eggs and bacon, taking care that the cream and coffee and tea are *good*". She was delighted to hear that "you and Lord Derby cuddle"* and she wrote in Glynnese of the most idiomatic variety that a proof of William's forthcoming pamphlet on the Vatican Decrees would be *breakissimus.**

Meanwhile May Lyttleton hung between life and death. The affection between May and Mary Gladstone had never slackened in spite of their gentle rivalry over Arthur Balfour. Mary now came down to Hagley and was allowed a very brief visit to the sick-room, but Balfour himself never saw May again. She died on Palm Sunday, March 21st, and the emerald which he had intended to give her as an engagement ring was buried with her in her coffin.

May had been a curiously vital creature, unforgettable and unforgotten by those who loved her. Catherine wrote sadly to Harry in India, "Perhaps May might be said to be the very last person who seemed likely to die, everything about her was so full of energy and life and power."

But 1875 was not a time of unmixed sadness, "an April year", Mary called it in her diary. If it was overshadowed by May's death, and less deeply by the death of Robertson Gladstone, it also had its moments of shining brightness. Foremost among these was the birth of a daughter to Agnes Wickham, an event joyfully chronicled by Catherine in a letter headed "Darling Grandpapa". In June Catherine was writing delightedly to Harry, "Willy gives me the idea of thinking of marriage", and a month later his engagement was announced to Gertrude Stuart, daughter of Lord Blantyre. "It is too little to say she is lovely and striking," wrote Catherine, "she is good, modest, simple yet has what Willy needs in a wife—decision." "May the bride learn the noble ways of her mother-in-law" was William Gladstone's wish for his son's wife.

Willy had once been thought to be courting another Gertrude, one of the Glynne cousins from the Rectory. This Gertrude was as beautiful as her cousin Mary Gladstone was clever; Spencer Lyttelton, when asked where he would like to sit at dinner, promptly replied, "Next to Mary, but of course, opposite Gertrude." Now she too announced her engagement, her choice being George Pennant, heir to Lord Penrhyn, the only drawback, according to Catherine, being that "he is thirty-nine and has seven children". She found herself almost equally concerned with this wedding as with Willy's, having long acted the part of a mother to the Glynne girls.

The celebrations which were to have marked Willy's marriage had to be postponed because of the death of his uncle Robertson, but the return from the honeymoon was greeted with great local festivities. Catherine and William met the married pair at the Glynne Arms amid scenes of much rejoicing, and drove home with them "along the road by which we went to our own wedding". Nevertheless Catherine's joy was not unalloyed—"Ah, who can marry a son and not be turned inside out?"

The next year saw another cause for family rejoicing in Herbert's First Class in his Final Schools at Oxford. "The surprise is great, the pleasure enormous," Catherine wrote in congratulation. "As *The Times* newspaper arrived Papa rushed to it; I felt all shaking and had not the courage to look. In came Papa to the dining-room calling me. My heart in my mouth I heard the word 'First'. . . . I know the pleasure you have given your father is one of your chief delights; you should have seen that countenance all lighted up!" The happiness of Hawarden seemed more precious in contrast to the sorrow that once again hung over Hagley.

George Lyttelton's suicide in the spring of 1876 was a grim shock to the whole family, not least to Catherine and William, to whom he had been as a brother. Nineteen years earlier Catherine had quietly taken upon herself the responsibility for George's motherless children and now, as she stood by his grave, she could feel that her task was accomplished and her duty towards her dead sister discharged. Mary's children were all grown men and women, and the birth of a daughter to Lavinia Talbot marked the advent of a new generation. In the year of George's death Lucy Cavendish wrote a touching letter of thanks to her aunt: "I have read your dear words on my birthday; you have never let the poor old dozen feel quite motherless all these nineteen years. Oh, you are right about the sight of the little children reminding one more consolingly than anything else of the new blessings and mercies which spring around the very graves at which we weep."

That letter was typical of the generous and self-forgetful Lucy whose great grief was her own childlessness. George Lyttelton left three little daughters by his second wife and to these children, as to the elder family, William and Catherine were to be a much loved aunt and uncle, although affection for Uncle William was somewhat tempered with alarm. "I hope I see a nest of little Liberals," he would boom genially at three awe-struck little girls perched in a decorous row on the drawing-room settee. As William grew older he lost the happy man-to-man touch with children that had so much endeared him to his own family. Some years later his daughter Mary made friends with a highly intelligent small boy whose ambition it was to have one word with his hero Gladstone. Mary good-naturedly arranged to bring him into the Presence, but bitter disappointment followed. "Well, my little man," said the Grand Old Man, "do you know how many sides there are to a plum-pudding? No? Two, of course, the outside and the inside." Not one other word of wisdom fell from the lips of the oracle and away went a sadly disillusioned young enthusiast.

All through these busy years Catherine continued steadily with her works of charity. The separations from husband and family which these commitments sometimes entailed seemed to her to be the heaviest of sacrifices, but she would not shrink from it. "Oh the delight of being with you at home," she wrote to William in 1874, "but I don't shut my eyes to the fact that when one has begun a work of considerable delicacy it is not right to run away." Her attitude towards the various institutions in which she was interested remained refreshingly unconventional. She presented the Woodford Convalescent Home with a cow, price £25, not in order to ensure a supply of fresh milk but for the much more exciting reason that "animals are first-rate to interest people". Similarly she gave another institution a canary costing half-a-crown, and later, "a pianoforte and some seeds for the garden", delighting always in the small personal touches which made for homeliness. Her heart went out especially to those who were both helpless and hopeless and in 1875 she wrote joyfully, "Our tiny Incurables' Home is begun, a little seed." Out of this grew a home for old ladies at Hawarden, occupying one of the houses in the yard, and this charity remained one of Catherine's greatest interests until the very end of her life.

All these charities cost money, and on their behalf Catherine became a shameless and most successful beggar. On one occasion she wrote to a rich friend asking for £1000. A cheque came back for £500. Nothing daunted Catherine promptly returned this cheque with a letter pointing out that £500 was not the sum for which she had asked. She received £1000 by return of post. Though their resources were very limited the Gladstones themselves were generous to a fault. Not only did they give endless donations to charities but they were always ready with help for distressed individuals.

One instance deserves quotation. When Gladstone was Prime Minister for the second time he offered a poor Manchester parson a Crown living. In the end the man was unable to accept the offer but he had already undertaken an expensive and fruitless journey to Cornwall. Knowing this, Gladstone wrote to a mutual friend enclosing a cheque large enough to cover all travelling expenses with instructions that it was to be slipped into the parson's pocket as from an anonymous well-wisher. Very few are the busy statesmen who would have given not merely money, but time, thought, and delicacy of feeling to the affairs of a perfect stranger.

When money was not needed Catherine could always be relied on for practical help, sympathy and encouragement. On Boxing Day, 1874, Lucy recorded that "poor Auntie P. was knocked up with wet feet and over tired after rushing off through the slush to see the poor Potters whose stables caught fire last night", and many are the entries that record similar acts of kindness. Like her husband Catherine would stop in the street to speak to a prostitute. In the middle of a letter to Lucy, full of distress at William's impending retirement, comes the sentence, "Yesterday I took a poor young thing to the new House [of Mercy], picked her up in Windmill Street and left her safe."

So the months wore on, Catherine occupied with her charities and with family affairs, William apparently perfectly content with his forestry and his book, his mind full of Homer and the iniquities of Ultramontanism. In the summer of 1876 Mary Gladstone could look round her and feel the happiness of her home as something almost tangible: "Last Thursday at the flower show at the Rectory everything was so lovely and bright and happy I could quite have cried from the pure pleasure of mere existence. It all rushed over me in a moment what blessings we had, and as I looked round all seemed so unbroken and beautiful, Agnes and Edward with their baby, Stephy, Herbert, Willy and Gertrude, Mama and Papa—such moments are rare and so precious." William Gladstone's lot would be cast in pleasant places should he persist in his determination to retire from politics. But did he in his heart really wish his retirement to be permanent? Catherine, for one, preferred to think of him as a prophet withdrawn into the wilderness, awaiting his call.

Chapter Eleven

GLADSTONE did not have to wait long for a sign. A month after
Mary had written her ecstatic description of the peace and
happiness at Hawarden he was on his way to London to start his
campaign against the Turkish atrocities in Bulgaria. "This," he
said to Catherine, "is the most extraordinary moment in my
recollection," and Catherine herself cast grammar, punctuation
and even sense behind her in her excitement: "I leave it to your
imagination, his state of righteous indignation and his energy
and pluck, a pamphlet nearly written he has been boiling over at
the horrors and at the conduct of the Government very proud
that England's voice is speaking its great heart throbbing and
in this pumped-out[1] moment with no backing it speaks." No
wonder that Catherine should describe herself as being "brimful
of Bulgaria". She had set her heart on being present on the great
occasion of the monster meeting at Greenwich: "I consider that
this speech of yours may be one of the most interesting chapters
in your life. No musical festival, no treat, can compare to being
with you at Greenwich."

She had her wish, as was only proper, for the moment was
decisive for her as for him—"this is indeed a moment in our lives
for your life feels mine". The Greenwich meeting over, they set
out on a private holiday in the North of England which turned
into a triumphant political progress—"such a feeling among these
Northerners for Uncle William". At Ford Castle William amused
himself by cutting down an ash, and as soon as the tree crashed
to the ground an eager crowd of spectators surged forward to
snatch up the chips as relics. At Alnwick enthusiasm was so great
that it was almost impossible to maintain any show of privacy,

[1] Is this a translation into not very plain English of the Glynnese "pompé"?

169

but much as Catherine delighted in this appreciation of William she was bored by the grand company and disappointed in her innocent scheming to introduce daughter Helen to some suitable young men—"we could not have fallen in with more grey beards and hair". The grand tour ended at Castle Howard. Lucy and Frederick, who were waiting on the doorstep to welcome the Gladstones on arrival, saw a great crowd come surging up the avenue into the courtyard between the wings of Vanbrugh's tremendous building. In the middle was a carriage drawn along by willing arms, and in the carriage sat William and Catherine, bowing in acknowledgement of a welcome that any king might have envied.

The family, however, were not unanimous in echoing this enthusiasm. Catherine's niece, Gertrude Pennant, had married into a "toryissimus"* family and Catherine had to endure a very awkward visit to the Pennant home at Penrhyn Castle, where she found the assembled company anything but sound on the Eastern Question. Soundness on the "E.Q." was henceforward to be her shibboleth. She derived consolation, however, from Lady Penrhyn's declared dislike of Disraeli, and she was much amused to find herself, at the mature age of sixty-five, solemnly invited to dance with Lord Penrhyn himself.

More serious trouble arose with the Cavendishes. At Gladstone's request Hartington had reluctantly assumed the party leadership together with Granville, and now Hartington found himself not at all in sympathy with Gladstone's zeal on behalf of the persecuted Bulgarians. Frederick and Lucy Cavendish were torn in two between conflicting loyalties, and Catherine was almost distracted. "To Harley Street after dinner," Lucy noted; "poor Auntie Pussy looked worried to death and Freddie is nearly wild." Catherine was not above hinting to Lucy that Hartington had been less than generous in his speeches: "Of course Lucy dear I should have liked a little reference to Uncle William considering all, I do see what great difficulties there were but one cannot live with Uncle William and not be impressed by his humility and generosity, never thinking of himself." The implication that Hartington had been neither humble nor generous was an unfounded slur on a man acting with great loyalty in a very difficult situation. Where William was concerned Catherine was beginning to lose

both her sense of proportion and her sense of justice. Nobody
was allowed to stand comparison with him, and she was particularly hard upon their old friend Sir Stafford Northcote, "poor Sir
Stuffy", as he was known to the Gladstone family. She reported
him as making "a very poor beginning as Leader [of the House],
no dignity, no statesmanlike bearing, small, fussy. Certainly he
has a difficult case, and he stood up in a plucky way for his chief.
Then when Uncle got up, oh, the contrast! So dignified, so noble,
the voice like music upon the waters."

Extraordinary demonstrations of popular enthusiasm continued
throughout 1877. Day after day during that wet, cold summer
there would be two or three thousand people haunting Hawarden
Park on the chance of catching a glimpse of their hero, or flocking
into the church in order, as Mary Gladstone put it, "to worship
his seat". A private visit to Hagley provoked similar demonstrations and a holiday in Ireland produced an extraordinary outburst
of popular interest. All this Catherine took simply as William's
due, but she much disliked the attendant newspaper publicity—
"really, too provoking, although I am not blinded as to him being
Tomkins", Tomkins being a family term for a nonentity. During
this same summer Catherine came into contact with that flam-
boyant and rather foolish character, Madame Novikoff, known as
"the Russian Spy". "I went to Novikoff and delivered your
letter," she wrote on July 3rd; "she very nearly devoured me with
kisses, gushed beyond* and went off into raptures about you, in
which I fully agreed, said that you are the only man in whom the
Emperor really places confidence, that his Ministers are ——.*"

Gladstone's popularity was not to last and next year the fickle
crowd changed its tune. He remained popular as ever in the
North, but in the South of England public opinion veered round
to the opposite point of view. On February 24th, 1878, a crowd
gathered outside the Gladstone house in Harley Street, and although Catherine with her usual nonchalance made light of the
incident her description shows plainly that the mood of the mob
had been very ugly. She wrote to reassure Herbert about alarming
newspaper reports and to give him her own account:

"You may get exaggerated accounts of yesterday's proceedings but they were indeed notable, a great crowd gathering and

increasing like a snowball. Mary was very brave and saw it all; I was at church. You may think the numbers were very formidable when I tell you seventy policemen were on the ground and that in spite of this they had hard work to keep the peace until mounted police arrived who did their work splendidly. The window over our hall door is broken, and in Papa's little study. My feelings is that there has been a so-as-to-speak smouldering going on, abusive letters without end, and perhaps it is as well it has come outside, but what with ingratitude without and deep and real anxiety as to the E.Q. within one lives in a bathing-feel*.''

The feeling against Gladstone ran high indeed among those whom he was soon to castigate as "the upper ten thousand". Even the Prince of Wales displayed distinct chilliness although he had the grace to be much annoyed when Queen Victoria, with deliberate and studied rudeness, omitted to send the Gladstones an invitation to the wedding of the Duke of Connaught. "I dare say you boiled over at Papa not going to the wedding", Catherine wrote to Herbert, adding wisely, "Our line is to say nothing." In spite of this strong feeling Catherine remained on the most friendly terms with various ladies in the opposite camp. She was much cheered when Lady Derby exclaimed in her hearing that there was "a dark spirit working underneath" in oblique reference to Disraeli, a curious sentiment from the wife of Disraeli's ex-Foreign Secretary. Lady Salisbury, "fat and cheerful", the wife of Lord Derby's successor in that position, took up a different point of view. "Well," she remarked, "if the Russians will tell lies we must fight; after all, we ought to think of British interests", a platitude which provoked Catherine into exclaiming, "I am sick of that kind of talk." However, kind Lady Salisbury refused to be offended and steered the conversation into the safe channel of Convalescent Home doings.

The Convalescent Home and other charities continued to occupy a large part of Catherine's time in spite of renewed political excitement. The various Homes at Hawarden sheltered some curious inmates; there is talk in her letters of the children of a murderer, and of a boy, who, having no arms, fed himself with his feet. Some of these sad waifs and strays were lodged in the

Castle itself; in the summer of 1879 the dining-room was fitted up as a room for a tired schoolmistress in need of rest and good food, and when this poor woman developed consumption Catherine threw up all other plans in order to stay by the invalid until she could see her cheerful and comforted with some provision made against the future. Catherine took an active part in local church work and in January of the momentous year 1880 she played a somewhat unexpected role in a parish mission—"Mamma is to do pothouses," wrote Mary, "she is to walk in and address the men sitting over their drink."

At the Castle the family circle, so long inviolate, was at length breaking up. Willy had brought his bride to live under the parental roof, but her father, Lord Blantyre, was now pressing for a separate establishment for the young people, a not unreasonable demand which nevertheless gave great offence.

Stephy, ordered abroad for the sake of his health, had set out for South Africa, accompanied by Herbert, who had not yet settled upon a profession. At one time he had thought of becoming a Land Agent, and now he planned to work for a while under Edward Talbot at Keble, but his thoughts were turning seriously to politics. Young Harry had lost his place in the family firm on the death of Uncle Robertson, but he was now safely established with another company in India.

Catherine was always generous with money for her children, and she had supplemented Harry's allowance out of her own pocket so that he might enjoy a holiday in Italy on his way out East. "*Never* be afraid of asking me for money, I have such a horror of you not having any", she had once written to this same son.

The quiet and retiring Helen was making history as one of the very first women students at Cambridge. Helen owed her chance of a University education to her sister Mary who had persuaded her parents to allow Helen to enter the newly-established Newnham Hall, where Arthur Balfour's sister was Principal. Mary's nickname was "von Moltke" in laughing but rather rueful reference to the iron way in which she ruled and organised her family. As Mrs. Masterman puts it, "Mary sometimes gave her less energetic friends the feeling that they were being managed for ends not their own."

Mary was now the only child living permanently at home, and her influence with her parents was considerable although a gentle authority could still be exercised by Catherine, "meek and almost in tears, but inexorable". Elderly and famous men found Mary a most attractive young woman. Ruskin and Tennyson were frequent visitors at Hawarden and both of them flirted with her more or less decorously. Ruskin's behaviour was only to be expected but Tennyson's admiration left Mary surprised and disconcerted. It was embarrassing to find the Poet Laureate stroking your nose and describing it as *"un petit nez retroussé* meaning all sorts of naughty things", or staring hard in your face to determine the colour of "those wonderful eyes". "I put all this down," Mary confided to her diary, "because I am unused to personal remarks and it is so *very* odd."

News from Hagley gave Catherine a curious reminiscent pleasure. The young Lord Lyttelton was taking to himself a wife. "Little Mary Cavendish" was neither rich nor beautiful, and so desperate was the financial situation that even the unworldly Catherine sighed over her lack of fortune, but in every other respect she was a worthy successor to that other Mary Lyttelton. "I seem to see in the name a continuation of her sweetness", wrote Catherine, and her first visit to the newly-married couple was a joyous moment. It was delightful to find that the great house at Hagley was no longer a grievous place "where one seems to be waiting and watching for someone who does not come".

Disraeli had returned from the Berlin Conference bringing "peace with honour", and he now filled the place of popular idol which had been Gladstone's a year ago. It must be admitted that the attitude of the Gladstone family towards Disraeli now began to pass the bounds of decency and common-sense. "I shot* Dizzy in a brougham, looking more horribly like a fiend than ever, green, with a glare in his eye", wrote Lucy with horrid glee, and when Catherine arrived at Hawarden in August 1878 she wrote, "I feel as if out of d'Izzy's atmosphere, and the air is so fresh and so sweet." When he chanced to meet Catherine in society Disraeli was all charm and compliments—"I need not ask how *you* are! And those eyes!" Catherine was not to be mollified; she regarded these pretty speeches as foolish and fulsome and stigmatised the

speaker as "a wretched old man". Even when forced to admit
that the signing of the Treaty between Russia and Turkey was a
great event she could not resist a dig at Disraeli: "The Talbot
argument is curious"—the Talbots were unrepentant Tories—
"owning that d'Izzy wishes for war but is *sat upon*; therefore is a
P.M. to be a P.H.?" She could hardly have made a more scathing
comment; the letters P.H. stand for "phantod" which in Glynnese
signifies "an imbecile person, one incapable of serious and rational
behaviour".

The late summer of 1879 was spent on holiday abroad, visiting
sister Helen, staying with Lord Acton at Tegernsee, and from
there travelling to Venice and home through Paris. Mary struck
up one of her intense intellectual friendships with Lord Acton,
who was meditating his great History of Liberty. "It is extraordinary, the way he tingles with it to his finger tips," wrote
Mary, "and yet can be patient and quiet and wait and wait another year before he writes it." Acton's patience was to be the
world's loss for the book was never written.

On arriving home Gladstone accepted an invitation to stand as
Liberal candidate for Midlothian, and a whirlwind visit to his
constituency at the end of November became famous as "the
Midlothian Campaign". Catherine accompanied him to stay at
Dalmeny, a house which awoke memories of that long ago
Scottish tour before her marriage, where she and Mary had
arrived dressed in green plaids and escorted by brother Henry.

Now the grandson of the Lord Rosebery of those distant days
reigned at Dalmeny, a brilliant young aristocrat, immensely rich,
immensely gifted, yet touched with the blight of that accidie which
is not the least deadly of the seven deadly sins. Rosebery lived
very much *en grand seigneur* and the Gladstones' progress through
the mining villages of Midlothian was attended with almost royal
pomp. First came a single horseman, then the candidate's carriage
drawn by four perfectly matched horses and attended by out-
riders, followed by a string of carriages containing such lesser fry
as relations and secretaries. Everywhere they met with a welcome
that was almost frightening in its enthusiasm, and Catherine found
herself half bedazed with the cheers, the torches, the bonfires,
above all, with the faces, tens of thousands of faces all turned
towards William Gladstone as to a saviour.

175

Catherine came in for her full share of the crowd's devotion; she was patted, stroked, thumped on the back, had her hand shaken so many times that she felt as if it must fall off, received presentations of clothes, books, linen, table-cloths, accepted innumerable bouquets, and all the time her heart was overflowing with the awestruck conviction that the Almighty had indeed laid His hand upon her William. "Is it not a Providence," William remarked to her after the last great speech of the campaign. "Here am I, close on seventy; I hope I am not wrong in feeling as if a special power was sustaining me for the work." Catherine herself wrote to Herbert: "I think of my children in all this, and pray, I hope more and more, that they and I may be much more worthy of such a father and such a husband", then to her niece, in lighter vein, "Bless you, Lucy; I feel as if I must burst."

Catherine may have attributed her husband's remarkable resilience to supernatural aid but some of the credit was her own. The perceptive Rosebery watched, half-touched, half-amused at her sometimes comic manœuvres to save her husband from strain in small things as in great. He was specially delighted at her sleight of hand when she threw a particularly noxious brew of tea out of the window and returned an empty cup to William's saucer under the very eyes of their hostess who had observed nothing of this little episode. Such actions were typical of Catherine; grey-haired though she might be she still kept about her something of the *espièglerie* of a mischievous child.

Catherine's efforts were rewarded. At the end of the campaign William Gladstone returned to Hawarden in fine form, giving no sign of strain either physical or mental. It was Catherine herself who collapsed exhausted and took to her bed suffering from her old enemy, erysipelas. It was very seldom that she gave way to illness. A few months earlier Lucy had recorded that "Auntie Pussy" was suffering from "a horrid grievance" in the form of a broken blood-vessel in her eye, which was seriously affecting both her health and her sight, "but she has all her fine courage and pluck to help her and won't give way". This time, however, Catherine had to admit to being ill, and she was unable to accompany William when he hurried out to Germany to the death-bed of his sister Helen. Catherine had never liked Helen, but nevertheless she grieved not to be able to go to her now, feeling it unnatural that any member of the family should be ill and she not there to nurse and comfort.

A General Election followed the dissolution of Parliament in March 1880. Catherine accompanied William through the exciting Midlothian Campaign, which was a repetition of the triumphs of the first, ending with his return at the head of the poll. The Election was a victory for Liberalism and for William Gladstone in particular. Three Gladstones were now members of Parliament, for Herbert, though defeated at Middlesex, finally won a seat at Leeds and came home to a village triumph; "Flags wave, bands play, and he is drawn into Hawarden a hero." William was delighted with the success of this youngest son, whose presence he once described to Catherine as "being to him like a fresh wind off the sea", whilst Catherine herself wrote ecstatically, "Oh, Lucy, Lucy, I long to give you such a big hug!"

Lucy might well describe herself as being "in great perplexity", for the question of the leadership had now become acute. Four years ago Gladstone himself had insisted on handing over the official leadership to Hartington and Granville, and they had gallantly borne the heat and burden of the day. The popular cry, however, was all for Gladstone, and the country was in no mood to be put off with a lesser man. That kindly realist, Granville, was not likely to stand in the way but Hartington was another matter. Gladstonian zeal sorted badly with Cavendish detachment and the two men were not personally sympathetic. Gladstone insisted that the first move must come either from the Queen or from Hartington, and as Hartington himself gave no sign the Gladstone women decided that he must be prodded. Lucy Cavendish was clearly the connecting link. Catherine was a singularly ingenuous intriguer, and she may not have intended her incoherent letter to be read by anyone except Lucy. Doubtless, however, Lucy showed it to Frederick, and Frederick passed on its contents to Hartington. It is dated April 10th, 1880:

"Can Father, having brought up his soldiers, run away? Now, however excellent Hartington and Granville are, would it not be cowardly to think of self when the giant's hand is needed? Were there ordinary, simple work, the answer would be simple; Father might rest. But, look! See the rocks, Finance, Foreign matters! Supposing Father is called for and Hartington and Granville desire it, I feel certain he would take the Chancellorship [of the Exchequer] and the headship. But his vision would be only for a short time, perhaps a year, putting things as I believe only *he* could do into proper train for younger hands. . . . In the meantime he sits silent, dignified, avoiding demonstrations. All the time the admiration for Lord Hartington is enormous, but if the country calls for Father and Lord Hartington wishes it——! Surely it would be no disparagement of Lord Hartington to compare him with an experienced giant of power. What a work for Father, for how many would be nasty! And what a position he holds without any effort! But there lies in my heart—would one not die for one's country? I never looked upon Father but that he was the nation's. I have seen him go forth ill, I have seen him going forth exhausted night after night, leaving home, wife, children. Shall he fail now in his country's cause? The mighty, the brave spirit, if he is wanted, shall he shrink now? No."

To this curiously high-flown effusion Mary Gladstone added a much more explicit postscript: "Will you burn this when read, please? The reason I said that about Papa's taking the first step was because Mr. Brett told Arthur[1] as if it were meant to reach a Gladstone ear that Lord Hartington was waiting for some hint from Papa and that he would not ask Papa to lead unless he knew first that Papa would not refuse. This was, I think, in January."

"Von Moltke" Mary was very much in her element at this crisis. She enjoyed pulling strings and never before had she had her hands on strings attached to such important puppets. Gladstone might be still undecided, still hankering after the will-o'-th'-wisp of retirement, but his daughter was determined that he should once again become Prime Minister and she was working behind his back to bring about that desirable result. A carefully careless letter in pencil went addressed to Lucy, its contents clearly intended for Hartington:

"What I want really to write about is the great question as to who heads the next government. Every person I meet, every

[1] Arthur Godley?

letter I open, says the same thing, 'He must be Prime Minister'. But no one seems to see it is no good saying it to *him*; they must say it to the Queen, Lord Granville, and Lord Hartington. There is one thing I am certain of and that is that Papa will never take the smallest step *towards it*. The steps must be taken *towards him*. I have never doubted that in the event of a huge crisis of this sort he would never let personal longing for rest and retirement affect his coming forward again if he saw that the general feeling was in favour of it. Except among the Pharisees the whole mass is frantic for it, and something ought to be done soon for you see there is this huge stir as to giving him a glorious reception in London and I don't see that he can accept it until something definite is settled. You will think it so silly, my writing to you and saying all the things everybody knows by heart, but I have always rather understood Lord Granville was the difficulty, that he longed to be Prime Minister. And now I hear he would dread it excessively. And so I don't see what the obstacle is. Lord Hartington would no doubt be considered very much aggrieved by a certain party, but he's too big a man to suffer by that in any way. I mean, he is the man after Lord Granville and Papa have gone, and he would never lose by behaving with splendid humbleness, so as to speak. I think it would be glorious, Papa forced by England to become Prime Minister, and bringing the ship once more into smooth waters and then retiring in prosperity and leaving it to Lord Hartington. This is a private ebullition."

There is no indication that Gladstone himself knew anything about this correspondence. The letters of both mother and daughter would leave a more pleasant taste behind had they been content to state that Gladstone was willing to become Prime Minister without harping on the unselfishness of this attitude. To most people it must have appeared as if the unselfishness were all on the side of Hartington and Granville. Lucy Cavendish herself inclined to this point of view; she recognised, as her aunt would never do, that Hartington was fully capable of filling the position of Prime Minister, and she gave due importance to the Queen's dislike of Gladstone, a difficulty always soft-pedalled by Catherine. In the end, of course, Gladstone became Prime Minister, a result which everyone except Queen Victoria and Gladstone himself had known to be inevitable from the first. As he was setting out for the fateful audience at Windsor Catherine asked casually if there was anything she could do for him whilst he was away. "Pray for me", came the answer. It was a reply that Catherine well understood; in a letter written two or three years later she remarked, "You are speaking, I am off to church to pray."

Whilst William worried over the delicate task of cabinet-making Catherine worried over the equally delicate matter of Willy and Herbert. Willy had previously held minor office but his heart was clearly not in politics and now he was to be passed over and Herbert made a Commissioner of the Treasury. Catherine was always jealous for her eldest born, but Willy himself was perfectly content. He recognised that his true sphere was Hawarden, as Herbert's was the House of Commons, and no ill-feeling arose.

The Gladstones were this time to inhabit the official Downing Street residence, and in the middle of the business of house-moving in walked Harry, home on leave from India, to be greeted with great rejoicings. The house overflowed with people; in every room somebody was holding an interview or a private conference so that the servants were at their wits' end to know what to do with the distinguished callers who continued to pour in. Lord Granville was shown in on young Harry eating a hurried supper off a tray and the climax came when the Prince of Wales walked in upon Mary as she sat scribbling notes in the unlit and untidy drawing-room.

Mary was to act as supernumerary private secretary to her father, her especial business being ecclesiastical patronage, a curiously amateur method of dealing with Church affairs. She had her finger in many pies, for friends would write to her as an indirect means of approach to Gladstone himself. Catherine was never a wholly satisfactory channel of communication because she remained fundamentally uninterested in politics, but Mary was political to her finger-tips. On May 26th she wrote to Lavinia Talbot: "It is rather appalling, finding myself this time so much in the position of 'a political intriguer'. I mean people like Mr. McColl, Lord Rosebery, Lord Reay, and Lord Acton write me heaps of letters, suggestions, questions, things to mention if possible to 'the Dictator' as Lord Rosebery calls him, papers, general opinions etc., etc. Just now I was saying to Papa I would retire to another table at the breakfast and he answered I was not to as Lord Rosebery would be disappointed. Mama said, 'Oh, no, he only uses her as a *pis-aller* when he can't get our ear.' Papa was amused."

Gladstone's triumph had flown slightly to the heads of his womenfolk. Mary was seeing herself in the role of a "Grey Eminence" and Catherine, who had no thought of self at all, was seeing William as a major prophet. She was in no way boastful, but rather "grave and awestruck" as a person would be who believed, to use Lucy's words, that "the whole bit of history has been guided to its present crisis by the hand of God". Catherine was not to be blamed for seeing her husband as more than life-size; he was a colossus but a colossus is not necessarily always right. Gladstone would have been better served at this period by a more discriminating affection than this blind devotion which pushed aside other people's rights and opinions as being of no consequence. Hartington's claims went for nothing in Catherine's eyes; it was almost blasphemous to put forward any leader save the one upon whom the Almighty had so clearly laid His hand. In private life she was not afraid to laugh at and even to contradict her husband; when the company were wilting under the strain of one of his very learned, very courteous and almost interminable discourses she would interrupt with scant deference and switch the conversation into more lively channels. Where public affairs were concerned, however, her attitude was very different. She had always, and with good reason, regarded William as the greatest political figure of the age, but the extraordinary scenes she had witnessed in Midlothian seemed to have confirmed her in the opinion that he was little less than inspired.

During the first two years of its existence Gladstone's second ministry was chiefly concerned with the problem of Turkey, and when at length the Sultan yielded to the threat of force great was Catherine's jubilation. "If only the Sultan does not again bolt!" she wrote to Lucy. "I have had to bury Smyrna deep down in the recesses of my heart.[1] But now how grand is the Government policy, the coward frightened to death by the aspect of strong

[1] Britain had threatened to attack Smyrna if Turkey did not fulfil treaty obligations towards Montenegro and Greece.

measures! You may fancy the hope springing in Uncle William's heart of hearts; I copy his words, 'Praise to the Holiest in the height'."

Another and even greater problem than Turkey was looming on the horizon. "The Irish soup thickens," said Gladstone in the autumn of 1880, to which his new Private Secretary Edward Hamilton added the comment, "It is becoming what the brewers call Treble X." Over the issue of the Irish Land Act Gladstone lost the support of the Duke of Argyll, an old friend whose defection was a particularly bitter pill for Catherine. Three years earlier the ailing Duchess of Argyll had been taken ill at a dinner-party given by Lucy Cavendish, and had died in Catherine's arms. About this time another old acquaintance fell from grace, even more seriously than the Duke of Argyll. Baroness Burdett-Coutts had been a personal friend as well as a munificent benefactor of many of Catherine's charities. When she announced her intention of marrying her young and penniless secretary the Gladstones were horrified and William stigmatised her conduct as "loathsome", refusing absolutely to see her or listen to her explanation. Very reluctantly, Catherine agreed to deputise for him when the Baroness begged an interview, but, much to her relief, the lady failed to put in an appearance.

In August 1880 William fell ill with congestion of the lungs. He was ordered a complete rest and accordingly accepted Sir Donald Currie's offer of a cruise in the *Grantully Castle*, a ship so big that even the Gladstones, bad sailors though they all were, could hardly feel seasick. This was the first of those cruising holidays which Catherine and William so much enjoyed as providing an escape from work and publicity, though even on board ship they were not always free from the attention of pleasure steamers crammed with sight-seers. When a proper holiday was not to be had Catherine was always a believer in the efficacy of a day or two spent out of London in "fine air" at Brighton, or perhaps St. Leonards. On one of these occasions William was much amused to discover that the engine which drew their train back to London bore the name "Beaconsfield". Sometimes they would spend a week-end at a small country house which Lord and Lady Aberdeen had taken at Mill Hill. It had originally been built by Charles II for Nell Gwynne, and the Gladstones found themselves somewhat incongruously ensconced in a tiny gold and white drawing-room decorated with the entwined cyphers of Charles and Nell. Summer Sundays were now the most decorous of days in this Stuart love-nest. Between church services the Prime Minister was frequently to be found at the bottom of the kitchen garden for where strawberries were concerned Gladstone was always as greedy as any schoolboy.

The prospect of strawberries had always been one of the baits used by Catherine to lure her husband out of the summer heat of London to the quiet coolness of Hawarden—"Oh, the strawberries *are**—and cry aloud for you so much!" Not that William ever needed much persuading for Hawarden was always the most beloved of places. Catherine went down there alone in the summer of 1881 and wrote to tell him of its beauties: "Rodos [*sic*] gorgeous, foliage grand, I feel ready to burst over them, but the drawback is your not being by me. God bless you; I could not enter the Cabinet and give you a kiss."

At Hawarden the day followed an ordered and not too strenuous pattern. Long before breakfast husband and wife, the one already in his seventies, the other only three years younger, would be out of bed and off on the mile-long uphill walk to early service in Hawarden church. On their return there would be letters to open and a brief glance at the *Pall Mall Gazette*, the only paper Gladstone cared to read, all to be done before breakfast, which was always a cheerful meal with the great man at his best. From breakfast to lunch he worked in the Temple of Peace, where Catherine also habitually wrote her letters, and back he would go there after luncheon until it was time to sally forth axe in hand to lop and chop the trees in garden and park. Tea at five was a favourite meal, followed usually by an hour or so with a book until it was time to dress for dinner, a business which both husband and wife accomplished at incredible speed. After dinner came a family evening round the fire, with conversation or reading aloud, or the music in which the whole family delighted. Gladstone had been a founder-member of the London Bach Choir, and many famous musicians frequented their London house, including Jenny Lind and Joachim.

At Hawarden the family circle did not grow less though Harry might return to India and Helen take up permanent term-time residence at Cambridge, where she had accepted the post of Vice-Principal of Newnham, a step which Catherine regarded with rather mixed feelings. Their places would be taken by Willy and Gertrude, come down from the new house they had built for themselves at the other end of the village, or Stephy from the Rectory full of parish news, or Molly Glynne from "Glynne Cottage". Among passing visitors there would be Wickham grandchildren and, of course, Lytteltons galore, including the beloved Lucy. Frederick was now acting as Financial Secretary, chief assistant to Gladstone at the Exchequer, and making himself yet more dear and indispensable every day. As Lucy was in the position of a daughter to Catherine so to William Gladstone Frederick had become "the son of his right hand".

In the spring of 1882 the resignation of Lord Cowper as Viceroy and Forster as Chief Secretary left the most important Irish posts vacant. Gladstone was contemplating a rearrangement of the Cabinet and he was engaged in negotiations with Lord Derby through the medium of their respective wives. Catherine wrote "A Memorandum of a conversation with Lady Derby" dated May 1st, 1882. The writing of memoranda was not an art at which she excelled but the drift is clear enough:

"Lady Derby and I had a very friendly and very interesting conversation today. I gathered from it how [much] they had both felt all the kindness and how deeply interested they had both been in the offer. Seeing an opportunity I tried to bring her out and ventilate the matter. I spoke of the tremendous difficulties of the moment, did not duty speak in a case like this? She warmed up and seemed to feel this [illegible] and gradually we got more and more confiding in one another. I have certainly gathered that time might do something. Lady Derby most frankly spoke of her husband's indecision, and I left her feeling it would be worth while, if possible, not to shut the door now. She had been so touched by your last letter, she had not dared to show it to him, he was quite unhappy. Now I spoke of the old days when you acted with his father, and, if I venture to say so, of the value of acting with one like you, and she warmed up still more. She said the Indian Office was the very thing for him. I believe his being told he must make up his mind at once had a bad effect. It was Lady Derby's speaking of his indecision and of the matter being so hurried which led me to say 'Of course I know nothing but what if the matter could be delayed by the Chancellorship of the Exchequer being kept by my husband?' "

Lord Derby did not in fact join the Government until the following December when he became Colonial Secretary, but the two Irish posts had to be filled immediately. Lord Spencer was a fairly obvious choice for Viceroy, and Gladstone was determined to offer the difficult and dangerous position of Chief Secretary to Frederick Cavendish, who was not at all eager to take it. For two days there was great perturbation, and then on May 3rd, when aunt and niece were sitting together after a meeting of the Convalescent Home Committee, Frederick walked into the room and announced, "Well, I'm in for it."

Three days later on May 6th, Lord Northbrook gave a grand evening party at the Admiralty. The Cavendishes had of course been invited but as it chanced neither of them was present; Frederick had already gone over to Ireland on a brief visit, intending to return the next day, and Lucy, in typical Lyttelton manner, had mislaid her card and forgotten all about the invitation. Hartington, however, was among the guests and so was Frederick's sister, Lady Louisa Egerton. Rumours began to circulate when these two disappeared into a private room with their host; nobody had any definite news but the air was heavy with a sense of foreboding.

Meanwhile, the Gladstones had been dining at the Austrian Embassy, and Catherine was on her way alone to the Admiralty, William having elected to walk home. She had already spent a long and tiring day at the Woodford Convalescent Home and at the official opening of Epping Forest Park, followed by the Embassy dinner, and now she must show herself for half-an-hour or so at the Northbrooks' party.

As she drove up to the Admiralty door her host hurried out to meet her in great agitation. She must not come in, but must go at once to Downing Street; there was bad news. Her mind at once leapt to William; she knew the Irish were on his tracks for he had been obliged much against the grain to accept police protection.

Reassured on that point she next supposed that some fanatic had shot the Queen but during the brief drive to Downing Street some instinct warned her of the truth and she spoke with deep anxiety of Ireland and the beloved Frederick. As she entered the hall of Number Ten she saw Edward Hamilton waiting for her and cried out that she must know the worst at once. In a very few words he told her the shocking truth; Frederick Cavendish had been murdered that afternoon in Phoenix Park. She had no time to recover herself before the door opened and in walked William Gladstone. For a brief moment Hamilton saw the two old people break down completely but almost immediately the unselfish habit of a lifetime reasserted itself. They must go to Lucy to bring what they could of help and comfort, and tired as they were they set off at once for Carlton House Terrace.

In the small hours of the morning they returned home, but not to sleep. William found relief in composing some memorial verses to go with a long letter to Lucy, and Catherine was very early astir seeking a messenger to take these over to Carlton House Terrace. The next night she herself spent with Lucy and the following day she was in her place in the Ladies' Gallery of the House of Commons. All around her women were weeping and the House itself had the air of a funeral. She was growing an old lady now, past her seventieth birthday, and worn with sorrow and sleeplessness, but her husband was determined to speak, and if he could summon up the strength to face that ordeal she too would not fail. Those who watched her knew she bore a double burden, grief for Frederick, and acute anxiety for the old man who stood leaning heavily on the despatch box as he forced himself to utter his tribute to the dead. But he did not break down, although he could not bring himself to mention Frederick by name, and before leaving the House Catherine scribbled a note to Lucy, describing the scene and telling her of the sympathy expressed on every side.

There was still one more trial to face; on May 11th William and Catherine made the long journey down to Chatsworth to attend Frederick's funeral although, as Hamilton noticed, it was to both of them "a frightful effort". It is worthy of mention that on May 9th, whilst Frederick still lay unburied, Catherine had occasion to remark to Hamilton that her usually discreet husband had exclaimed, "The Queen will never be happy until she has hounded me out of office."

It might have been supposed that respect for an old and grief-stricken man might have induced the Queen and "the Upper Ten" to cease their vilification of Gladstone, but the bitterness seemed only to increase. In an inspired moment Labouchere referred to William as "The Grand Old Man". The Tories fastened on the name, trying to turn it into an abusive jest, but the nation at large were soon using the initials G.O.M. as a term of respect, almost of endearment. Catherine, in her turn, was known to her friends as the G.D. or *Grande Dame*. The masses were true to "the people's William" and of a Sunday the Gladstones would be followed by admiring crowds as they walked across the Park on their way home from church. In society, however, feeling ran so high that faithful Gladstonians found it unpleasant to attend parties in certain of the great Tory houses, and Catherine, of course, came in for her share of abuse. The question arose as to whether she should be expected to entertain politically during this year of private mourning. The suggestion that she should give parties was considered unfeeling yet the idea of giving none was stigmatised as stingy. In the end other notable Liberal ladies came forward to take her place but it was noticed that their parties were poorly attended, many people staying away to mark disapproval of all things Liberal and Gladstonian.

Gladstone was not visibly altered by the shock of Frederick Cavendish's death, but Catherine saw him in unguarded moments and knew that he was beginning to feel the strain. In July 1882 she wrote to Lucy, "I have seldom seen Uncle William so tired. As he got into the victoria at the House of Commons his face and his words really made me feel that I must ask him nothing but pour oil." For Catherine too the strain was great: "I thought as one grew older that one would not feel the intense anxiety one *does* feel as to one's husband and the dread of seeing him suffer." She had aged visibly since Frederick's murder but she still went as usual about her busy life, attending the official opening of the Law Courts, welcoming Sir Garnet Wolseley on his return from his successful Egyptian campaign, or entertaining the Zulu chief, Cetewayo, "a curious sight, very interesting as he sat in his glory, a striking pleasing-looking person". In the New Year, when she rushed up to Glasgow to launch the new ship, the *Hawarden Castle*, for their friend Donald Currie, Edward Hamilton stood astonished at her energy and pluck.

Nevertheless neither she nor William was in good health; they were both sleeping badly, so that they welcomed an invitation to spend some weeks in Lord Wolverton's villa at Cannes, going there in a family party with Spencer Lyttelton to act as secretary. Catherine, however, did not find herself immediately cured. "It would have been too bright for me, too heavenly," she wrote to Lucy, "with sleep and all the loveliness of this place if I had been in full force." As her strength began to come back to her she grew bored with the enforced inaction and she was soon yearning for home and the excitements of political life.

The men implicated in the Phoenix Park murders were brought to trial whilst the Gladstones were still at Cannes, and Catherine wrote pathetically to her niece: "Oh, I have yearned to be at your side during this fresh revelation! I well remember you always told me, 'There is the sad reality that nothing can make worse.' Oh, how comforting the noble effort for another,[1] the last act of Frederick's life crowning the act of self-sacrifice in going forth to help Ireland!" From the time of Frederick's death Catherine's letters to Lucy become more and more concerned with Irish politics. To Lucy Ireland was almost a sacred subject; she had never lost sight of the hope held out to her by Gladstone in her darkest hour, that somehow the sacrifice of her husband's life would avail to bring peace. Again and again Catherine echoes this thought. "One cannot doubt that Irish hearts will be more and more touched by these confessions," she wrote during the trials. "Ah, his life will not be offered in vain and so I feel strongly that you will be permitted to see beyond black clouds into glorious rays of light and comfort and even thankfulness." She took delight in pointing out any signs of improvement in the Irish situation. "First let me tell you that the agrarian troubles and outrages have fallen considerably," she wrote in August 1882, "further that when the land question settles down all seems to quiet down [also]. This will be a little balm for you."

Any scrap of news that held promise of improvement in Ireland

[1] Frederick Cavendish was killed in trying to protect his companion, Burke.

was indeed balm to Lucy. She could also find pleasure in other people's happiness; "One clings to the sight of happiness or brightness," said Catherine, whose own laughter still bubbled up irresistibly. Only a month after Frederick's murder she ended a letter of solemn, religious comfort with the unexpected remark, "It is to be written on my tombstone that I have kissed Lord Hartington."

The gentleman in question was regarded by the Gladstone family with respect not unmingled with alarm, but Catherine prided herself on getting on very well with his taciturn lordship. On one occasion she made bold to urge him to read more, and to read more seriously. She even went so far as to advocate marriage, which was indeed pressing boldness a little too far as she was very well aware of the obstacle in the way in the shape of the Duchess of Manchester. "The *nasty* Duchess has sprouted a double chin", Catherine once wrote of the lady in question whom William referred to shortly and simply as "*She*".

On his return from Cannes William spoke in support of the Affirmation Bill and Catherine was right in supposing his speech to be something far beyond the ordinary: "Oh, Lucy, it lifted one up higher, so much higher! Read it! Only you would not have the tones of that voice. It certainly carried people away and the rapt attention even of the Opposition was extraordinary. Two notes came immediately, overflowing, one from Lord Rosebery."

This gesture on Rosebery's part was the more generous because the relationship between the older statesman and the younger one was sometimes slightly strained. In private life the Gladstone and Rosebery families were on terms of almost affectionate intimacy but where politics were concerned Gladstone was curiously slow to give due recognition to the younger man's undoubted abilities, whilst Rosebery, too proud and too sensitive to put forward his own claims, suffered acutely from a sense of impotence and neglect.

Hannah Rosebery was no less devoted a wife than Catherine Gladstone and this same year a curious passage of arms took place between these two women, each of them so entirely absorbed in their own husband's interests as to be completely blind to the other's point of view. After touching on the difficulties with the

Queen and with the republican-minded Sir Charles Dilke, Catherine proceeded to attack Sir William Harcourt, who was stoutly defended by Hannah Rosebery, and then passed on to dismiss Rosebery's own claims in somewhat too casual a manner. "It is all right now," she persisted in repeating. "He must not be in a hurry to mount the ladder, he is very young," forgetful perhaps that her own William had been a cabinet minister at the age of thirty-three. "It is Scottish business, not himself, that he is anxious about," came the reply, but Catherine refused to be convinced that Rosebery was fundamentally uninterested in a political career. After a not too tactful reference to his passion for horse-racing, she returned to her original argument, "He is so young." "Not of head or heart," retorted the faithful wife, who ended her description of this stormy interview with the somewhat acid remark, "Mrs. Gladstone went downstairs and I had no need, thank God, to kiss and shake hands."

The Gladstones spent their summer holiday of 1883 cruising to Scotland, Norway and Copenhagen, the company on board including the enchanting Miss Laura Tennant, who was soon to marry Catherine's nephew Alfred Lyttelton. In Norway Catherine was pleased to discover how "people take in Papa and touching presents arrive". On his return Gladstone started work on his new Reform Bill which was to have a rough passage owing to the determined opposition of the House of Lords. Catherine noted his "calm happy appearance and inward content" in the very middle of the battle and she herself took comfort from the fact that if the Lords Temporal were stubborn Tories at least some of the Lords Spiritual were on their side—"Is it not something to have had so many bishops?"

In the end it was not Reform but the crisis in Egypt and the Sudan which destroyed Gladstone's popularity and wrecked his government. As usual, Catherine was over-optimistic. "We had our cares as to the subject of finance," she wrote on February 2nd, 1884. "All has ended well. Harmony, sweet harmony, reigns in the Cabinet. . . . Fancy the day before yesterday the receiving three deputations, requiring important and varied speeches to each, between acts writing the Queen's Speech, I pass by the variation of sitting for his bust, the wretched sculptor prancing in and out as deputations or Cabinet members came in—then the

Cabinet itself. . . . Tories rabid, they are watching Egypt *like cats.*"

Catherine's blindness to everything except William's interests made her curiously insensitive to public opinion over the fall of Khartoum and almost callous in her attitude towards the tragedy of General Gordon. Her letter to Herbert gives no hint of shock or sorrow for the dead, only intense preoccupation with her husband's reaction to the situation:

"Poor old Herbert, I know by myself how you would be turned right inside out! It was so sudden; as Lord Hartington said, we had actually ceased to be anxious, whilst a month ago quite the contrary. Now I am fairly upon the spot and have seen most of the Cabinet Ministers and have found poor Father's sleep uninterrupted I feel stiffened. It is far better for our nerves and I have been sorry for you at a distance reading beastly newspapers, but it was interesting being with Father and Lord Hartington and hearing their fresh remarks and speculations. One good thing is it happening a fortnight before Parliament met to get rid of some of the angry nay furious excitement. After the Cabinet meeting yesterday I was cheered, or rather, made less sad by seeing some of the Cabinet Ministers and hearing they were all in unison, and [by] the fact of Father's continued good sleep and wonderful conduct all answering to the lovely text, 'As thy day so shall thy strength be'. He always rises to the occasion, does not he? I shiver to think if he had now been at Cannes, all out of sorts, not sleeping. Oh, we have had such mercies! I would not have been away from him for worlds now."

There is some excuse for this unfeeling letter when the attitude of another woman is taken into account. On February 5th, 1885, Catherine, William and Lucy were all at Holker, one of the numerous country houses belonging to the Duke of Devonshire, when news arrived of the fall of Khartoum. Two telegrams arrived almost simultaneously; one was to Lucy from Edward Hamilton, "Make him come up, his colleagues wish it and the country expects it", the other was to Gladstone, containing Queen Victoria's famous and unforgivable rebuke written *en clair* for all the world to read. A gloomy and irate Prime Minister travelled up to London, not to be the slightest cheered until his devoted wife had him cosily installed by a roaring fire eating a supper of eggs and mutton chops.

Devotion was all very well but it would have been better mixed with a little discretion. Whilst the whole country seethed with grief and indignation Catherine was foolish enough to urge her husband to attend a theatre. In vain the Private Secretaries pointed out to her the unwisdom of such a course; the party was already arranged and nothing worried William so much as a last-moment change of plan so to the theatre they would go. The result was as might have been expected; the little incident exacerbated public opinion and a spate of anonymous and abusive letters descended on William.

The rift between the Queen and Gladstone was widened by their difference of opinion over the wisdom of appointing Lord Wolseley Governor-General of the Sudan. Whilst this matter was still under discussion the Gladstones were invited to dine at Windsor. The party cannot have been a very happy one and even Catherine was made to feel the weight of the Royal displeasure. "I told Mrs. Gladstone," the Queen wrote in her Journal for March 11th, "when she began lamenting over all the trouble and anxiety I had had, that I should have been far less distressed had I felt that the right thing had been done, which would have prevented all this, and she shook her head, saying she hoped not, whereon I told her I was sure of it."

Political troubles had been slightly sweetened by private rejoicing over Stephy's marriage, which took place at the end of January. The bride was Miss Annie Wilson, the beautiful daughter of a Liverpool doctor: "Though this sounds uninteresting it is anything but, so good, so charming, young, tall, fair and healthy." The bride was one of a bevy of sisters all famous for their good looks, and a typical story is told of the wedding of one of the other girls. An hour or so before the ceremony, when the church decorations were finished and the bouquets all ready, an enormous hamper arrived from Hawarden containing one hundred and nine camellias. Consternation reigned; Mrs. Gladstone had sent this generous but slightly belated gift, she was coming to the wedding and willynilly the camellias must be displayed, so a flurry of bridesmaids rushed to the church and pushed armfuls of camellias into every available nook or cranny.

To all outward appearance Gladstone appeared unmoved by the catastrophe at Khartoum, but those who knew him intimately could see small signs that told of strain. Once more he began to speak of retirement, and some of his colleagues approached Catherine to beg her to use her influence to keep him in office, believing with Hamilton that "her *réchauffées* of arguments often tell more than direct reasoning with him in person". Catherine, however, had at last decided to reconcile herself to the inevitable and she had already begun to pack in preparation for the move from Downing Street. In the event, however, that move was not a dignified voluntary retirement but an enforced retreat.

Late on the evening of June 8th the Government were defeated on the Budget. So unexpected was this vote that even Catherine, who was never absent from her seat in the Ladies' Gallery when anything interesting or exciting was going forward, had not thought to attend the House that night. Instead, she had gone to bed, only to be awakened by Herbert dashing in at two o'clock to break the news. To her, as to Gladstone, the reverse came as "a clap of thunder". Perhaps they were the only two people of those nearly concerned on the Government side who did not welcome this release from a situation that was daily growing more difficult and intolerable. Ministers as a whole could not conceal their glee but Catherine was frankly and openly distressed: "I think of the country, of the danger from Russia, of much else! You see, I do think more of country than of party and in the midst of all Ireland is very deep down in my heart." Most of all, she might have added, did she think of William Gladstone. But there was nothing for it but to accept defeat, and on June 24th the Gladstones left Number Ten Downing Street to take up their temporary abode in a pleasant house at the end of Richmond Terrace.

Chapter Twelve

"MR. GLADSTONE is not so relieved at the prospect of escape as he always thought he would be"—thus Edward Hamilton. The Gladstone family had made the garden of the Richmond Terrace house into an *al fresco* library, where everyone met to read the papers, write letters or exchange news, and as they sat enjoying the fine summer weather the talk was not of retirement but of plans for future campaigns. Lucy Cavendish considered that the time had now come to give Hartington his turn, and she was perturbed to discover that her Uncle William intended to stand again in Midlothian, a decision which implied his continuance at the head of the Liberal Party. In justification of this step Catherine wrote a letter half-explanatory, half-defiant, arguing that great pressure had been brought to bear upon Gladstone, especially by Sir William Harcourt, to persuade him of "the necessity not to shirk". She declared that Hartington himself had made it quite clear in private conversation that he was prepared to serve again under his old leader.

In another letter written a few days later she enlarged upon the uncertainties of the situation and the difficulty of coming to any decision: "Perhaps the last fortnight has been in many respects as trying as any time. To say what is best, to give courage or to soothe? I think I seem to know a little of a soldier's life; all the time different feelings, different and conflicting circumstances arise. Now I seem brave, now cowardly—things changing, and changing enough to make one swear!" Again she stresses, "the tremendous pressure—the country is turning its eyes towards him", and argues that Lord Hartington is entirely acquiescent, "what really pleases him most is that Lord Hartington's conversation was very genial".

These two letters to Lucy were written from Oxford, a place

dearly loved by Gladstone. Catherine mentioned that he was toying with the idea of buying a house there, a frame of mind which seemed to point definitely in the direction of retirement. As late as August 1885 Catherine confided to Hamilton that "Mr. Gladstone had never felt more embarrassed as to what to do and he can't even now make up his mind", but meanwhile she herself was writing to Lucy as if it were almost certain that he would retain the leadership: "Two things Uncle William is very strong upon, (first) that he should not go on without a cry—he never has yet—or (secondly) without old colleagues, but there is no doubt at all that deep down in his heart the Irish legislation is there." From Ireland she passes to the position of the newly-enfranchised voters: "Is he to run away just as the Franchise comes into play and leave new and unruly sheep without a shepherd?" Then she returns to the real problem: "After the Midlothian letter Lord Hartington received a serious letter in which he [W. E. G.] opened his whole heart to him as to his Irish policy."

If Gladstone had indeed opened his whole heart Hartington must have been well aware by this time that his leader was committed to a crusade for Home Rule. Although Home Rule was not yet an official part of the Liberal programme Ireland was always uppermost in Gladstone's mind and in Catherine's also. Sometime in the course of 1885 she wrote Lucy a revealing letter: "Oh, Lucy, I am often longing to be together as the gigantic question unfolds more and more, the tremendous interest and the tremendous difficulties, you and I and Uncle William, who all have the same feeling as to Ireland! He did not indeed exaggerate when he spoke months ago of Ireland as the question of the hour. He has never budged from this. How one manages to keep one's proper balance these times I don't know, but surely the number of prayers offered up and the blessing of his good health—oh, these are indeed mercies!"

On July 14th private rejoicing broke happily in upon political preoccupation when a son was born to Willy and Gertrude. Catherine was especially delighted with the appearance of an heir apparent to her beloved Hawarden. Mercifully she could not read the future nor see the end of her high hopes. William Charles Glynne Gladstone grew up into a young man of singularly attractive character, who entered the House of Commons early in life and gave promise of political ability beyond the ordinary. He was killed in action at Laventie in June 1915, leaving no child to inherit the property. Out of respect for his grandfather's memory permission was given to bring his body home to England to be buried in Hawarden churchyard.

Catherine and William spent their summer holiday on board Sir Thomas Brassey's yacht *Sunbeam*. Even on holiday William's mind was running on the problem of Ireland and Catherine wrote to Hamilton "in her curiously erratic style" that "he sees everything with his eagle eye" and that "his mind is largely surveying".

One of the greatest difficulties in the way of any Home Rule scheme was the opposition of Joseph Chamberlain on the one hand and old John Bright on the other. During the month of October, when the Gladstones were home again, both Chamberlain and Bright were invited to Hawarden. Catherine is always believed to have been very antagonistic to Chamberlain, being jealous, for William's sake, of the younger man's popularity with the working classes. This view is hardly borne out by the facts. She wrote to Lucy, "Chamberlain has to be reckoned, one feels, as clever, yet he does lack tact and a certain good taste", a judgement which, if unfavourable, was neither imperceptive nor unjust. Gladstone actively disliked Chamberlain, and it was Catherine who persuaded him to fall in with G. W. E. Russell's suggestion and invite "Our Joe" to Hawarden. Chamberlain duly arrived, laden with a gift of beautiful orchids, and the visit passed off most successfully, but unfortunately it resulted in no sort of political *rapprochement*. Chamberlain was followed by John Bright, who persisted in losing himself in the not very confusing corridors of Hawarden, his lack of any bump of locality being a standing joke.

In November came the third Midlothian Campaign, a repetition of its predecessors with its cheering crowds, thronged meetings, banquets and receptions, all enveloped in an atmosphere of almost idolatrous enthusiasm. Catherine had always revelled in these demonstrations but this time she appeared curiously depressed. The Election went against the Liberals but Gladstone himself scored a personal triumph in Midlothian. On the night of November 29th the moon shone brightly down as Hawarden prepared to welcome "the dear veteran champion", to use the words of

Auguste Schluter, Mary Gladstone's highly impressionable Ger-
man maid. It was a quarter to one in the morning before the sound
of wheels was heard approaching. As William and Catherine
drove up every window of Castle and orphanage was suddenly
ablaze with lights, and a little group of servants and well-wishers
standing by the front door struck up "Home Sweet Home".

Amid all this political excitement Catherine may have been
excused for not observing the surprising fact that at the age of
thirty-eight her daughter Mary had at last fallen in love. Two
years previously a handsome young curate called Harry Drew
had arrived at Hawarden. A penniless parson, eight years her
junior, might not seem much of a match for the daughter of a
Prime Minister, but Harry Drew was a man of parts, "excellent
and charming, with every good gift except money", and worldly
considerations weighed as nothing with Catherine when it came
to the question of her children's choice of husband or wife. She
might, however, have objected to the marriage on other grounds;
Mary had made herself almost indispensable at home and her marriage must inevitably disturb William's peace of mind and settled
routine. Instinctively Catherine put her husband's convenience
before everything else, even the interests of her children. When
Agnes Wickham developed a lameness which was to handicap her
for life, Catherine's reaction was almost comic: "Supposing it had
been me instead of Agnes, oh, what should we have done?" Such
was her apparently selfish comment. Far better that poor Agnes
should be permanently disabled than that Catherine should be
hampered in her great task of caring for and cherishing the Grand
Old Man.

Though taken by surprise Catherine professed herself delighted
when on Christmas Day, 1885, Mary became engaged to Harry
Drew. "We have had our darling Mary with us for many years,
her happiness is ours", she wrote, and again, "I try to bask in
the sunshine of her happiness." She might congratulate herself
that for much of the year she would still have Mary with her
for the married pair were to take up their quarters in Hawarden
Castle. In fact the only person to object was Auguste Schluter,
who considered that a curate was no fitting match for her young
lady: "When I saw Mr. Drew I felt like a tigress wishing to hurl
herself upon the enemy." Mary herself had no qualms; she was

o   197

prepared to enjoy the adventure of life on £300 a year and although all the greatest names in England were on the list of guests invited to her wedding she persisted in choosing a dress of plain white muslin, arguing that a clergyman's bride should not look over-smart.

Among the congratulatory letters was one from Queen Victoria, who took the opportunity to express the hope that Mary's father would not over-tax his strength, a sentiment with which Catherine was rather less than pleased, choosing to read into it a hint that it was time for him to retire from politics. Gladstone was still labouring under the delusion that the Conservatives might be persuaded to bring in a measure of Home Rule, but if his conversations with Lord Salisbury should fail to produce the desirable result Catherine for one was determined that no one but he himself should succeed Salisbury as Prime Minister. In this crisis she described him as standing "like a giant, all calm with thought though with a burning desire to help the great question deep down, almost life-long". It was a difficult, uncertain moment and Catherine's own spirits began to flag in the cheerless January weather—"It has been too grubous* for words, the dirty snow, the Irish party, Harry's going,[1] Mary away."

At last the introduction of a Coercion Bill made the Conservative position perfectly plain and gave Gladstone the signal to turn them out of office. Lucy Cavendish had lent the Gladstones her London house, which Catherine described as being "brimful of secretaries and wedding-cake", as political planning went on side by side with preparations for Mary's marriage. She wrote to Lucy describing the perturbation into which the Liberal leaders had been thrown by their opponents' action:

"I have sought shelter in your bedroom having made the drawing-room comfortable for Ministers. In came Lord Hartington and Lord Richard Grosvenor; they will discuss this sudden change, a dodge beforehand to get power or aid to bring in the Crimes' Act, I suppose in fullest force, the conclusion only arrived at today as a pistol to the head. If passed, imagine the loss of time before anything can be done for Ireland, the fury of the fighting such a measure would arouse . . . time

---

[1] Harry Gladstone returned to India in January 1886.

lost, and Ireland in danger, and through our fault. All is very, very trying, and here I sit brooding over it all and feeling so deeply for Uncle William who meekly answered to me, 'It is God's will, the break and the difficulties.'"

"Very, very trying" the matter certainly was, involving an inevitable split in the Liberal Party on the question of Home Rule, but meekness was not the characteristic of Gladstone's behaviour that was most apparent to anyone except his devoted wife. He rushed into the fray like the old war-horse that he was, and in spite of the defection of Hartington and Goschen, he succeeded in defeating the Government on an amendment to the Queen's Speech. Catherine took an unjustifiably optimistic view of Hartington's action in voting with the Conservatives. Always sanguine, she found it impossible not to believe that "things will right themselves in due course". As brother to the beloved Frederick, Hartington was almost a member of the family, and a family split was to her inconceivable:

"For something of a bad business light streams through it all. Of course one had a *mauvais moment* that Lord H. should have felt obliged to go against us. But if it was to be done it could not possibly be done in a nicer way, or a more tender way; this will comfort you and dear Lady Louisa.[1] I was sent to Devonshire House and had armed myself with a short note which I had written to Lord H. We waited at the door; out he came, and in a genial way, not in one of *his*——*! He came according to invitation here, and he and Uncle William had an hour's talk. I went a drive afterwards and Uncle William had been greatly pleased and said it had been one of the nicest talks he had had. Since then Lord Granville has been in and told Uncle William how much he liked the talk. Oh, may it please God that Uncle William may keep Lord H.!"

It was unfortunately only too clearly apparent that William was not to be allowed to keep Lord H. In the midst of difficulties and dissensions Catherine remained confident, living, as Hamilton put it, "too much in the neighbourhood of fools' paradise". On January 30th, 1886, Gladstone took office as Prime Minister, on

[1] Lady Louisa Egerton, Lord Hartington's sister.

February 2nd he gave away his daughter Mary at her wedding in St. Margaret's, Westminster, and the next day he announced the formation of his third ministry. Their tenure of office was to be far from easy. All the "great world" was rabid against Home Rule and even such a responsible person as a Governor of the Bank of England could declare with absolute certainty that he knew Gladstone to be out of his mind.

During the next few years stories of his insanity circulated freely; it was believed, for instance, that his mania showed itself in buying hats by the dozen and neckties by the hundred. Catherine, however, was not merely unmoved but oblivious; Society might choose to insult her husband but she neither noticed nor cared. When Herbert was riding one day in Rotten Row a group of fashionable people lined up along the rails and "hissed like cobras". Gladstone himself was hissed on the occasion of one of his public appearances, yet all the time Catherine was writing cheerfully, "people in the streets are very enthusiastic". And in fact she was right, although appearances might point in the opposite direction; "the man in the street" was now, as always, heart and soul with Gladstone, no matter how "the Upper Ten" might behave. Only when the Duke of Westminster turned Millais' great portrait of Gladstone out of the picture gallery at Eaton did Catherine really show signs of feeling hurt; the Grosvenors and the Glynnes had been friends and neighbours for generations back, and this unfriendly, unneighbourly act succeeded in piercing the armour of her indifference.

When Gladstone introduced his first Home Rule Bill on April 8th, 1886, Catherine was in the Ladies' Gallery accompanied by Lucy Cavendish, who was making her first visit to the House of Commons since her husband's murder. The Bill was defeated on June 8th and a General Election followed. Catherine remained in London for the beginning of the campaign, driving down to the East End with G. W. E. Russell, who was standing for Stepney, and even making a little speech at Mile End, much to her own amusement, but Gladstone, who had been returned unopposed for Midlothian, had taken up his headquarters at Hawarden and as soon as she could Catherine joined him there: "My place was by his side after I had done the little I could do, and here is the power of daily [church] service, and the roses all running races as to bursting forth, and today a fine bracing air with brightness to revive after yesterday, when elections and tremendous heat pulled me almost to pieces."

The result of the Election was a defeat for the Home Rule cause. On July 20th Gladstone submitted his resignation to the Queen and a month later he set out for Bavaria to spend a holiday with Lord and Lady Acton and Doctor Döllinger. Mary Drew was unwell, and much against her inclination Catherine remained behind. Rather than disturb William's peace of mind Catherine kept from him the alarming nature of her fears for Mary, who fell seriously ill shortly after his return. For a while anxiety was intense and it was Christmas Day before the invalid was even allowed to be carried downstairs.

Through all the private and political anxieties which filled the autumn of 1886 Catherine remained characteristically buoyant and hopeful. Although the Liberal-Unionist schism was now an accomplished fact she still deluded herself that Hartington might return to the true fold: "That was a pretty bit of Lord Hartington's about Uncle William. It is difficult to think that all may not yet come right. Meanwhile, the Ex-P.M. is so thankful and so happy, full of hope but in no hurry. He sits waiting, praying, patient." It was well into the New Year, after the failure of the Round Table Conference between Liberals and Liberal-Unionists, before Catherine would admit that William was indeed beginning to despair of Hartington.

The house in Harley Street had now been given up and when in London the Gladstones made their home either with Lucy or in a villa at Dollis Hill lent to them by the Aberdeens, an abode which was much disapproved of by political supporters and friends because of its inaccessibility. This type of consideration never weighed with the Gladstones who were much attached to the place and put up cheerfully with the inconvenience. On one foggy night when returning late to Dollis Hill after a dinner party their carriage came to a full stop against the railings of Hyde Park and they were obliged to alight and walk back to their London lodging. On hearing of this adventure Hamilton commented truthfully, "There are probably not two other people of their age who would set out on a cold foggy night to drive five miles in an open carriage."

Mrs. Gladstone

Distance from London did not prevent the Gladstones from giving parties, which were as usual sadly mismanaged. On one such occasion a purely social gathering came into collision with a political deputation, and Ambassadors and similar grandees were considerably annoyed to find themselves drinking tea in company with Irish Americans come to present Gladstone with a testimonial in recognition of his championship of Home Rule.

Gladstone disliked large, formal dinners so that Catherine was obliged to go alone to various banquets held to mark Queen Victoria's Jubilee, a renewal of the practice she had so much disliked in the early days of her marriage. Week-ends were sometimes spent at The Durdans, Lord Rosebery's house near Epsom. Wherever they might be William and Catherine never relaxed their strict observance of Sunday. Lucy describes a typical London Sunday: "Uncle William had been to the full service [Mattins and Holy Communion] at the Chapel Royal and again in the afternoon, and had only worked two and a half hours between whiles, topping up with reading a sermon." When on a visit, if it should not prove possible to attend church twice in the day, William and Catherine would solace themselves by collecting together their ladies' maid and valet and reading aloud an improving book or sermon. To Catherine one of the greatest joys of a Sunday spent away from home was the walk to and from church. She delighted in the surprised signs of recognition, the whispered comments, the respectful greetings of the groups of worshippers gathered in porch or churchyard. At such moments she could feel that her William was appreciated at his true worth—"I never can make him think himself a great man! Which everyone else thinks, or should think."

Best of all she loved to be at Hawarden in the centre of a happy circle of children and grandchildren: "Yesterday we had tea in the garden; the bees are humming, the magnolia has taken a fresh start and scents the whole air, the children are charming—bright, good and well." To both Catherine and William a big Jubilee dinner for neighbours and tenants was a function infinitely preferable to any London celebration. Great and famous names filled the Visitors' Book but elderly relations would also arrive to be petted by Catherine and to delight William with "interesting fits of Italian literature talks". (Somehow the younger generation

were not quite so appreciative of Dante as they might have been.)
The estate prospered under careful and devoted management of
Willy, who lived at the Red House with his wife and family, whilst
Stephy and Annie inhabited the Rectory and Harry and Mary
Drew remained in the Castle. This arrangement, which might
have given rise to much trouble, worked admirably on the whole,
thanks to Harry Drew's strength of character and to Gladstone's
profound respect for the calling of a clergyman. In 1890 the
birth of a daughter to the Drews was a cause of great rejoicing.
Dorothy, or "Dossie", became the especial delight of her grandparents, and also, it must be admitted, of the pressmen and photo-
graphers who were not slow to exploit the picturesque possibili-
ties of golden-haired babyhood and hoary old age.

Catherine, who always preferred men to women, found sons-
in-law easier to deal with than daughters-in-law. She had been
for so long the Queen of Hawarden, almost as much in control
at the Rectory as at the Castle, that she could not be expected
to abdicate with entire good grace in favour of her sons' wives.
She did not succeed in turning a sufficiently blind eye to what she
considered to be their errors and omissions and they in their
turn were inclined to consider her interfering and over-critical.
"Mrs. Gladstone's zeal and habits of management", to quote the
words of Lord Blantyre, Gertrude Gladstone's father, sometimes
provoked storms, but these were only the surface disagreements
inevitable in any family, however devoted, and fundamental respect and affection remained unshaken.

It was a matter of slight importance that Catherine should be
over-anxious to manage the affairs of Hawarden or of her own
family, but it was unfortunate that she should have allowed her
old tendency towards "bossiness" to come again to the fore where
her husband was concerned. Most of Gladstone's friends and contemporaries were dead, and among his relations no one of his own
generation remained except the morose and difficult Tom. Only
Catherine could speak to him with the complete freedom born of
shared memories of youth, and it was becoming clear to such men
as Rosebery and Hamilton that her influence was daily increasing
and that her husband would sometimes listen to her when he
would listen to no one else. Undoubtedly her influence helped to
keep him in politics long after his personal inclination would have

taken him into retirement. Both Hamilton and Mary Drew agree in maintaining that Catherine would have preferred to see her husband die in harness rather than in the semi-obscurity of private life.

No one can say how far Gladstone was influenced by her determination and how far by his own conviction that he himself was the only man alive who had any chance of carrying a measure of Home Rule, but if Catherine kept him in political life longer than was desirable at least she devoted herself untiringly to the business of helping him in his task. He is reputed to have said, "If anything should happen to Catherine, then indeed, I should close the volume and close it for ever", and lacking her watchful care he could never have survived the strain of political life.

As they grew older separations between husband and wife grew less and less frequent till by the end of the eighteen-eighties they were seldom if ever apart. At political meetings she was his faithful shadow as described by a spectator at a meeting at Marylebone:

"He is followed by a simply-dressed woman who busies herself in warding off the hands of enthusiasts eager to touch him. This is Mrs. Gladstone, with the soft face, high-coloured like a girl's, and tremulous mouth, intent on one thing only in this life—her husband. They step up to the platform by a reporter's stool. A dozen willing hands would aid him but it is hers which grasp his ankles to steady him lest in his eagerness he should slip. She begs a seat immediately behind him. Forth he stands and begins at once, 'Mr Chairman!' She pulls at his overcoat and one sleeve comes free; impatiently he stops whilst she tugs at the other sleeve. Two more sentences and he is fairly launched upon a sea of passion regardless of Mrs. Gladstone who sits behind, placidly folding her husband's overcoat."

A spectator at another meeting, this time in Glasgow, reported a little incident when Gladstone had wished to read something aloud, but could not find his eye-glass: "Mrs. Gladstone jumped up, tried the back of his neck, and at last, at the end of about five minutes, fished it up from under his coat, at which the whole assembly cheered and the success of the meeting was made." She was supremely unselfconscious and never found the slightest embarrassment in these small comic mishaps.

Catherine's devotion to her husband and unswerving belief in his mission made her take an over-sanguine view of the political situation. It was ridiculous to suppose that the Liberal-Unionists were "a miserable remnant, feeling their position very badly". She was always apt to give people the benefit of the doubt, to put almost too kindly a construction on their actions, and now as she grew old those around her combined to keep from her anything distressing and to encourage her to look at the world through rosy spectacles. But it is hard to call her optimism a fault since it was part and parcel of her indomitable courage. She had faced Frederick Cavendish's murder, Hartington's defection, the bitter hostility of old friends and the irresponsible behaviour of the Irish, always their own worst enemies, without wavering in her determination or ever thinking to give up the struggle, but even she recognised the fact that there was one enemy who could never be defeated. "Time is on our side", Gladstone had once cried with triumphant defiance, but now time was against him. Yet even this inevitability of defeat Catherine greeted with courage, scorning to regard the years of opposition from 1886 to 1892 as altogether wasted. She, who could so little afford to wait, accepted that necessity with proud patience. "I always remember now that you told me we should have to wait," she said one day to Hamilton. "It has been a very happy wait and if political events had marched differently they might have marched much worse."

Soon she was to have need of all her high courage. Fate had two bitter blows in store, one political, the other personal. To Catherine, as to William, Ireland was the greatest of political interests and the cause of Ireland was incarnated in the person of Parnell. If he fell, Home Rule fell with him. Catherine was passionately interested in the affair of the Pigott forgeries. Day after day she attended the sittings of the Special Commission, and on one occasion she persuaded her husband to accompany her against his better judgement. The Gladstones were convinced that Parnell spoke the truth when he denied writing the incriminating letters and to mark their support they invited him to dine with them one night at a time when feeling against him ran very high.

Pigott's exposure established Parnell's innocence as far as the authorship of the incriminating letters was concerned; the political sky cleared, but the calm was deceptive. Neither William nor Catherine, however, had any premonition of the coming storm. On July 26th, 1888, a group of friends presented husband and wife with their own portraits. At the touching little ceremony the company as a whole were inclined to be tearful and William himself had difficulty in controlling his emotion, a rare thing for him, but Catherine returned thanks in a few admirable sentences. The presentation marked not the actual golden wedding anniversary but the entry into the fiftieth year of married life, the donors perhaps thinking that it would be unwise to risk the delay of another year in the case of two old people of seventy-nine and seventy-six. Catherine, however, had recently described William "like a three year old in vigour and movement", whilst she herself was reported as being "radiant and hopeful as ever".

By a bitter irony of fate the son was to be taken and the aged parents left. On March 1st of the golden wedding year of 1889 Willy Gladstone was suddenly seized by a mysterious illness. The doctors were puzzled, supposing it to be some form of stroke, but there could be no doubt at all as to its serious nature. A week after Willy was taken ill William was summoned to Fasque to attend the funeral of his brother Tom, which was to take place in the chapel whose building had been a great interest and delight of earlier days. The first Gladstone to be laid there in the family vault had been little Jessy, and when Catherine wrote to William she spoke gently of this long-ago grief. Now, after an interval of forty years, death again threatened one of their children. In their anxiety over Willy they found some comfort in the sympathy all around them: "It sometimes seems as if dissentients and tories, to their credit, like to have this opportunity of showing kindness", William wrote to Catherine from Fasque. Political differences did not always preclude private friendship; the Gladstones could still go to tea with Lord and Lady Salisbury, and enjoy what Catherine described as a "spicey" afternoon.

The golden wedding year was brightened by Harry Gladstone's engagement to the daughter of the Gladstones' great friend, Lord Rendel, "Maud", as Catherine described her, "with those beautiful loving eyes, so original and full of fun". The actual golden wedding anniversary was spent in London, with presents and greetings pouring in from all over the world. Whilst the family were at church their good friends, Lord and Lady Aberdeen, slipped into the house to supervise the hanging of the new portrait of William with grandson Will, and to see that the table for the wedding breakfast was properly decked in white and gold with a posy of flowers beside each plate. A week later the celebrations were crowned by a Hawarden home-coming which echoed the festivities held at that double wedding fifty years ago. After the presentation of addresses the horses were taken out of the carriage and William and Catherine were drawn up to the front door of the Castle, where they saw standing before them in all its glory the most exciting of all the presents, a handsome stone porch built to replace the wooden erection long known to the family as "the bathing machine".

Among all the rejoicing the aloof attitude of Queen Victoria struck a jarring note. Other old friends were not so hard-hearted, in spite of long estrangement. Cardinal Manning wrote a charming letter to which Catherine replied with equal warmth: "Your letter has touched us very much—old days have come back and back as the old friendship is revived although it has never been extinct, and it was indeed pleasant upon the Golden Wedding to read your words as to 'the long climb up of nearly sixty years', though I feel hardly worthy of them. Will you add to your kindness by praying for our precious son? Willy is better, but there must still be an anxious waiting and watching—he often uses the book you gave him. May all the real blessings be yours, my dear friend, we hear with great pleasure that you are in good force."

When Catherine asked the prayers of her old friend for his god-son Willy she was touching on "the only cloud on a perfect golden sunset". In the autumn husband and wife took a trip together to Paris, enjoying everything "with their usual freshness", and the year ended fittingly with the celebrations held to mark the Grand Old Man's eightieth birthday.

The year 1890 opened with a deceptive period of calm, William chiefly occupied with the arrangement of his books in a new library that he was giving to Hawarden village. But now on this aged couple, already overshadowed by the tragedy of Willy's illness, fell the devastating blow of Parnell's divorce and disgrace.

The chief actors in this drama were only slightly known to Catherine personally. There is no record of any meeting between her and Mrs. O'Shea, although in May 1882 she had invited O'Shea to a dinner party which was cancelled because of the Phoenix Park murders. (The party, had it been held, would have been a curious gathering, the other guests including Lord and Lady Cowper, Lord and Lady Granville, and "that libidinous old fire-eater" the O'Gorman Mahon.) One thing is certain; Catherine had no idea of the relationship existing between Parnell and Mrs. O'Shea.

Victorian ladies were not unduly innocent, least of all Catherine Gladstone; she was very well aware of Hartington's liaison with the Duchess of Manchester, "the Twopenny Duchess", as she once remarked, and in early letters she referred quite as a matter of course to stories current about Palmerston. Where Parnell was concerned, however, a most unfortunate ignorance seems to have enveloped the entire Gladstone family, for even Herbert, essentially a House of Commons man familiar with all the gossip of the lobbies, knew nothing whatsoever about the "notorious and recognised fact" of the liaison between Parnell and Mrs. O'Shea.

Parnell himself was not personally familiar with the Gladstones —Lucy Cavendish maintained that her uncle had never had more than five intimate conversations with him—but he was on sufficiently friendly terms to send them a present of game and in December 1889 he was invited to Hawarden on a brief visit. Catherine's only comment was a heart-felt wish that he would not fall in with one of their more conservative friends who had also proposed herself to stay, but Mary Drew was much impressed by his personality and wrote of him as "a most mysterious man of compelling power".

Catherine had always misread his character; as early as 1882 she wrote to Lucy, "I think you have hit the word as applied to Parnell—cowardice, and, I would add, ambition." Now once again she stressed that characteristic of ambition which would have been more properly interpreted as pride. On December 31st, 1890, when the storm was at its height, she wrote to Hamilton that her husband "stands firm and patient, thankful that what seems so sad may be for the purifying of dear Ireland, and that it has been discovered what Parnell is. Surely it is as well before too late that we know his character, throwing up his country's good for ambition". Catherine was never one to cast stones where sexual immorality was concerned, and it is typical of her that what she held against Parnell was not his sin with Mrs. O'Shea but his sin against his own country, and, she might have added, against William Gladstone.

Even at the height of the crisis Gladstone himself preserved a certain detachment of mind. Lucy described his reception of Parnell's manifesto, an unfair and tendentious document which charged him personally with gross perfidy towards the Irish nation: "On the morning when this production appeared I went over to Carlton Gardens and found Uncle William so astonished by its *owdacity* and falseness as to be almost amused. He had his answer written by about 11.30 but he sat down at the study table and went through the manifesto again, marking the notable passages in it with very black dashes. As Spencer [Lyttelton] and I stood opposite him something in Parnell's words reminded him of *The Bride of Lammermoor* and he suspended operations for a while to look up and say to us 'The more I read that book the more admirable do I think it'."

It is astonishing that two old people, the one past eighty, the other approaching her eightieth birthday, could bear up under the double strain of the political tragedy of Parnell and the private tragedy of Willy Gladstone without showing signs of physical or mental collapse. Worn, haggard, more untidy than ever, Catherine still went about her many avocations with untiring zeal and energy. She had time to spare for Edward Hamilton, suffering from a long and trying illness, and in company with William, she busied herself with the thankless task of trying to straighten out the matrimonial entanglements of their old friend, Lady Stepney. Catherine never spared herself and ill-health was seldom allowed to turn her from her purpose. In December 1889 she fell ill when staying in Manchester but nevertheless persisted in travelling to Liverpool and giving away prizes to two hundred and fifty schoolgirls, no mean effort for an old lady only a week or two short of her seventy-seventh birthday. Some of her other forms of activity did not recommend themselves to the more judicious of Gladstone's supporters. During the summer of 1890 large crowds flocked to Hawarden, and it was noticed with surprise that when William addressed a few words to these excursionists Catherine, usually so silent in public, now occasionally chimed in of her own accord.

In addition to all her other occupations Catherine had recently undertaken a new, and, to her, most uncongenial work. On May 29th, 1891, Hamilton noted "that wonderful woman Mrs. Gladstone, is frisking up to London to attend a charity concert and a political female gathering". These "political female gatherings" were in fact the bane of her life. Catherine had never, in all her long experience of politics, taken any part personally in public life, but in 1887, against her better judgement, she had accepted the Presidency of the newly-formed Women's Liberal Federation. The position was distasteful to her but she would not shrink from anything she could do to help forward William's cause. The devoted Lady Aberdeen was at hand to save her from all avoidable work and worry but even so the strain was great. Whenever she had to make a speech her nervousness was painfully apparent, and nothing in her experience of small charitable committees had taught her how to deal with large public meetings. Trouble soon arose within the fold.

In 1890 and 1891 the Federation was rent asunder by a controversy over Women's Suffrage. The storm-centre was Rosalind, Countess of Carlisle. When this formidable lady had been a difficult, somewhat unattractive young woman Catherine had, in typical manner, endeavoured to say a good word for her. "There is something to like about Rosalind," she had written some twelve years previously, "and something to be done about softening her, I think." But nothing had availed to soften Rosalind. On the subject of teetotalism she was hardly sane, pouring all the priceless contents of the family cellar into the fountain at Castle Howard, and where Women's Suffrage was concerned she was equally fanatical. Caring nothing for Liberalism or the Liberal Party she schemed to use the Women's Liberal Federation to further her own ends, and in doing so she split that Federation from top to bottom.

As soon as Rosalind gained even partial control the old stalwarts believed that Catherine ought to have resigned, and they bombarded her with grieved and angry letters when Lady Aberdeen persuaded her that it was her duty to remain. Even the Liberal leaders became involved in the quarrel, John Morley taking one side, and Sir William Harcourt the other, and Catherine found herself entangled in complications and animosities beyond her comprehension. It had been folly to expect an old lady of seventy-seven to undertake so trying a post but not until the autumn of 1893 could she resign her office as President.

On Christmas Day 1890 Willy was sufficiently improved to be able to attend church, and Catherine's heart swelled with thankfulness as she saw her son apparently better and her husband "so brilliant in mind and strong in body". But there was no real sign of permanent improvement in Willy's condition, and at last the doctors decided on an exploratory operation. Very early on the morning of July 1st, 1891, Catherine left Hawarden for London, persuading her husband to stay behind in company with John Morley. As was then customary the operation took place in Willy's London house, where wife and mother waited together to hear the result. It fell to Sir Andrew Clark, the Gladstones' old friend and family doctor, to break the news to Catherine; the tumour on the brain was inoperable and nothing could save her son.

At once she sat down to write Willy's father a letter, even now too pathetic for the cold light of print, very quiet and gentle in tone, wholly concerned with the grief she must cause her husband and not at all with her own heart's agony. Yet she loved Willy as his father had never loved him; deeply devoted as Gladstone was to his son his love held none of the intensity of passion which Catherine felt for her first-born. Her letter has neither the clamorous sorrow nor the determined struggle for resignation which filled the letters written so long ago by Mary Lyttelton's deathbed; she is an old woman now and acceptance of loss comes more easily to her. She comforts William and herself also with the remembrance of their son's sterling goodness and the happiness which had been his in full measure. Other people, she says, have trials even worse than this that they must bear and at least the doctors expect the operation to bring some temporary relief.

This hope was to be disappointed for two days after the operation Willy died without regaining consciousness. As long ago on the occasion of Jessy's death it was William who broke down whilst Catherine remained "astonishing in courage and bearing". "Willy ever was a treasure," she wrote in reply to a condolence letter from Queen Victoria, "perhaps I loved him too well." Sir Robert Peel had once enquired genially of baby Willy, "Well, will you ever be as clever a man as your father?" Willy had never striven to emulate his famous parent; rather, he had found contentment in mountains and in music, in the work of caring for his beloved Hawarden, and in the society of his wife and children. Catherine found comfort for herself in comforting that bereaved family. From now onwards her letters are full of plans for her daughter-in-law and news of her doings. One little granddaughter, a sensitive child of an age to be particularly affected by her father's death, clung especially to her grandmother, and Catherine took a touching pleasure in the child's dependence on her.

Sorrows and anxieties had borne heavily upon Catherine so that it was not surprising that when John Morley saw her in the autumn of 1891 he should find her looking very aged and haggard. But now that the blow had fallen she was at least released from the wearing strain of anxiety and hope deferred. For a little while her health did indeed appear to suffer, but she was soon herself again, having seemingly shaken off the deafness which had recently grown upon her. Looking back over the past four years, with all they held of frustration and sorrow, she could yet declare with a high heart that they were to be numbered among the happiest years of her life. The truth was that she still looked forward instead of backward, talking confidently of "what may be expected of William in 1892 at the age of eighty-two". Through all sadness and disappointment she was buoyed up by one confident hope, the hope of seeing William Gladstone once more Prime Minister.

Chapter Thirteen

A GENERAL ELECTION was approaching, and in November 1891 Gladstone went up to Newcastle to deliver himself of that ill-digested hotchpotch of Social Reform known as the Newcastle Programme. Catherine accompanied him as she had done on that triumphant visit thirty years earlier, and found herself as usual delighted by the success of the meeting and the way in which William's voice stood the strain of a long speech. But inevitably the years were beginning to tell and those about them noticed a change in both husband and wife. That winter a great gale blew down a beech tree that had been a special favourite with Willy, and the little incident left Willy's father saddened and depressed. As for Catherine, though she showed a brave face to the world, at heart she grieved bitterly for her dead son: "Oh I try to be good, but I am not, I fear." It was to Lucy that Catherine turned especially for consolation because Lucy herself had experience of grief: "You have been called to suffer deeply as few are, and have come out of the suffering—is it too much to say?—as one to be envied." She begged Lucy to look upon Hawarden as her own country home, coming and going just as she wished, and from the time of Willy's death when writing to this beloved niece she signed herself as "Mother".

The Gladstones spent part of the winter of 1891-2 at Biarritz as the guests of their generous friend, George Armitstead. Parliament was dissolved in the following summer and Gladstone went to stay with Lord Rosebery at Dalmeny for the last of his Midlothian campaigns. Catherine as a matter of course went with him, but for once she might have done better to stay at home. All her life she had been liable to occasional unexpected "blind spots" in her judgement of character and unfortunately those "blind spots" usually coincided with a similar failing of understanding on the part of her husband. She had once expressed sympathy for one of the Lyttelton relations, pitying the lady in question because "she has trial of a constitution, a sort of natural discontent". Just such a constitution did Rosebery possess, and at this period of his life the nervous depression natural to him had been intensified by the shock of his wife's sudden death and by the insomnia which made his nights a misery.

Neither William nor Catherine could understand a character that was essentially melancholy and introspective, nor would they see that a subtle nature like Rosebery's required especially subtle handling. The pity was that Catherine had a real liking for Rosebery, and a real sympathy with him in his sorrow. When inviting him to stay at Hawarden in November 1891 she had thoughtfully included one of his young sons in her invitation, and Rosebery was deeply touched by her kindness to the motherless child. Yet now, when Rosebery's support was essential, both Gladstones treated him with a total lack of tact and comprehension and in particular Catherine's behaviour during the Dalmeny visit strained his already over-taut nerves almost to breaking-point.

The Election went in favour of the Liberals. "The old man, and still more, the old woman, are bent on fighting *ad desperandum*", wrote Hamilton when it became clear that against the wishes of everybody except his own family Gladstone had decided to become Prime Minister for the fourth time. Without Rosebery there was no forming a Liberal administration, and Rosebery now refused to take office. Neither William nor Catherine had perceived that anything had been amiss at Dalmeny, and on their return Catherine cheerfully asserted that William and Rosebery had got on famously together. She maintained that William had done everything possible to conciliate Rosebery, and that it was "monstrous" of the younger man to make such difficulties; "I should like," said she, "to give him a bit of my mind." Rosebery's behaviour may have been perverse but the Gladstones had both treated him with marked lack of understanding, and in the end the Prince of Wales had to intervene personally before he could be persuaded to take office as Foreign Secretary.

Of Gladstone's other colleagues Catherine particularly disapproved of Harcourt and approved of Lord Spencer, whom she described as behaving "like an angel". In the dark days of 1883, when Lord Spencer had been feeling the strain of his dangerous and difficult position as Viceroy of Ireland, Catherine took great delight in any occasion that might come her way "to *pet*, as it were, dear Lord Spencer". Among the younger men she had a great liking for John Morley and for G. W. E. Russell, and some unkind persons saw her finger in the appointment of Russell as Under-Secretary for India. She was also much exercised over the rival claims of Arthur Acland and Edward Marjoribanks for the position of Chief Whip, and in fact the Prime Minister's new Personal Assistant, Sir Algernon West, had good cause to complain of her interference. Catherine herself was coming to rely more and more upon the judgement of her son Herbert, who had an inside knowledge of the political situation, and could also be relied upon to keep an unobtrusively watchful eye upon his father. "Each day I expect a letter from you to Father," Catherine wrote in an undated letter of this period, "be very firm in it, for I do want you to be about his path and about his bed."

Gladstone took office for the fourth time in August 1892. The responsibility for persuading an old man of eighty-two to undertake so tremendous a task must rest with Catherine, aided and abetted by son Herbert and daughter Mary. As he grew older Gladstone became more and more dependent upon his womenfolk. It was a dependence that sometimes irked him a little; in 1890, when he spent a week in Oxford as the guest of All Souls College, observers noticed that he was particularly gay and spritely, and rather unkindly attributed his high spirits to his escape from petticoat government. Yet between husband and wife there was entire mutual devotion and dependence; they could never be long content when apart, and during a last visit to Hagley the incident which most moved the onlookers was the reunion between husband and wife after a brief temporary separation. In 1893, when Catherine was at Hawarden and William perforce in London, this old woman of eighty-one ended a letter with words which might have been written by the youngest and most devoted of brides: "You never saw such a day, brilliant sunshine, clear views, but I am longing to get back to *somebody*. Who can that be? God bless you. Be very good."

The return to Number Ten Downing Street felt to Catherine

like a real home-coming, and she cared little that the house was most inconveniently cramped now that family and secretariat had all to be housed under the same roof. She had never been one to worry overmuch about the niceties of domestic routine or creature comfort. Even in old age she maintained her Spartan outlook. Until she was eighty she took a cold bath every morning of her life, even on the occasion when she rose early in the small hours to attend a mission service beginning at four o'clock in the morning. Carpets were one of the luxuries she preferred to do without. When Harry and Herbert clubbed together to buy a handsome carpet for her London bedroom she was put in a terrible quandary, for she hated to hurt her sons' feelings or to seem ungrateful for "your attention and pretty, pretty kindness". At length she summoned up courage to write to Herbert: "I have a confession and it is beastly because it has been too pretty of you to think of me so much, combining with Harry to give me the present of a carpet. I have a very strong feeling against carpets in bedrooms; carpets, like curtains, exhaust the air. You will not be hurt, but I adhere to having my floor scrubbed constantly with soap." The handsome, unhygienic carpet went into some back room at Hawarden and Catherine continued to enjoy fresh air and bare boards.

She had, in fact, made very few concessions to old age. Visitors were surprised to see her invariably run rather than walk upstairs. Every morning at Hawarden husband and wife set off before breakfast on the mile-long uphill walk to church, he throwing sticks for the amusement of Petz the pomeranian, she dropping a trail of envelopes and letters behind her as she opened her post. Anything in the least unexpected or adventurous delighted her intensely, as when she wrote home from the seaside an account of a boating expedition with Stephy's family, "We could not land so behold Annie and me taking off our shoes and stockings and tramping through the sea!"

She was curiously unlike the accepted notion of a Victorian grandmother, being completely without the lesser pruderies. Young Talbot nephews staying at Hawarden would be surprised to find their great-aunt wandering about the upstairs corridors on her way from bedroom to bath draped in nothing but a large towel. Odd stories about her eccentricities circulated freely. Many were the legends attaching to the egg-nog, made with her own hands, with which Gladstone was wont to refresh himself in the very chamber of the House of Commons. In defiance both of parliamentary convention and the usages of polite society he would pause in the middle of a speech to put a thick-necked pomatum bottle to his lips and to take a long pull at this heartening concoction. A particularly persistent rumour had it that every night Catherine filled her husband's hot-water bottle with soup which he would drink at two o'clock in the morning, the origin of this tale being a chance remark of Gladstone's to the effect that soup retained heat longer than water.

Other stories, in which there was an element of truth, concerned her habit of carrying off from any grand dinner some particular titbit, a sweet perhaps or a particularly luscious fruit, with which to regale a child or protégée at home. Always a great person for sharing, she was prepared to go to any lengths to see that other people enjoyed at least some part of her own pleasures, and she would arrange, for instance, that her lady's maid should be admitted into some inner sanctum of Buckingham Palace to enjoy a view of the smartly-dressed guests at a Drawing-Room. Her devotion to her husband produced another crop of comic tales. One such story has it that Catherine was sitting with some friends in the drawing-room when a theological question was being discussed without a satisfactory answer being found. A pious lady remarked, "What a comfort to know there is One above who is able to tell us!" "Yes," Catherine replied, "I think William will be down in a few minutes."

The Gladstone family hotly denied that she ever passed notes round the dinner table asking guests to change the subject or to refrain from contradicting the Grand Old Man, but the story is too well authenticated to allow of disbelief. "I met the G.O.M. at dinner in 1889," writes one unimpeachable authority,[1] "and had a dispute with him about the opium question. He got very angry and changed the subject. A slip of paper was put into my hand; on it was 'Do not contradict the Prime Minister. Signed, Catherine Gladstone.' He was not P.M. at the time."

Her overflowing spirit of charity still kept her busy both with

[1] Brigadier-General Sir James Edmonds to Thomas Jones, December 19th, 1949. *A Life and Some Letters*, by Thomas Jones, C.H.

committees and with individual cases and she grieved greatly if she was obliged to give up any of the work which had been so long her duty and her delight. "It goes to my heart to have to give it up", she wrote pathetically about a Home for Girls, where, in her usual manner of killing two birds with one stone, she had installed one of her "lame dogs" as Matron. She was as full as ever of sound common-sense; before sending out a personal appeal for funds for one institution she insisted on knowing the exact financial position, and she urged the appointment of a proper accountant, laughing gently at Lucy Cavendish for her lack of money-sense, "You, whose only want of bump is finance!" She was still collecting for the House of Charity which had been the first of all her interests, still begging from her friends on behalf of the blind, as long ago she had begged of Palmerston.

At Hawarden she now had a Home for old ladies, as well as the boys' orphanage, and visitors to the Castle would be packed off to entertain the inmates: "Nobody has said a word as to our Orphanage and Home, will you shine on them one day?" Her sympathy with individuals was as quick as ever; "Was glad I went by that train," she wrote to William in December 1893, "was of some use in trying to comfort a hysterical woman." On another occasion, when she was well over eighty, she rushed to the rescue of a nurse stricken with typhoid, and spent the whole day trailing round Chester from hospital to hospital, meanwhile supporting and comforting the sick woman, never resting until she saw the patient safely tucked up in bed, when she herself at length had leisure to remember that she had forgotten all about her own mid-day meal.

Two incidents of the year 1893 show Catherine as touching hands both with the past and with the future. In August, when William was staying in Birmingham, he wrote to Catherine to describe a visit to the house which had once been the home of Sir Robert Peel: "We have been driving over to Drayton Manor which I had not seen for sixty years and you never. It is only seven miles off and I had no idea of the whereabouts and gladly accepted the proposal to go. I very clearly recall the most import-ant rooms and the collections of busts and portraits. . . . There is a portrait of me painted by Lucas in 1843 for Sir R. Peel, which is hung in a bad light, but appears to be extremely clever and is thought well of there." To this Catherine replied: "I rather envy you seeing the poor old Peel house, having had a curiosity to see the place. I suppose the pictures are still there; I remember the one of you is poorissimus*." In her own person Catherine spanned the distance between Peel and Asquith.

A few months after William's visit to Drayton Manor, the Gladstones' young friend, Margot Tennant, announced her engagement to H. H. Asquith, Home Secretary in Gladstone's administration and one of the most promising of the younger politicians. After dinner one night at the house of Sir Henry Campbell-Bannerman the older ladies present, headed by Catherine, endeavoured to give Margot some advice as to her conduct as the wife of a possible Prime Minister. Humility under instruction was never one of Margot's characteristics and she complained that she had been bidden to give up dancing, riding and acting, but surely Catherine could never have been so imperceptive as to suggest that any young woman should abandon the three pleasures which had been specially dear to her own youthful heart.

It had become customary for the Gladstones to take a holiday abroad every year, a cruise in the summer or a winter trip to some warmer southern climate. This year of 1892 Catherine for one would have been well content to remain at home at Hawarden with the children and grandchildren, but the other members of the family decided that a trip abroad was necessary for the Grand Old Man's health, so to Biarritz they went with the assistance of the ever-helpful Armitstead, in spite of loud protests on the part of Cabinet colleagues and private secretaries.

Gladstone returned apparently restored to health and to all seeming more spritely than ever, but in fact his powers had begun ever so slightly to fail. His colleagues would have been thankful to have him retire, and Hamilton even went so far as to note, "Come what may, he must be got out of office this year." He had gone very deaf, one eye was entirely blind, and the other was rapidly failing, but his family were prepared to do everything they could to conceal these defects from the general public. The truth was that Catherine's mind, like William's own, was concentrated on the great question of Ireland. She believed implicitly in his divine mission and she was sure that old and tired and ailing though he might be, strength would be given him from above to carry through his Home Rule policy in spite of a divided House of Commons and a solidly hostile House of Lords. In the face of this belief there was no arguing with her and indeed Gladstone's bearing and behaviour might have been held to justify her opinion.

The Home Rule Bill was introduced on February 13th. All through the spring and summer Gladstone piloted the measure through the House of Commons almost unaided, fighting every inch of the way and obviously in high enjoyment of the battle. Those who met him at the various social functions he chose to attend—and these were many considering how little time he had free from the demands of the House of Commons—noticed that he was looking as fresh as a youngster and Randolph Churchill was moved to remark that the Grand Old Man would probably reach his real prime about the middle of the next century. Catherine, however, appeared to be ageing and very deaf; perhaps the strain told more on her than on him, for to her fell all the anxiety and none of the excitement.

Victory came at last on the first night of September. In the thirty-six years that had passed since Mary Lyttelton's death Catherine had never failed to write a letter for Lucy's birthday on September 3rd, and this year her greeting was jubilant indeed: "The never-to-be-forgotten birthday comes close to that tremendous evening when the third reading of the Home Rule Bill was passed with acclamation. It was a never-to-be-forgotten night, the victory. You won't be surprised whilst my heart is overflowing that your birthday comes to force me to express some thoughts. Shall we not feel that your precious husband, our beloved Freddie, comes vividly before us, and all that you have suffered?" Catherine herself had every right to be triumphant. She had been prime mover in persuading her husband to take office for the fourth time, and if she is to be blamed for the difficulties of his last administration she must also be praised for its victory.

An empty victory, some called it, since the Bill was certain to be rejected by the House of Lords, "that dead mass of peers", as Mary Drew had once remarked. And rejected it duly was, a week after that glorious victory in the Commons. But Catherine was not downcast; she rejoiced that her husband had been allowed to do all that in him lay for the cause of Home Rule, and to demonstrate to the Irish nation that whatever might be the attitude of the House of Lords, the people of England were at last ready to grant Ireland her freedom.

It was not really the Lords who had defeated Gladstone, but time, that adversary who must always have the last word. Gladstone might be "in staying mood", he might even urge a dissolution and an appeal to the country against the decision of the Upper House, but it was clear that a blind old man of eighty-three could not lead the nation through the major constitutional crisis that such a course of action must provoke. Clear, that is, to everyone except his wife and family. Catherine still struggled to prevent any news of his failing sight from becoming public, believing, as she told Hamilton, that William with hardly any eyes at all was worth more to the country than any other man equipped with a pair of sound ones. William himself was old, blind and at last a little tired, although he could still spare enough energy and eyesight to translate the Odes of Horace. Now, for the first time, he consented to see a London oculist and he even consented to go on holiday to Brighton with George Armitstead, leaving Catherine herself to spend Christmas in bed in London, ill with erysipelas. "The thought that you were out in such air seemed to waft some of its freshness to me," she wrote, her thoughts as always concentrated upon him rather than upon herself, "don't pity me too much, it is quite enough break* to be really better."

This month of December 1893 was saddened by a domestic tragedy. William had been forced to dismiss his trusted valet and factotum, by name Zadok, for gross drunkenness, and ten days later the unfortunate man's body had been found in the Thames. Zadok was a family servant of many years' standing; long ago, during a visit to Whittingeham, Catherine herself had taught him to read, and she was greatly shocked by this sad ending to his story.

On his return from Brighton Gladstone faced his final battle. The rest of the Cabinet wished to increase the Naval Estimates, but true to the policy of a lifetime he refused to sanction a step which he regarded as contrary to his two basic principles of peace abroad and economy at home. Over this matter Gladstone stood entirely alone, even his son Herbert taking up the opposite point of view. It is typical of the hold that Gladstone women had come to have over their men that Herbert Gladstone should have made Mary his spokesman with his father. "Herbert spoke to Mary very seriously about this, in grave opposition to his father," Lucy wrote in her journal on January 6th, 1894; "Mary did her best to put Herbert's views before the G.O.M. but was entirely smashed." Contrary to his usual habit Gladstone seems to have said little to Catherine about the true state of affairs and he now left it to John Morley to explain the position fully. In his autobiography Morley describes the scene which took place on January 9th after a dinner at Number Ten Downing Street:

"After dinner in the drawing-room Mr. Gladstone at once sat down to a game of backgammon with Armitstead. Mrs. Gladstone carried me to a sofa behind a glass screen and I then found that I was to tell her the fatal news. Mr. Gladstone had said to her on his return from the House of Commons that he was fagged and that I could tell her how things stood. It was as painful as any talk could be. I told her the reign was over, and the only question was whether the abdication should be now or in February. The poor lady was not in the least prepared. Would not the Cabinet change when they knew the perils with which his loss would surround them? I was obliged to keep to iron facts. What a curious scene! I breaking to her that the pride and glory of her life was at last to face eclipse, that the curtain was falling on a grand drama of fame, power, acclamation; the rattle of the dice and the laughter and chuckling of the two long-lived players sounding a strange running refrain."

Even now Catherine would not give way without a last struggle. The Gladstones had planned to go on another holiday to Biarritz, taking with them Mary Drew and little Dorothy. Morley, Harcourt, Hamilton all urged Gladstone to resign before he left for abroad, but he refused, according to Lucy Cavendish, his reason being the fact that two bills were still before the House of Commons, one dealing with parish councils, the other with employers' liability. It is hard to believe that the Grand Old Man took a very serious interest in either of these subjects but his family were pressing him to remain in office till the last possible moment, and now that the time had actually come, he himself was curiously reluctant to retire.

When the Gladstones left for Biarritz on January 13th Gladstone was still Prime Minister and still in a minority of one in his own Cabinet over the question of the Naval Estimates. In these circumstances it was not surprising that the holiday was not entirely a happy one. "We are the better for this place," wrote Catherine, "but where is peace to be found?" Gladstone himself was moody and excitable whilst Catherine and Mary were hoping against hope that some means might yet be found to keep him in office and catching at any straw which seemed to point in that direction. So preoccupied were they with this one absorbing question that for once they forgot the ordinary civilities and their kind host Armitstead had to put up with a great lack of consideration. Only the child Dossie, unconscious of strain and stress, provided a ray of cheerfulness to which everybody turned with relief from the prevailing gloom. To the onlookers the situation was both ridiculous and pathetic. Gladstone would listen to no one but his wife and daughter, and it was tragic to see the Prime Minister of England dependent in this crisis on the advice of an old woman of failing understanding supported by a younger one who, although intelligent, was yet remarkably obstinate.

On his return to England Gladstone agreed to put forward his age and failing eyesight as reasons for quitting office rather than expose his difference with his Cabinet. Catherine was bitterly grieved that he must go out "on a lie"; she would have liked the truth to be known, and she was convinced that when the whole story came to be told the verdict of history would be for her husband. Meanwhile his family must keep silence. "The misery is that his position must not be known," wrote Lucy, "his case must not be pleaded, at least till history is being written in some distant future."

Many of Gladstone's friends feared that temptation would prove too great and that the secret would inevitably come out, but Catherine's discretion had always been absolute and it did not fail her now. Unhappy though she was at the prospect of retirement she was as usual certain that her husband's course was the only right and sensible one. Again and again, with the tenacity of old age, she repeated that William had never gone against his conscience and that he would not do so now, not even for Ireland's sake. Maybe she was remembering those days fifty years back when a rising young politician had thrown up office because of a high-flown scruple about the Maynooth Grant.

The various ministers coming for consultations with Gladstone found her always at hand, sometimes sitting in the room all through their conversations, unhappy but inflexible. She was under the delusion that members of the Cabinet would wish him to remain in office and she was sadly puzzled to understand why they appeared to be so little eager to meet his advances half-way. Especially was she grieved by Rosebery's chilly manner and lack of deference to Gladstone's opinion, little thinking how much she herself was responsible for the coldness between the two men.

The evil day could be put off no longer and on March 2nd, 1894, Catherine accompanied her husband to Windsor, where he was to hand in his resignation to the Queen. Victoria's dislike of Gladstone amounted to hatred, but she still cherished some remnants of her former kindness towards Catherine. Between the two women there was the bond of shared memories. "Many, many years have rolled on since I have had the honour and privilege of knowing Your Majesty," Catherine wrote on May 5th, 1893, in a letter of congratulation on the engagement of the Duke of York, "they are years never to be forgotten by me, and I cannot refrain from saying how deep down you ever are in my heart, whether sorrows or joys touch Your Majesty." "It is indeed a very long time that I have known you," the Queen replied. "At York, in '35, I saw the two very beautiful Miss Glynnes and have not forgotten it. How much of weal and of woe has happened since then!"

When Victoria had to receive Gladstone in audience during his last ministry she invariably treated him in her chilliest and most distant manner, but she would sometimes unbend sufficiently to enquire after Catherine "with evident sincerity and perhaps a touch of warmth" or to ask "somewhat kindly" after her health, to quote Gladstone's pathetically truthful phrases. Before the final interview with Gladstone Victoria sent for Catherine and saw her privately. No account of this interview exists except in the Queen's own journal. If Victoria is to be believed Catherine broke down in tears, pleading that whatever his errors may have been her husband had always been devoted to the Crown, and begging permission to tell him that the Queen indeed believed this to be true. Lacking as it does any further confirmation this account may well be regarded as suspect; it is hard to believe that even to "the dear Queen" Catherine would have admitted to any errors on the part of her husband, much less apologise for them.

On March 12th the final farewells took place. Number Ten Downing Street was all of a bustle, Gladstone still at work up to the very last minute, Catherine, with tears in her eyes, bidding goodbye to servants, friends, officials. "You know", wrote Mary, "how she loves being inside the main spring of history and all the stir and stress and throb of the machine is life and breath to her." Now it was as if her own mainspring was broken and she herself left without purpose in life. In the midst of all the sadness of farewell small Dossie struck the one cheerful note as, dressed in bright green cape and bonnet, she wandered from room to room shrilly and incongruously chanting "Alleluia".

One final episode completed the story. Queen Victoria had made no sort of sign of recognition to Gladstone himself in reward for his sixty years of public service, though in fairness it must be said that she would have given him a peerage had he been disposed to take one. The College of Heralds had long ago suggested that Catherine should claim the extinct baronies of Percy and Poynings to which she stood entitled, but she had declined to take any steps in the matter. Now, through Rosebery, an enquiry was made as to whether she would take a peerage in her own right. This offer was also declined; to Catherine it was unthinkable that she should ever be known by any other name than that of Gladstone.

*   *   *

Four years were still to be theirs, a happier time perhaps for William than for Catherine. Even now she could not bear to feel totally withdrawn, finding it impossible to believe that the affairs of the nation could go smoothly on without William's magic touch. Only a few days after Rosebery had taken office as Prime Minister a snap division in the House of Commons resulted in a governmental defeat. It was a matter of no importance, but Catherine at once wrote off in agitated manner to Herbert: "Father has been greatly perturbed at the late proceedings. Oh,

Herbert, we little thought that such immediate calling out for Father's hand would arise directly! How thankful I am that he is still in Parliament! Between ourselves he is taken out of* at the handling of affairs; he wrote to Harcourt but it will arrive after the Cabinet." It was Catherine who had kept him in Parliament, much against his own wish, if Morley speaks true, and against the unspoken wishes of his late colleagues. "*All* Mamma's heart is fixed on him remaining in Parliament", wrote Mary, and in fact he did not resign his seat until the Dissolution in the summer of 1895.

Gladstone himself at first found the enforced inactivity a trial. "Father is better but weakened and things do worry and set upon him perhaps more than they should. It is only to be expected that this most sudden change from the power of putting things right when he sees they are wrong is working seriously to depress and retard calm recovery." Fundamentally, however, he was reconciled to the change and he submitted humbly to all the cramping disabilities of old age, thankful to have time to devote to his classical studies and to his projected edition of the works of his beloved Bishop Butler. Catherine, however, could not give up so easily, nor accept so simply the ministrations of friends and children. She hated to be dependent on other people, hated too her inability to continue with her innumerable works of kindness and charity—"I long to give less trouble and to visit the poor". There were no more letters now to her husband because she seldom if ever left his side, and the few she wrote to friends and relations were pathetically wavering and brief.

In May 1894 Gladstone underwent an operation for cataract. At first all went well; then came a period of disappointment and the threat of a further operation but by September Catherine was writing joyfully, "When Father has mounted his four pairs of spectacles he will see by their aid the smallest print, distant views, and the human face divine!" Now that Gladstone had recovered his sight there was still much that husband and wife could enjoy together. There was a cruise to Germany for the opening of the Kiel Canal, there was a visit to Cannes and a last meeting there with Queen Victoria, who thawed not at all in spite of all Catherine's efforts, there was one last outburst of William's old crusading zeal, this time on behalf of the persecuted Armenians, and a great meeting at Liverpool where Catherine could once again revel in the warmth of the reception accorded to her husband and listen to the music of his speaking voice.

Visitors still flocked to Hawarden, including such famous characters 'as Burne-Jones, General Booth, Arthur Balfour, and the Chinese Li Hung Chang. Best of all was a visit from the Prince and Princess of Wales whose warm and faithful friendship had done something to heal the wound made by Queen Victoria's unkindness. In their turn the Gladstones called at Marlborough House to pay their respects to a small baby who was one day to be King Edward VIII. One visit of old friends to Hawarden ended in sadness when Archbishop Benson collapsed and died as he knelt at Catherine's side during morning service in Hawarden Church.

Little Dorothy Drew left Hawarden in 1897, when her father took a neighbouring living, but even so the Castle was seldom empty of children. Grandpapa was an impressive and much-beloved figure, who could send delicious shudders down the spine with his blood-curdling recitation of "Fee-fi-fo-fum". In his Temple of Peace there were many treasures for small visitors to inspect, in especial a small round box which, when opened, displayed a most realistic red lobster with tail and claws all a-quiver. The thought of Grandmamma was always linked with the sweet smell of the scented verbena which grew in the nooks and crannies of the old Castle ruins. Even in old age Catherine's beauty shone like a lamp, and a fifteen-year-old niece, meeting her on Christmas Eve, 1896, carried away an unforgettable impression of the outline of a still lovely profile and the sparkle of a pair of deep blue eyes.

The happiness of old age is inevitably brief, and in the autumn of 1897 Gladstone developed symptoms of serious illness. Catherine herself had been ailing but now she forgot her own illness completely in her absorption in her husband's health. For a while Mary Drew deluded herself into supposing that her father's troubles were chiefly imaginary: "The real misfortune is that he has been allowed to drop all occupation and work, and the whole of his great unimpaired mind is turned on to his own ailments . . . if he had some malignant disease it would be different. Because there isn't one that one knows of or has any reason for suspecting the public will imagine a mystery." Six weeks after these letters were written the doctors diagnosed cancer of the jaw.

The Gladstones were staying at Bournemouth when the nature of his illness became known. He could wish for nothing except a quick release, but Catherine was growing increasingly feeble and the family trembled to think what might happen when she was left alone. Lucy and her uncle talked the problem over very frankly and at the end of their discussion he declared, "I shall ask no more for instant dismissal."

On March 20th, 1898, on a golden evening, William Gladstone came home to Hawarden Castle to die. Catherine's intellect was clouding over and her sons and daughters supposed her to be ignorant of the true state of her husband's case, but however that might be from now onwards she hardly left his side. When young Will came to bid farewell to his grandfather Catherine put her arms round the boy and spoke to him clearly and urgently of the past with all its effort and achievement and of the future which would now lie in his own hands. On one of the rare occasions when she consented to allow Mary to take her place in the sick-room for a little while, the dying man turned to his daughter with the words, "Carry my blessing to my wife—for fifty-eight years."

During the last two days and nights Catherine was constantly with her husband, lying on a sofa alongside his bed or kneeling close by his head holding his hand. She was kneeling by his side when he died quietly after long suffering on the morning of Ascension Day.

Three days later a man was killed in one of the collieries on the Hawarden estate. Catherine insisted on driving over to see the poor young widow, and the two women, alike in nothing but their grief, knelt down on the rough cottage floor and prayed together. The cloud had lifted from her mind and something of her old strength and resilience had come back to her so that her bearing and self-possession throughout the long funeral ceremonies astonished all who saw her. As she drove in an open carriage behind the hearse which carried her husband's coffin from Hawarden church to the railway station, she bowed right and left like a queen towards the silent masses of working people, all in their mourning black, come in their thousands from the industrial towns of the North to pay their tribute to "the people's William".

The huge congregation gathered in Westminster Abbey for the funeral rose to their feet as one man when she entered by the great West door. Her place was at the head of the grave, surrounded by her family, nearest of all being the two beloved grandchildren, Will and Dorothy. At the end of the service the Prince of Wales paused for a moment by her chair and stooped to kiss her hand. He was followed by all the other pall-bearers and for each of them she had a word of greeting, then, supported by Harry and Herbert, she walked slowly down the aisle, smiling as a bride might smile, as she recognised, one after another, the faces of her husband's friends.

Lucy Cavendish took her back to that house in Carlton House Terrace which had for so long been to her a second home. Friends and relations were there to comfort her and letters came from the Presidents of France and America, the Italian Parliament, the King of Greece, amongst countless others. She insisted on writing herself to those who were especially near and dear, such as the saintly eccentric Albert Lyttelton, to whom she sent a touching letter, scribbled, as so often, on a messy half-sheet of paper. "Now I thank God," she wrote, "for does not the whole world know the truth and cannot I with humble heart echo the glorious words which flow from all?" The letter ends with a childishly simple sentence, echoing words written long ago to William, "You will pray for me and not believe that I am half as good as I ought to have been." "How I am to live without him I can only leave to God," she wrote in reply to a somewhat chilly letter of condolence from the Queen.

She had two twilight years still before her but all that counted of life was finished. Her mind was failing, but she could still enjoy the visits of friends, and particularly those younger men who had loved and revered her husband, John Morley, Henry Scott Holland, George Russell. When she drove with Russell through the Hawarden lanes or along the park roads made long ago at the time of the Cotton Famine she would talk to him not of the recent events already blurred in her memory but of distant days, to her still crystal clear, when Stephen and Henry, Pussy and Missykins, shot their arrows and rode their ponies about these same woods and fields. She would speak of Sir Robert Peel as if it were but yesterday that she had met him at a London dinner-party or listened to him speaking in the House of Commons. She did not lack for affection and support; Mary lived nearby, Lucy came on frequent visits, and Miss Phillimore, a relation of her old friend and admirer, was often at hand to cherish and care for her. There was to be one farewell visit to the relations at Penrhyn Castle and in the autumn of 1899 a last holiday at Penmaenmawr, where she had spent so many happy days. After that she was never again to leave Hawarden. There she had been born and in that beloved place she was to die.

At the end of May 1900 she caught a slight cold which quickly turned to pneumonia. Ever present in her conscious mind had been the wish that she might quickly rejoin her husband, and though she lingered a little her unconscious body made no great resistance. She died quietly without pain on the evening of June 14th, 1900, and three days later she was buried in the same grave as her husband. He had been four times Prime Minister of England, one of the most famous figures of his age and generation; she had simply been his wife, but those who knew them both might judge that she too was not unworthy a place in Westminster Abbey.

Extracts from "The Glynnese Glossary"

ADDLE—To be *addled* about a subject is not to be in a vacant state about it, but to be confused and perplexed about it and so to be in an irresolute and undecided state of mind; the reverse of the nut or egg of the comparison.

ANTIC—Any small thing or object which, from whatever reason the speaker will not or cannot define in precise terms.

BATHING-FEEL—A significant description of the state of mind previous to some rather formidable undertaking, resembling that of a child about to fall into the arms of the bathing-woman.

BEYOND—A simple form of ellipsis. Mrs. Gladstone might say, "Really, teaching Stephy is beyond."

BREAK—Any event or circumstance that breaks or tends to break the monotony of existence.

CARES, TO HAVE THE—To be anxious and uneasy about something in which one is much interested, and which one fears may go wrong, but which is more or less beyond one's control at the time.

CUDDLE—To associate constantly together.

EBB—Anything, especially any occupation, that is low, loathsome, degrading to a sad and even ludicrous degree.

FALSE FLASH—Any sham appearance of splendour, power, or the like when the substance is wanting.

GAUNT—Lugubrious.

GRUBOUS—Dingy, dirt-coloured, mud-and-water-like.

HIGH GEE—In full fling.

HUMAN—Very absent, for the time, for some particular reason. Example: Mrs. Gladstone, in a letter from London: "I was

231

not human last night talking to Alick Wood, having the cares of William in his new tights."

ISSIMUS—Latin adjective superlative. Sets rules at defiance with characteristic audacity.

MANNERS—The habit of, or things done by, particular people with inferences to particular seasons and circumstances. "What are your *manners* before lunch here? Do you go out, or what?"

MAWKIN—Unknown individual.

NOTE—What was observed. A Glynnese would say after a visit to a disagreeable place, "My note was that everybody quarrelled with everybody."

ONE OF MINE ⎫
ONE OF HIS ⎬—Peculiarities or habits.
ETC. ⎭

PASSING PIGMAN—Any casually-met person—the first person that may come by and therefore probably of a low and scrubby description.

PHANTOD. PH.—An imbecile person, one incapable of serious or rational behaviour.

POMPE—The French participle *pompé*, properly *pumped out* and so in Glynnese jaded or exhausted.

POOR—Short, bald, disproportionate in means compared to the end, an anti-climax, denuded of due and decent decoration, etc. Examples: The hinder part of a French poodle. A pig without a tail.

REBOUND—The impression or opinion about A., communicated by B. to C.

SHOOT—Suddenly to discover or hit upon.

SITTING TIGHT—In eager anticipation.

TAKE—"My take" signifies "my particular way", "the course I consider best".

TAKE OUT OF—The painful sensation, which most persons must have felt, as if some part actually was taken out of one's stomach.

TAKE RANK—To be proud of, to plume oneself about a thing.

TOTTERTON—Imbecility from second childhood, or premature old age.

UMS—Termination in. To be much occupied with, to devote much of one's conversation to something.

UNEARTHLY—Something strange, mysterious, or again, something nasty and revolting.

USE OF THE VERB TO BE—In peculiar and very emphatic ellipse, always uttered as if it were a singularly full and perfect statement.

WHO'S WHO AND WHAT'S WHAT—A general bewilderment of the faculties and universal suspicion of the identity of men and things.

Index

235

Index

Index

Gladstone, Catherine (*contd.*):
Separations from W. E. G., enforced, 46, 48, 52-4, 70, 90, 99, 147; W. E. G.'s reply to her complaints, 53-6
Social obligations, slipshod over, 97-8
Speechmaking nervousness, 210
Travel, methods of, 120
Untidy and unmethodical, 36-8, 64, 119-20

Gladstone, Catherine Jessy (daughter), 77-8; death (1850), 82-5, 99, 111, 116, 206, 211

Gladstone, Gertrude (earlier Gertrude Stuart) (daughter-in-law), 165, 168, 184, 195, 203

Gladstone, Helen (sister-in-law), eccentric nervous invalid, 22, 69; W. E. G.'s attentions to, 23; Catherine's attitude to, 40, 59, 65; her drug-taking; reception into Roman Catholic Church, 59; W. E. G.'s missions to Germany to persuade her to return home, 59-60, 73, 162, 175; death (1880), 176

Gladstone, Helen (Lena) (daughter), birth (1849), 78; at Hagley, 86; mother's anxiety over scripture lessons, 108; governess, 137; acts as secretary to father, 144; at Hawarden, 147; visits Germany, 161-2; holiday in North of England, 170; enters Newnham Hall, Cambridge, 173; Vice-Principal of Newnham, 183-4

Gladstone, Henry Neville (Harry) (son), birth (1852), 99; childhood at Hawarden, 123; illness while at Eton, 132, 139; prepares for business career, 144; in India, 162, 164, 173; home on leave, 180, 183; returns to India, 198; engagement, 206; gift of carpet to mother, 216; at father's funeral, 229

Gladstone, Herbert John (later Viscount Gladstone) (son), quoted, 71; birth (1854), 102; at Hagley, 109; opinion of Downing Street, 118; mother's love for, 123; delicacy, 125; illness while at Eton, 132, 139, 144, 147, 150; end of schooldays, 143; taken

Gladstone, Herbert John (*contd.*):
ill in Wales, 147; Queen asks about health, 150-1; mother's letters to, 151, 155, 158, 171-2, 176, 191, 225-6; recites at "Speeches", 152; success at Oxford, 165; at Hawarden, 168; uncertainty about choice of profession, 173; elected to Parliament, 177; minor office, 180; informs mother of Government's defeat, 193; hissed in Rotten Row, 200; and Parnell, 208; persuades father to take office, 215; gift of carpet to mother, 216; opposes father on Naval Estimates, 221; at father's funeral, 229

Gladstone, Sir John (father-in-law), served in family corn store, 4; helps to finance railroads, 14; character, 22; wealthy man, 31; Catherine's relations with, 39; gift of house to W. E. G. and Catherine, 41; advocates selling of Hawarden, 62; disapproves of Free Trade, 67-70; pride in his son, 71; death (1851), 98, 116

Gladstone, John (brother-in-law), 39, 124-5

Gladstone, Kate (niece), 144

Gladstone, Mary (daughter): *see* Drew, Mary

Gladstone, Robertson (brother-in-law), 39, 136, 158-9, 173; death (1875), 164, 165

Gladstone, Stephen Edward (Stephy) (son), birth (1844), 49; first lessons, 70, 78; characteristics, 77; mother's hope for Holy Orders, 77; illness, 83; at Hagley, 86; goes to school, 95; welcome-home to mother, 116; father's help in upbringing, 123; eye-trouble, 125, 143, 144; ordained deacon, 143; Rector of Hawarden from 1872, 153, 168, 184, 203; health, 162; ordered abroad, 173; marriage (1885), 192

Gladstone, Tom (brother-in-law), Catherine's relations with, 39, 98, 153, 203; and Free Trade, 69; head of family, 98; illness, 137; votes against W. E. G.'s party, 158; death (1889), 206

Index

Lyttelton, Lavinia: *see* Talbot, Lavinia (niece)

Lyttelton, Lucy (niece): *see* Cavendish, Lady Lucy

Lyttelton, Mary, Lady (earlier Mary Glynne) (sister), childhood, 2, 4, 6; nickname "Missykins" and with sister Catherine "The Pussies", 11; compared with Catherine, 11, 12; visits Paris (1829), 13; relations with Catherine, 14, 15, 46 80; men admirers, 16; refuses Lord Gairlie, 16; on jilting of Catherine by Colonel Harcourt, 19–20; Scottish tour (1837), 21, 175; continental tour (1838), 21, 23; engagement to Lord Lyttelton, 32–3; marriage (1839), 34–5; honeymoon, 38–9; exchanges visits with Gladstones, 40; Carlton House Terrace as London headquarters, 41; daughter born (1840), 41; devotion to Catherine, 45–6; Catherine's letters to, quoted *en passim*; and Oak Farm crash, 61–2; 65–7; and mother, Lady Glynne, 65–6; seventh child born, 79; and Catherine's illness, 90; and the Talbots, 94–5; illness (1855), 107–8; eleventh child born, 108; twelfth child born (1857), 109; last illness and death (1857), 33, 109–10, 211; effect of her death on Catherine, 111, 112–13, 116, 220; and Queen Victoria, 127

Lyttelton, Mary, Lady (earlier Mary Cavendish), 174

Lyttelton, May (or Mary) (niece), 145, 154, 163, 164

Lyttelton, Meriel (niece): *see* Talbot, Meriel

Lyttelton, Neville (nephew), 154

Lyttelton, Sarah, Lady (earlier Lady Sarah Spencer), 33, 34, 40–1, 48, 49, 110, 146

Lyttelton, Spencer (nephew), 165, 188, 209

Lyttelton, Sybella, Lady, 145–6

Lytton, Lord (Bulwer Lytton), 113

Macaulay, Lord, 29

McColl, Mr., 180

Magdalene College, Cambridge, 45

Magnus, Sir Philip, cited, 163

Mahon, The O'Gorman: *see* O'Gorman Mahon, The

Manchester, Duchess of, 189, 208

Manners, Lord John, 43

Manning, Henry (later Cardinal Manning), meets W. E. G. in Rome (1838), 24–5; godfather to Willy Gladstone, 41–2, 207; Catherine's liking for, 41–2; Catherine's letter to on W. E. G.'s accident (1842), 47; W. E. G.'s opinion of, 68; Catherine's vision of him presiding over a penitentiary, 75; and Gorham Judgement, 84; reception into Roman Catholic Church, 88; correspondence with Catherine on her golden wedding (1889), 207; mentioned, 48, 61

Manzoni, Alessandro, 24

Marjoribanks, Edward, 215

Marlborough House, 151, 227

Masterman, Mrs., 173

Masterman, C. F., 37

Maynooth Grant, 56–8, 224

Melbourne, Lord, 30, 43

Mendicity Society, 52

Midlothian campaigns, 194, 195, 196, 200, 213

Mildmay, Sybella: *see* Lyttelton, Sybella, Lady

Mill Hill, 182

Millais, Sir John, 200

Milnes, Monckton, 94

Monsell, Mrs. (Mother Harriet), 89, 104, 129

Monsell, William, 89, 155

Morley, John (later Lord Morley), description of W. E. G., 1; on bad handwriting, 38; and W. E. G. and untruthfulness, 124; and Women's Liberal Federation, 210; sees Catherine after Willy Gladstone's death, 212; Catherine's liking for, 215; explains to Catherine W. E. G.'s differences with Cabinet (1894), 222; visits Catherine in later years, 229; quoted, 40, 73, 145, 222, 226

Morocco Loan question, 122

Motley, J. L., 149

Mytton, Charles, 17

Index

Index

Talbot, John (junior), 94, 95, 117, 125

Talbot, Lavinia (earlier Lavinia Lyttelton) (niece), 145, 166, 180

Talbot, Meriel (earlier Meriel Lyttelton) (niece), 41, 45, 77, 107, 109–11, 116, 117

Teck, Duchess of, 151

Tennant, Laura: *see* Lyttelton, Laura

Tennant, Margot: *see* Asquith, Margot

Tennyson, Alfred, Lord, 174

Thackeray, W. M., 119

Theatricals, private, 108–9

Times, The, 99, 112, 165

Tories: *see* Conservatives

Tractarianism, 31, 105

Trimmer, Mrs. 6

Turkey 175, 181–2

Tyneside, W. E. G.'s visit (1862), 125–6

Vale Royal, Cheshire, 6, 14

Vatican Decrees, pamphlet on, 164

Victoria, Queen, visits Hawarden when Princess Victoria, 18; popularises Highland holidays, 39; admiration of Willy Gladstone when a child, 49; Catherine and her children at Windsor and Buckingham Palace, 50; invites W. E. G. to Windsor (1845), 57–8; early attitude to W. E. G., 58, 126; at Great Exhibition (1851), 92; friendship for Catherine, 98, 128, 150, 224–5; Queen of Greece's enquiry regarding (1859), 115–16; at Chester (1860), 119; W. E. G.'s visits to Balmoral, 126–7, 146, 150, 155; Catherine's account of party at Windsor, 126; increasing weight, 126–7; seclusion in mourning for Prince Consort, 127–8, 146, 150; telegram to W. E. G. (1868), 140; Lucy Lyttelton's relations with, 146; changing attitude to W. E. G. (1869), 146; relations with W. E. G. become and remain unfriendly, 150–1, 172, 179, 187, 191–2, 198, 207, 224–5, 226; interest in Agnes Gladstone's marriage, 155; omits to invite Gladstones to Duke of Connaught's wedding (1879), 172; and Hartington, 177, 179; W. E. G. becomes Prime Minister (1880), 179–80; rift with W. E. G. widens

Victoria, Queen (*contd.*):
after Gordon tragedy (1885), 191, 192; letter to Mary Gladstone on her engagement, 198; jubilee (1887), 202; aloof attitude to Gladstones' golden wedding (1889), 207; condolence on death of Willy Gladstone (1891), 212; receives W. E. G.'s resignation (1894), 224–5; makes no sign of recognition of W. E. G.'s services, 225; W. E. G.'s last meeting with, 226; condolence on death of W. E. G., 229

Vidler, Canon A. R., 29

Wales, Edward, Prince of, dress as child, 50; Bishop of Oxford and, 94; and Willy Gladstone, 114; effect of Queen's secluded life, 127; illness, 150; attitude to W. E. G., 151, 172, 227; visits Gladstones at Downing Street, 180; intervenes between Rosebery and W. E. G., 214; Gladstones exchange visits with, 227; at funeral of W. E. G., 229

Wales, Princess of, 151, 227

Walmer Castle, 148–9

Walpole, Lord, 73, 75

Ward, W. G., 68–9

Wellington, Duke of, 50, 92

Wenlock, Lady, 14

West, Sir Algernon, 215

West Bromwich, 8, 9

West Indian question, 72, 73

Westminster, Duke of, 200

Whigs, Government resigns but returns to office (1839), 30; W. E. G.'s relation by marriage to "The Grand Whiggery", 33; mentioned, 42, 102, 138

Whitby, 143, 153

Whittingeham, 154, 163, 221

Whittingham Mr. (butler), 9, 35

Wickham, Agnes (earlier Agnes Gladstone) (daughter), birth (1842), 48; childhood, 49, 64, 75; plays with royal children, 50; first lessons, 70; illness (erysipelas), 71, 77, 83; character, 77; visit abroad (1850), 86; help during Crimean War, 103; accompanies parents to Corfu (1858), 113, 115, 119; men ad-

Wickham, Agnes (*contd.*):
mirers, 116–17, 139; illness (1859), 118; visit to Scotland, 136; and Disraeli, 140; proposes taking up nursing (1871), 143–4; marriage (1873), 155; letter from mother written on sandwich paper, 164; daughter born, 165, 168; children visit Hawarden, 184; lameness, 197; describes mother as "the genius of charity", 51

Wickham, Edward, 155, 168
Wilberforce, Bishop Samuel, 94, 142
Wilbrahams of Delamere Hall, 17
Williams, Miss (governess), 9
Willis, Professor, 45
"Willy": *see* Gladstone, William Henry (son)
Wilson, Annie: *see* Gladstone, Annie (daughter-in-law)
Windsor Castle, Gladstones' visits, 50, 57–8, 140, 192, 224; Sabbath

Windsor Castle (*contd.*):
observance at, 113; Catherine's accounts of parties at, 126, 155; Lucy Lyttelton at, 146
Wiseman, Cardinal, 24–5, 88
Wolseley, Lord (earlier Sir Garnet Wolseley), 187, 192
Wolverton, Lord, 188
Women's Liberal Federation, 210
Women's suffrage, 210
Wood, Sir Charles, 118
Woodford Convalescent Home, 133–4, 139, 162, 167, 185
Wyndham (family), 33

Yonge, Charlotte Mary, 89
York, Duke of, 224
Young, Lady, 115
Young England Party, 43

Zadok (valet), 221